The
Ministry
of the Word

Vol. 15, No. 4 • April 2011

The Ministry of the Word (ISSN 1938-1921)
is published monthly by Living Stream Ministry,
2431 W. La Palma Ave., Anaheim, CA 92801.

Unless otherwise noted, all Bible quotations and footnotes are taken from the Recovery Version, published by Living Stream Ministry.

The Ministry of the Word is a monthly publication of Living Stream Ministry dedicated to the continuation of the ministry of Watchman Nee and Witness Lee. Each issue includes the printed messages from a recent conference or training held by Living Stream Ministry.

This magazine is intended for the fellowship and supply of the churches under the ministry in the Lord's recovery. It is not intended to be disseminated to the public at large.

The Ministry of the Word is available either by subscription through our "direct mail service" or by direct order. Please direct all inquiries to:

Book Section
Living Stream Ministry
P. O. Box 2121
Anaheim, CA 92814

Letters to the editor are welcome. Those considered for publication must include the writer's name and address and may be edited for the sake of space and/or clarity. Correspondence may be sent to the following:

The Ministry of the Word
P. O. Box 2121
Anaheim, CA 92814
www.lsm.org

About This Issue

This issue of *The Ministry of the Word* contains the first eight messages given during the fall 2003 term of the full-time training in Anaheim, California, on the general subject "The Divine Economy in the Book of Isaiah." This is a continuation of the series of messages published in the November and December 2010 issues of *The Ministry of the Word*. The concluding nine messages of this series will be published in the next issue.

The book of Isaiah, the chief book among the prophets, has as its central focus the divine economy. Isaiah 40 is concerned with God's manifestation. Verse 5 says, "The glory of Jehovah will be revealed," and verse 9 says, "Behold your God!" When Jehovah appeared, He came as Jesus, Jehovah the Savior. Jesus is the very Jehovah God come in the flesh as the manifestation of God. The wonderful Christ who is the glory of Jehovah is Himself the center of the gospel, which is the gospel of the glory of Christ. The issue of the Christ of glory as the center of the gospel is the new creation.

God's expression is a matter of His glory. God desires in His economy to have a corporate expression of Himself for His glory. He wants such a corporate expression so that He may be glorified. God's desire is to expand the revelation, the manifestation, the expression, and the glory from one person, God the Son, into many persons, God the sons.

In Isaiah 41—50, Cyrus, Israel, and Isaiah each typify Christ as the Servant of Jehovah, serving God to carry out His economy in three particular ways. First, Christ is the Servant of Jehovah in our spirit, releasing God's chosen people from Satan, sin, death, and Babylon. Second, Christ is the Servant of Jehovah laboring to build up God's house, the temple, which signifies the church as the house of the living God. Third, Christ is the Servant of Jehovah to build up God's kingdom, signified by the city of Jerusalem.

Isaiah 42:6 says, "I have given You / As a covenant for the people, as a light for the nations." This verse, as a prophecy concerning Christ, indicates that God has given Himself in Christ as a covenant for His people. This indicates that Christ Himself is the covenant. The new

covenant is a person—Christ Himself. A covenant and a testament are
the same, but when the maker of the covenant is living, it is a covenant,
and when he has died, it is a testament. God has bequeathed to us the
unsearchable riches of Christ in His written will, the Bible. He came in
Christ through incarnation, passed through human living, died an all-
inclusive death, and resurrected to become the life-giving Spirit. He
died to satisfy all the righteous requirements of God's law, and in resurrection He became the life-giving Spirit as the reality of the new
covenant. By His death Christ enacted the new covenant, and by His
resurrection He became the new covenant, the new testament. Christ is
all the blessings in the new testament. He is life, light, peace, joy, and
everything else that we need. He is the reality of all the unsearchable
riches of the Divine Trinity that are bequeathed to us in His will. What
is written in the Bible as our will is a reality in our spirit.

Isaiah prophesies that Christ will be the light of Jehovah, a great
light, and a light for the nations. He shines on those who dwell in the
land of the shadow of death. He opens the eyes of the blind and brings
those who dwell in darkness out from the prison house. Light is the
presence of God, and God's people can walk in the light. If we are in
God's presence, we are in the light. If we are not in God's presence, we
are not in the light. Darkness is the absence of the presence of God.
When we were converted, light entered into us. We then became sons
of light. Our Father is light, and His name is Light. When we were
begotten of Him, we became sons of light, children of light. Our spirit
is the lamp of the Triune God. When God came into us, a sevenfold-
intensified lamp came into our lamp. As we walk in the light, day by
day we corporately shine Him out in this dark age as the churches, the
golden lampstands. We thus will hasten the day of His coming, at
which time we will be fully prepared to be His bride, the New Jerusalem, the city of light and the kingdom of light, for the full expression of
God as light.

We need to see the relationship between Christ, the covenant, light,
righteousness, life, and God's full salvation. Isaiah 42:6 says that God
has given Christ as a covenant. Christ initiated and enacted the covenant; furthermore, He is the Mediator of the covenant, the bequests of
the covenant, and the reality of the covenant. Without Christ there
would be no covenant. Since Christ is the reality of the new covenant,
in the sight of God He is the covenant. A covenant is a matter of God's
righteousness. When a legal contract has been signed, the carrying out

of it is not a matter of love, grace, kindness, or mercy but of righteousness. God has entered into a covenant judicially, justly, and righteously according to His own righteousness, and He is prepared to carry out this covenant according to His righteousness. Isaiah 42:6 also says that Christ is the light to the nations. He is the true light (John 1:9), and those who receive this light are born of God (vv. 12-13). Light brings in life. We may be judicially and objectively righteous, but that is not God's complete salvation. Hence, Christ is light to bring in life. Life regenerates us, enlivens us, and makes us children of God. Only then can we have Christ as our full salvation. Christ is the covenant issuing in righteousness, and He is the light issuing in life for our full salvation.

Isaiah as the servant of Jehovah typifies Christ as a covenant of the people to restore the land (Isa. 49:1-9; 42:1-7). As the reality and fulfillment of the type, Christ is a covenant of the people to restore the land (49:8). In our experience the restoration and enjoyment of the land means that we enjoy Christ as the new covenant for His expansion in us. In order for Christ to expand within us, we need to enjoy Him as the bequests of the new covenant in its four major aspects. First, He is propitious to our unrighteousness and does not remember our sins; second, He imparts His laws into our mind and inscribes them in our hearts; third, He is God to us and we are a people to Him; and fourth, we all know the Lord. In order for Christ to expand within us, we also need to enjoy Him as the Servant of Jehovah in the following aspects— Christ is never discouraged; He is constituted with the Spirit of Jehovah; He is the Prophet of Jehovah to be His mouthpiece to speak forth His word; He does not cry out, lift up His voice, or make His voice heard in the street; and He does not break the bruised ones or quench the smoking ones.

Isaiah 51:9—53:1 is a prophesy concerning Israel's experience of Christ in the millennial kingdom as the arm of Jehovah, the reigning God, and the exalted Christ. As the New Testament believers, we should experience these aspects of Christ today in the principle of the restoration of life. We want to be those who change the church age, the age of grace, into the kingdom age. We want to be His dispensational instrument to change the age and to bring the Lord back to reign on this earth. In Isaiah 51—53, we see a scene of recovery, of revival, and of restoration. We want this to be our present reality so that we can become His bride and He can reign on this earth for a thousand years.

Eventually, He will reign for eternity through all of His chosen and redeemed as the New Jerusalem.

In the New Testament His burden is to release God's people from the captivity of Babylon, of Satan, of sin, and of the world in order that they would return to Jerusalem, the unique ground of oneness. God's intention is that on the genuine ground of oneness (Jerusalem) His people would build up the temple as the house of God and the city, especially its walls, as the kingdom of God. Our returning to Jerusalem, our coming back to meet on the genuine ground of oneness, the ground of the church, is for the Lord to gain Zion, signifying the overcomers. God desires and is calling for overcomers in all the local churches. He is calling for those who will live the life of a God-man and live in the reality of the Body of Christ. This is why Christ is the arm of Jehovah. When we are under God's throne, God's golden administration is within us, and we enjoy the divine light in the redeeming God for the application of God's judicial redemption with the life-river and the life-tree for the enjoyment of God's organic salvation. Under the Lord's headship and lordship, He is the preeminent One in our being. God shines in us as the light in the Lamb as the lamp. God is the light, but He shines in the Lamb. The light exposes and convicts us, but the blood of the Lamb cleanses us from every sin as the application of God's judicial redemption so that we can open to Him to partake of His holy, golden nature. By partaking of His divine nature, we enjoy the life-river flowing in us and the life-tree supplying us in order to become men of life to constitute the city of life.

The Reports and Announcements section at the end of this volume includes a report from South Africa and a schedule of upcoming trainings and conferences sponsored by Living Stream Ministry.

Outline of the Messages
for the Full-time Training
in the Fall Term of 2003

GENERAL SUBJECT:
THE DIVINE ECONOMY IN THE BOOK OF ISAIAH

Christ as the Glory of Jehovah—
the Center of the Gospel for the New Creation
(Message 18)

Scripture Reading: Isa. 40; 2 Cor. 4:3-6; 5:17; Gal. 6:15

I. In the Old Testament of thirty-nine books, the main thing covered is the old creation, and in the New Testament of twenty-seven books, the main thing revealed is the new creation—2 Cor. 5:17; Gal. 6:15:

A. God's two creations make the boundary between the Old Testament and the New Testament.

B. In the first thirty-nine chapters of Isaiah, the old creation is covered, including God's chastisement of Israel and His judgment of the Gentiles, whereas in the last twenty-seven chapters, the center of Isaiah's prophecy is the new creation.

C. The coming of the new creation does not involve the immediate end of the old creation:

1. After the new creation comes, the old creation remains for a period of time.

2. The end of the millennial kingdom will be the termination of the old creation as well as the completion, the consummation, of the new creation as signified by the New Jerusalem in the new heaven and new earth—Rev. 21:1-2.

D. First Corinthians 15:45 implies two creations:

1. The old creation is with man as a living soul to be the center—v. 45a:

a. Because God created Adam a living soul, his main

part was the soul, which is for the old creation—Gen. 2:7.

b. In principle, if we live in our soul, by our soul, or for our soul, we are in the old creation—1 Cor. 2:14:
1) The soul is the center and lifeline of the old creation.
2) A person may be moral, but if he lives in the soul, he still belongs to the old creation.

2. The new creation is in resurrection with the life-giving Spirit as the center and lifeline—15:45b:
a. Christ being the last Adam implies a termination and conclusion of the old creation.
b. The new creation comes into being by resurrection.
c. The germinating element of the new creation is the resurrected Christ as the life-giving Spirit.

E. In Isaiah 40 we have a comparison between Hezekiah, a godly man who was still in the old creation, and a regenerated and transformed person in the new creation—v. 31.

II. In Isaiah 40 Christ is revealed as Jehovah the Savior:

A. *Jehovah* means "He who was, who is, and who will be"—Exo. 3:14:
1. God's name is I Am; His name is simply the verb *to be*:
a. *I Am* denotes the One who is self-existing, the One whose being depends on nothing apart from Himself.
b. The I Am is also the ever-existing One; that is, He exists eternally, having neither beginning nor ending.
c. Apart from God, all else is nothing; He is the only One who is, the only One who has the reality of being—Isa. 40:12-18.
2. As the self-existing, ever-existing One, God is the reality of every positive thing; the Gospel of John reveals that He is all that we need—6:48; 10:11; 8:12; 11:25; 14:6.
3. God requires us only to believe that He is—Heb. 11:6.

B. Jesus is Jehovah—Exo. 3:14; John 18:4-6:
1. The Lord Jesus is I Am—the eternal, self-existing, ever-existing God, the One who is everything to us—8:24, 28, 58.
2. The name *Jesus* means "Jehovah the Savior" or "the salvation of Jehovah"—Matt. 1:21.

3. When we call on Jesus, the whole universe realizes that we are calling on Jehovah as our Savior, Jehovah as our salvation—Rom. 10:12-13.

III. Christ as the glory of Jehovah is the center of the gospel for the new creation—Isa. 40:5; 2 Cor. 4:3-6; 5:17; Gal. 6:15:

A. In the Bible, glory signifies the expression of God—John 1:1, 14.

B. Christ as the image of God is the effulgence of God's glory, and this effulgence is like the shining of the sun—Heb. 1:3:

1. Christ's first coming was the rising of the sun—Luke 1:78.

2. When Christ appeared, the glory of Jehovah appeared to be seen by the God-seekers and Christ-believers—Isa. 40:5, 9.

C. The gospel is the gospel of the glory of Christ, which illuminates, radiates, and shines into the heart of man—2 Cor. 4:4:

1. The illumination, the enlightenment, that makes the glory of Christ's gospel known to us issues from the shining of God in our hearts—v. 6.

2. The old creation came through God's outward shining in darkness, but the new creation is accomplished by God's inward shining in our hearts—Gen. 1:3; 2 Cor. 4:6.

3. God's shining in our hearts brings into us a treasure, the Christ of glory, who is the embodiment of God to be our life and our everything—2 Cor. 4:7.

D. Today, the glory of Jehovah is the resurrected Christ as the life-giving Spirit dwelling in our spirit—1 Cor. 15:45b; 2 Cor. 3:17.

E. If we would experience the Lord's shining, we need to have direct, personal, affectionate, and intimate contact with Him—Psa. 27:4; 2 Cor. 3:18.

CHRIST AS THE GLORY OF JEHOVAH—
THE CENTER OF THE GOSPEL FOR THE NEW CREATION

Prayer: Lord Jesus, we love You, adore You, worship You, exalt You, and praise You with our whole being. We begin this term of the full-time training by worshipping You, Lord Jesus, as Jehovah. We thank You that as Jehovah You have come in the flesh to be our Redeemer, our Savior, our salvation, our life, and our everything. Lord, shine as the gospel of glory and be glorified. We open our hearts and our whole being to You. Shine Yourself into us. Saturate, permeate, and constitute us. Make us the same as You. Hallelujah for Your prevailing blood that cleanses us from every sin! Hallelujah for the law of the Spirit of life that conforms us to Your image! Hallelujah for the divine dispensing! We are being filled with You to be Your corporate expression. Lord, we consecrate this term of the training to You. Lord, speak to us, speak Yourself forth, and speak Yourself into our being. May we hear the speaking of Jehovah. Praise the Lord! Amen.

In this term of the full-time training, we will continue the series of messages on "The Divine Economy in the Book of Isaiah" that we began in the previous term (see *The Ministry of the Word,* vol. 14, nos. 11-12). The divine economy is God's plan and arrangement according to His good pleasure, which is the desire of His heart, to dispense Himself into us in Christ as our life, our life-supply, and our everything to make us His corporate expression for His glory. The book of Isaiah, the chief book among the prophets, has as its central focus the divine economy.

In the previous term we presented seventeen messages primarily covering the first thirty-nine chapters of Isaiah. That term concluded with a message entitled "Christ as Jehovah the Savior—His Word of Comfort to His People," a marvelous and all-embracing message on the all-inclusive Christ as the salvation of Jehovah as unveiled in Isaiah 40 (no. 12). The first thirty-nine chapters of Isaiah may be rightly compared to the first thirty-nine books of the Bible—the

Old Testament. The remaining twenty-seven chapters, chapters 40 through 66, may be likened to the New Testament. Chapter 40 is the turning point. In its intrinsic significance it is the preaching of the gospel to the heart of God's redeemed people.

As a review of that concluding message, we will focus on one particularly lovely and glorious matter, which is indicated by the title of this message: "Christ as the Glory of Jehovah—the Center of the Gospel for the New Creation." When Jehovah appeared, He came as Jesus, who is Jehovah the Savior. Jesus is the very Jehovah God come in the flesh as the manifestation of God. The wonderful Christ who is the glory of Jehovah is Himself the center of the gospel. The gospel is the gospel of the glory of Christ (2 Cor. 4:4). Our gospel is the gospel of the radiant Christ, the gospel of the glorified, shining Jesus. God shines into dead, darkened, and empty hearts to enlighten and illumine them with the glory that is God Himself expressed. As He continues to shine in the believers, who are now children of light, He constitutes them not only with truth and life but also with the God of glory Himself, the Christ of glory. Eventually, the God of glory who has shined into them will shine through them and out from them into other dead, dark, and empty human hearts, thereby continuing the blessed cycle of the gospel of the glory of God. The issue of the Christ of glory as the center of the gospel is the new creation.

The New Testament speaks emphatically concerning overcomers, especially in Revelation (2:7, 11, 17, 26-28; 3:5, 12, 20-21; 21:7). All New Testament believers are priests as typified by the Old Testament priests (1:6). In addition, when the believers are in a normal condition, they reign in life as kings (Rom. 5:17), as typified by the kings in the Old Testament. Therefore, we need to consider what group of people in the Old Testament typifies the overcomers. The Old Testament prophets typify the New Testament overcomers. In the Old Testament the prophets were raised up in times of degradation. That was certainly the case with Isaiah, Jeremiah, and Ezekiel, who overcame the degradation at their time. Their speaking was an act of overcoming. They prophesied as the oracle of God with an authority to which even the kings had to attend.

Some Bible expositors call Isaiah the king of the prophets. The prophets typify the overcomers, and Isaiah was such a prophet; therefore, we can surely say that Isaiah was an Old Testament overcomer. The book of Isaiah breathes the prophetic spirit of overcoming. It is not a small thing to realize that prophesying is a major aspect of the God-ordained way. By prophesying we overcome the centuries' old clergy-laity system. We exercise the overcoming life by prophesying.

Isaiah released a breathtaking, exhilarating, and awesome prophecy. Hebrews 11:37 speaks of one of the witnesses of faith who was sawn in two. According to Hebrew tradition, Isaiah was martyred in this manner. This is the reaction of the world and religion to the prophesying of the Word of God. This should be an encouragement to us. We are studying a book written by a brother who was faithful unto death. He was faithful to the vision that he saw, and he was faithful to speak the word that was given to him by Jehovah.

IN THE OLD TESTAMENT OF THIRTY-NINE BOOKS, THE MAIN THING COVERED BEING THE OLD CREATION, AND IN THE NEW TESTAMENT OF TWENTY-SEVEN BOOKS, THE MAIN THING REVEALED BEING THE NEW CREATION

In the Old Testament of thirty-nine books, the main thing covered is the old creation, and in the New Testament of twenty-seven books, the main thing revealed is the new creation (2 Cor. 5:17; Gal. 6:15). The old creation was something created by God's power through His speaking. Although God created the old creation, it did not contain God. The new creation is essentially different from the old creation because the new creation has God wrought into it. The seventeen messages given during the previous term of the full-time training were on the section of Isaiah that corresponds to the old creation. Now we begin the remaining messages, which are on the new creation.

· God's Two Creations Making the Boundary between the Old Testament and the New Testament

God's two creations make the boundary between the Old Testament and the New Testament. In this training time, do you intend to merely polish, perfect, refine, and improve your old creation? Perhaps you are aware of certain defects and shortages in your old-creation being. Did you come here with the concept that you were coming to some kind of "reform school" or "finishing school" in order to be repaired and patched up, or did you come to learn how to become a new creation?

In the First Thirty-nine Chapters of Isaiah, the Old Creation Being Covered, Including God's Chastisement of Israel and His Judgment of the Gentiles, Whereas in the Last Twenty-seven Chapters, the Center of Isaiah's Prophecy Being the New Creation

In the first thirty-nine chapters of Isaiah, the old creation is covered, including God's chastisement of Israel and His judgment of the Gentiles, whereas in the last twenty-seven chapters, the center of Isaiah's prophecy is the new creation. We need to make our being a new creation, but this is easier said than done because our natural man is always lamenting over his sad state and is always longing to improve the old creation. We need to be aware that there is a danger of becoming subjective and even fixated on how natural we are and becoming discouraged to the point of despair because of our natural being. Therefore, we should be comforted with the real fact that we are becoming a new creation. Over the next six months, we will become newer than we are today. The new creation is the center and focus of this series of messages.

The Coming of the New Creation Not Involving the Immediate End of the Old Creation

The coming of the new creation does not involve the immediate end of the old creation. We should not expect our old creation to disappear any time soon. If the old creation were to disappear immediately, this would put us in great peril, for most of our being would be empty, making our latter state worse than the first (cf. Luke 11:24-26). We must realize that we are all in the "cocoon stage" and that the old creation is not going away in this age, neither will it ever get any better. Within the old creation, the new creation, comprised of redeemed humanity mingled with God, is increasing. Physically and psychologically, we are keenly aware of the old creation. By the infusion of the Lord's faith into us, we can stand against our feelings and declare the glorious fact: "If anyone is in Christ, he is a new creation. The old things have passed away; behold, they have become new" (2 Cor. 5:17). Not only a few things or some things, but all things have become new. This is our standing in Christ.

Experientially, we have the old creation outwardly and the new creation inwardly. We all need to receive grace to accept our complicated situation. We are all the same. Outwardly we have the old creation, and inwardly we have the new creation. The Lord wants not only to expose the old creation but also to reduce it to nothing so that there is room in our redeemed being for the Triune God in resurrection.

After the New Creation Comes, the Old Creation Remaining for a Period of Time

After the new creation comes, the old creation remains for a period of time. This period of time is our whole human life in this age. The last time that I visited Brother Lee in the last hours of his life, outwardly I saw a very elderly man dying in the old creation, but in my inner being I realized that within that dying, old-creation body, there was a splendid new creation. This is good news, particularly to those of us who are no longer young. We are going to have a brand new body that will never become sick or tired and will never die. This is our God-ordained destiny.

The End of the Millennial Kingdom Being the Termination of the Old Creation as Well as the Completion, the Consummation, of the New Creation as Signified by the New Jerusalem in the New Heaven and New Earth

The end of the millennial kingdom will be the termination of the old creation as well as the completion, the consummation, of the new creation as signified by the New Jerusalem in the new heaven and new earth (Rev. 21:1-2).

First Corinthians 15:45 Implying Two Creations

First Corinthians 15:45 implies two creations. This verse has two parts, implying two creations. "The first man, Adam, became a living soul"; this refers to the old creation. "The last Adam" implies the termination of the old creation. The life-giving Spirit is the unique element of the new creation in resurrection.

The Old Creation Being with Man as a Living Soul to Be the Center

The old creation is with man as a living soul to be the center (v. 45a). Many of those in the full-time training have testified of their decision not to improve, polish, refine, or perfect their old creation.

This means that they want to learn to not be "a living soul," that is, a soulish person who lives in the soul, by the soul, and for the soul. Overcomers have learned this to the point that they do not love their soul-life even unto death (Rev. 12:11). The fact is that we will lose our soul-life. In order to be delivered from the old creation, we need the new creation to be our center. However, the old creation is centered in the soul with the soul-life.

Because God Created Adam a Living Soul, His Main Part Being the Soul, Which Is for the Old Creation

Because God created Adam a living soul, his main part was the soul, which was for the old creation (Gen. 2:7). Not all our souls are the same size. Some of us have big souls, whereas others have little souls. First Thessalonians 5:14 exhorts us to comfort and console the fainthearted. *Fainthearted* here literally means "little-souled;" that is, "narrow and feeble in the capacity of mind, will, and emotion" (footnote 2). Some have big souls and are able to endure much, whereas some have narrow and feeble souls. God sovereignly brings all these kinds of different souls together in the Body of Christ. This helps us to learn to live in another realm, the realm of the mingled spirit.

In Principle, If We Live in Our Soul, by Our Soul, or for Our Soul, Our Being in the Old Creation

The Soul Being the Center and Lifeline of the Old Creation

In principle, if we live in our soul, by our soul, or for our soul, we are in the old creation (1 Cor. 2:14). The soul is the center and lifeline of the old creation. It is quite radical to not live in the soul. The sisters should not live in their feelings, and the brothers should not live in their will or in their reasonings. We must learn not to live by the soul and for the soul. By design, the full-time training does not appeal to the soul. For example, some of the food served here may not appeal to the soul. The aim of the training is to feed the inner man, that is, to feed us with God, with Christ, with the Spirit, and with *zoe*, the divine life.

A Person May Be Moral, but If He Lives in the Soul, His Still Belonging to the Old Creation

A person may be moral, but if he lives in the soul, he still belongs to the old creation. We may be those who are moral, ethical, and religious, but who still live in the soul. This means that we still belong to the old creation. It may be more difficult for the Lord to deal with our successes than with our failures, for we may be strongly built up and even self-righteous when we compare ourselves to others. It is not the Lord's intention to perfect our soul in the old creation. Nevertheless, our soul needs to receive a lot of shepherding for the new creation. We should not try to be Spartan stoics, heroes, or martyrs in our self. We all need shepherding. The Lord is the Shepherd of our soul (1 Pet. 2:25), but He is shepherding our soul into the new creation.

The New Creation Being in Resurrection with the Life-giving Spirit as the Center and Lifeline

The new creation is in resurrection with the life-giving Spirit as the center and lifeline (1 Cor. 15:45b). Resurrection is the key. We are all being shepherded into resurrection. Some of you may be quite intelligent, even brilliant. We would not hold that against you because that is the way God created you. However, God wants to bring your intellect into resurrection. Then your mind, when it is set on the spirit, will be useful. Some of you are naturally able to speak; you were born eloquent. While we do not blame you for being naturally eloquent, neither will we extol you for it. You must go to Babylon if you are seeking to be praised for your natural man. The Lord, however, wants to bring all of our faculties into resurrection.

Christ Being the Last Adam Implying a Termination and Conclusion of the Old Creation

Christ being the last Adam implies a termination and conclusion of the old creation. Termination must be applied to our old creation, not theoretically but concretely in the midst of actual situations. Eventually, after some years or even decades, we will learn not to resist the termination but to submit to the Lord under His mighty hand (1 Pet. 5:6). Until then, we will be Jacob, but eventually we will no longer be Jacob but Israel. We will simply humble ourselves under God's mighty hand and let Him do whatever is in His heart concerning us.

On one hand, you will all receive the same training, which is open, public, and consistent for all of you. On the other hand, you will each receive a particular training, not designed by the trainers but designed by God Himself. I hope that you will be willing to receive the training that God has prepared for you. John needed a different kind of training from Peter. John was impetuous, so he needed to be adjusted in a certain way. Peter also needed to be trained, but in a different way. We are not here in the way of a movement. On one hand, we are in something corporate, but on the other hand, we are also in something very personal according to the principle of John 21. We should not ask, as Peter did concerning John, saying, "What about this man?" (v. 21). The Lord's response was, "If I want him to remain until I come, what is that to you? You follow Me" (v. 22). It was as if the Lord were saying, "Do not ask me concerning anyone else; John may live until I come, but you will be martyred." Corporately, we receive the Lord's word, yet personally, we must contact the Lord day by day and let Him gain whatever He wants to gain in us. We are who we are; we will never be someone else. Eventually, we will say, as Paul did, "By the grace of God I am what I am" (1 Cor. 15:10). We need to let the Lord train us.

The New Creation Coming into Being by Resurrection

The new creation comes into being by resurrection. The more we touch resurrection life, the more we experience the new creation.

The Germinating Element of the New Creation Being the Resurrected Christ as the Life-giving Spirit

The germinating element of the new creation is the resurrected Christ as the life-giving Spirit. As *Hymns*, #1113 says, "Oh, He's the wonderful Spirit in us, / He's the wonderful Spirit in us! / God is in the Son, the Son's the Spirit now— / He's the wonderful Spirit in us!" He is wonderful, He is the Spirit, and He is in us. The life-giving Spirit is the very element that produces the new creation. Day by day, hour by hour, and eventually, even moment by moment, we must choose— "Will it be my soul, or will it be the mingled spirit?" Overcomers learn to deny the soul-life and live in the mingled spirit; furthermore, they are produced by denying the soul-life and living in the mingled spirit.

In Isaiah 40 Our Having a Comparison between Hezekiah, a Godly Man Who Was Still in the Old Creation, and a Regenerated and Transformed Person in the New Creation

In Isaiah 40 we have a comparison between Hezekiah, a godly man who was still in the old creation, and a regenerated and transformed person in the new creation (v. 31). Here is a comparison. Hezekiah was pious, godly, and a man of prayer, but he was altogether in the old creation (see *The Ministry of the Word*, vol. 14, no. 12, msg. 16).

In Isaiah 40 we see a person who is born again by the Word of God, a person who is transformed, and a person who has stopped himself and is waiting on the Lord. Those who are still in their twenties may find it quite difficult to wait. To them, having to wait for two years seems like an eternity. This is because the natural life is very active and cannot stand doing nothing. In Isaiah 40 we see someone who is waiting on Jehovah, which causes him to renew his strength and mount up on eagle's wings, typifying the power of resurrection. Then he runs and is not weary, and he walks and does not faint. Many of the brothers who serve as trainers are bearing one burden after another. They are here today, they are in Russia tomorrow, and then they are off to Singapore, Southern California, Israel, and Mexico. They are literally mounting up on eagle's wings. They are learning to run and not faint and to walk and not become weary.

Whom do you want to be like? Do you want to be a pious and godly Hezekiah who is still very much for himself? Or do you want to learn of Paul, a representative of the new creation, to be terminated, germinated, resurrected, transformed, and empowered by the resurrection life itself? Resurrection is not a doctrine; resurrection is a person and a reality. This person is the Spirit. With this as the foundation and the goal, we can go on to consider two intimate matters in Isaiah 40.

IN ISAIAH 40 CHRIST BEING REVEALED AS JEHOVAH THE SAVIOR

In Isaiah 40 Christ is revealed as Jehovah the Savior. First, this chapter reveals Christ as Jehovah the Savior. We need to see Christ as Jehovah the Savior. This is the first of two particular burdens in this section of the message. My speaking alone is not adequate; the Lord needs to touch you with something of His very Being. The book of Job reveals that Job was a man who had heard about God and who believed all that he had heard. Nevertheless, in chapter 42 he says, "I had heard of You by the hearing of the ear, / But now my eye has seen You; / Therefore I abhor myself, and I repent / In dust and ashes" (vv. 5-6). This is often the case with those who have grown up in the church life and have been blessed from their youth to hear many things in children's meeting, in junior high retreats, in high school mountain trips, and in college conferences. This is the Lord's preparation for them to have a great turn. Eventually, they also will be able to say, "I had heard of You, but now I see You."

I have a deep burden that we would know the Lord as Jehovah. It may take us some time to feel comfortable with using the name Jehovah for God. Perhaps it is because there is a well-known antichrist group that misuses this name. The following is a crystal clear word of testimony from the Introduction in the Recovery Version of the Bible as to why we use the name *Jehovah:*

> The reader will quickly note the use of the name Jehovah in this translation. In spite of the historical linguistic arguments against its use, no other rendering of the Tetragrammaton has the same heritage that Jehovah has in classic English literature. While our forebears in translation, based on a faulty understanding of the Hebrew vowel pointing, might have mistakenly transliterated the divine name, their great influence has firmly embedded the name Jehovah into the English language, as evidenced by its inclusion in our modern dictionaries. Our employing of the name Jehovah is motivated not by linguistic considerations but by a recognition of the heritage of the English language and, more importantly, by a desire to be true to our convictions as translators that the name of God, revealed and delivered to His saints (Exo. 3:16; 20:7), should be deliberately rendered in the translation of the Hebrew Scriptures. Deference to ancient religion and confusion from modern sectarians are no reasons to shrink back from the use and enjoyment of God's personal and revealed name.

We use the name *Jehovah* because we have a very solid basis in the language and in the proper understanding of the text. The Old Testament in Hebrew uses the word translated Jehovah over six thousand five hundred times.

I would like to fellowship four matters related to this name. First, Jehovah is a name of intimacy. God uses this name for His personal relationship with His people. The name *God,* a translation of the Hebrew word *Elohim,* is more general, denoting God in relation to His creation. However, when God reveals Himself as Jehovah, it means that He wants man to know Him as a person. The first mention of Jehovah is in Genesis 2:4. Then in 4:26 it says in relation to Enosh, "At that time men began to call upon the name of Jehovah." Nevertheless, the substance of this name was not revealed until Exodus 3, when God had brought Moses to the point where he could have an intimate, personal, direct, and face-to-face relationship with God Himself (vv. 13-14). It was then that God appeared to Moses as Jehovah.

Jehovah is God's name of intimacy, the name of God in His relationship with man. Married couples often have names for one another that they use only between themselves. No one else has the privilege of using or even knowing those names. Jehovah has opened up His Being to us. He desires to visit with us and be intimate with us. He wants to bring us into a relationship of intimacy with Him so that whenever we call, Lord Jesus, we touch a sweetness that has been lacking in our lives. We are not calling the air. We are calling on a wonderful person who comes to us not merely as Elohim, El Shaddai, or Adonai but as Jehovah.

Second, we need to be impressed that the name *Jehovah* comes from the Hebrew word *havah,* which means "to be," or "being." Jehovah's name means "I Am." His name is I AM WHO I AM (3:14). He confronts us with the stupendous reality that He is the unique self-existing Being. We cannot say that He is in the universe or even part of the universe; He simply *is.* Many years ago some students put up an advertisement for a Christian meeting on the college campus where I studied. An atheist (a rather rude one) wrote on their sign, "There is no God." A Christian, to counter the atheist, wrote under his statement, "So nice you could create yourself." Atheists are often clever in a devilish way. This one wrote in answer, "Who created God?" That Christian had no response. However, he should have quoted Exodus 3:14: "I AM WHO I AM." God, the Lord Jehovah, can say, "I am the only uncaused Being. I simply exist. I have the power to exist in Myself." Our mind buckles under such a thought, but eventually we must capitulate. If we need to struggle, it is okay until we experience the magnificent defeat. Then we will be able to truly testify, "O Lord, You are. You are who You are. You are the I Am."

Third, the name Jehovah is an incomplete sentence, "I Am...." He is what? He is the divine ellipsis. "I Am..." implies "I Am anything and everything." Jehovah is saying, "I, Myself, Am every positive thing. I want to be every positive thing to you. If you ask Me for health or healing, I may give those things to you, but in My heart I want to *be* those things to you." If we need strength, we should not ask the Lord to give us strength. Instead, we should say, "Lord, be my strength." We may say, "Lord, I cannot give this message. How can a man speak concerning the great I Am?" The Lord would say, "I am the message; I am the word; I am life; I am love; I am endurance; I am understanding; I am grace; I am faith; I am peace; I am authority; I am power; I am everything." He wants to be the I Am to all men. The sooner we realize this, the better. Many of the things that happen to us are actually His training us to realize that we need Him as our everything. As *Hymns*, #82 says, "O how I love Him! How I adore Him! / My breath, my sunshine, my all in all!" He is not only the I Am, the self-existing and ever-existing One, He is also the I Am as everything to us. Brother Nee was graced by the Lord at a young age to learn through his sufferings to know Jehovah, the I Am. We may continue, out of habit, to ask the Lord to give us this or that, but eventually we will all stop asking for things. We have the I Am as our everything. He is whatever we need.

Fourth, in times of great loss, we need comfort. The real comfort is our I Am. I have learned and am still learning this lesson in my human life. I had a personal experience of this when I sold my mother's house, an old four-room miner's house in a rural area of upper Michigan. My father died last year in January, and my mother followed him in September. Eventually, we sold all their possessions and also the house. By the end of that year, my father was gone, my mother was gone, all their possessions were gone, and their house was gone. This caused a sense of grief in me; it seemed that everything was gone, including the opportunity to see them every year. Yet I also had the realization that Jehovah is I Am. We cannot hold onto anything or anyone in the old creation. Some of these losses are deep and profound, but we know Jehovah as I Am. We know Him as the God of all comfort (2 Cor. 1:3). When we touch Him, we touch a person who is everything to us. He does not merely fill up the gap; He is the wonderful all-inclusive One.

Isaiah uses the name of Jehovah about four hundred and fifty times. Therefore, we may say that Isaiah was the prophet of Jehovah. In Isaiah 37:20 he says, "You alone are Jehovah." Isaiah reveals Jehovah in at least fourteen aspects:

1) Jehovah is the unique God (44:6b; 43:10).
2) Jehovah is the eternal God, the First and the Last (40:28; 44:6).
3) Jehovah is the Creator (37:16; 40:28; 44:24; 45:18).
4) Jehovah is the speaking One (1:2, 10).

5) Jehovah is the Judge, the Lawmaker, and the King (33:22). He is all three parts of God's divine government. The United States government seems to be modeled after Jehovah Himself. He is our King, corresponding to the President, the head of the executive branch; He is our Lawmaker, corresponding to the Congress, the legislative branch; and He is our Judge, corresponding to the Supreme Court, the judicial branch. As our Lawmaker, Jehovah makes the laws; as our King, He enforces the laws; and as our Judge, He interprets the laws.

6) Jehovah is the Holy One of Israel (30:15).

7) Jehovah is the Potter (64:8). This also indicates that we are the clay.

8) Jehovah is our Father (63:16; 64:8).

9) Jehovah is our Redeemer (47:4; 49:26).

10) Jehovah is our Savior and our salvation (43:11; 12:2).

11) Jehovah is our strength and our song (12:2).

12) Jehovah is our Husband (54:5).

13) Jehovah is God of all the kingdoms of the earth (37:16).

14) Jehovah will reign in Mount Zion and in Jerusalem (24:23).

Isaiah 66:23 says, "All flesh will come / To bow down before Me, says Jehovah." That day will come. The book of Isaiah is a marvelous revelation of Jehovah.

Jehovah Meaning "He Who Was, Who Is, and Who Will Be"

God's Name Being I Am; His Name Being Simply the Verb to Be

I Am *Denoting the One Who Is Self-existing, the One Whose Being Depends on Nothing Apart from Himself*

Jehovah means "He who was, who is, and who will be" (Exo. 3:14). God's name is I Am; His name is simply the verb *to be*. *I Am* denotes the One who is self-existing, the One whose being depends on nothing apart from Himself. If I were to ask, "Where were you thirty-five years ago?" you might say, "I was not here." If you are a young person, you did not exist. If you are older, you may say, "I was in such-and-such a place," but what if I were to ask, "Where were you one hundred years ago?" Jehovah is the self-existing and ever-existing One. He does not depend on anything apart from Himself.

*The I Am Being Also the Ever-existing One; That Is, His Existing
Eternally, Having neither Beginning nor Ending*

The I Am is also the ever-existing One; that is, He exists eternally,
having neither beginning nor ending.

*Apart from God, All Else Being Nothing;
His Being the Only One Who Is,
the Only One Who Has the Reality of Being*

Apart from God, all else is nothing; He is the only One who is, the
only One who has the reality of being (Isa. 40:12-18).

As the Self-existing, Ever-existing One, God Being
the Reality of Every Positive Thing; the Gospel of John
Revealing That He Is All That We Need

As the self-existing, ever-existing One, God is the reality of every
positive thing; the Gospel of John reveals that He is all that we need
(6:48; 10:11; 8:12; 11:25; 14:6). John 6:48 says, "I am the bread of life."
John 10:11 says, "I am the good Shepherd." John 8:12 says, "I am the
light of the world." John 11:25 says, "I am the resurrection and the life."

God Requiring Us Only to Believe That He Is

God requires us only to believe that He is (Heb. 11:6). Verse 6 says,
"He who comes forward to God must believe that He is."

Jesus Being Jehovah

Jesus is Jehovah (Exo. 3:14; John 18:4-6). This is a marvelous break-
through revelation. Jesus the Nazarene is Jehovah! He is I am. In
Exodus 3:14 God said to Moses, "I AM." In John 18 Jesus was in the
garden when some came to arrest Him. He asked them, "Whom do you
seek? They answered Him, Jesus the Nazarene. He said to them, I
am...When therefore He said to them, I am, they drew back and fell to
the ground" (vv. 4-6). Here is a Galilean who is about to give Himself
into the hands of the Jews and the Gentiles to be crucified. Those who
came to arrest Him said they were seeking Jesus the Nazarene, but He
answered, "I am." He is the only One who can say "I am" in an absolute
sense. This is a tremendous vision—Jesus is the I Am.

I do not advise arguing with the so-called Jehovah's Witnesses. It is
best to either ignore them, or exercise your whole being to look them

in the eye and say, "Jesus Christ is Jehovah, God come in the flesh. He is not merely a god created by Jehovah; Jesus is Jehovah."

We can give the devil a simple, three-word message: "Jesus is Jehovah." He is the great I Am. We really appreciate *Hymns*, #82, especially stanza 3, which says, "Without reluctance, / Flesh and blood His substance / He took the form of man, / Revealed the hidden plan. / O glorious myst'ry, / Sacrifice of Calv'ry, / And now I know Thou art the great 'I AM.'" We not merely believe but also know that He is the great I Am. The chorus continues, "The great Creator became my Savior." Jehovah became a Jew who was born in Bethlehem and grew up in Nazareth. The great Creator became a Galilean. We should shout again and again, "Jehovah is Jesus! Jesus is Jehovah!" When we call, "Lord Jesus," we are calling on Jehovah, the intimate One, the self-existing One, the ever-existing One, the all-inclusive One, and the comforting One. Because of our weaknesses in the old creation, there may be times when all we are able to do is say, "Lord Jesus." As Stephen was being martyred, his last words were, "Lord Jesus, receive my spirit" (Acts 7:59). What a wonderful way to pass from this life with our last words being Jehovah. Jehovah is the I Am, Jesus, and Jehovah my Savior and my salvation.

The Lord Jesus Being I Am—the Eternal, Self-existing, Ever-existing God, the One Who Is Everything to Us

The Lord Jesus is I Am—the eternal, self-existing, ever-existing God, the One who is everything to us (John 8:24, 28, 58). Verse 24 says, "Unless you believe that I am, you will die in your sins." To any antichrist who does not believe that Jesus is God—this is the gospel. Unless you believe that Jesus is the I Am, Jehovah, you will die in your sins. Verse 28 says, "Jesus therefore said to them, When you lift up the Son of Man, then you will know that I am." The One crucified on the cross was Jehovah in the flesh. In verse 58 He declares, "Before Abraham came into being, I am."

The Name Jesus Meaning "Jehovah the Savior" or "The Salvation of Jehovah"

The name Jesus means "Jehovah the Savior" or "the salvation of Jehovah" (Matt. 1:21).

When We Call on Jesus, the Whole Universe Realizing That We Are Calling on Jehovah as Our Savior, Jehovah as Our Salvation

When we call on Jesus, the whole universe realizes that we are calling on Jehovah as our Savior, Jehovah as our salvation (Rom. 10:12-13). When Stephen died, he was a duplication of Christ. His last words virtually were the same as two of the Lord's words on the cross. Stephen said, "Lord, do not hold this sin against them" (Acts 7:60). On the cross Jesus said, "Father, forgive them, for they do not know what they are doing" (Luke 23:34). Stephen also said, "Lord Jesus, receive my spirit!" (Acts 7:59). On the cross, Jesus said, "Father, into Your hands I commit My spirit" (Luke 23:46). Saul of Tarsus observed Stephen dying and calling on Yeshua, on Jehovah the Savior. We all can be overcomers, because we all can call on the Lord Jesus and be saved, "For the same Lord is Lord of all and rich to all who call upon Him" (Rom. 10:12).

The following is a simple new song that we can sing or declare in a sweet spirit of worship:

> He is I Am, He is I Am
> The only One, the One who's real
> He is I Am.
>
> His name—I Am, His name—I Am
> He's everything, He's all we need.
> His name—I Am.
>
> You are I Am, You are I Am
> Yes, I believe, believe He is
> You are I Am.
>
> O Jesus Lord, You are I Am
> Jehovah God, come in the flesh
> The Great I Am.

We can touch Him using His name of intimacy. He is I Am. He is the only One who is real. He is everything. He is all we need. We believe He is, and we can worship the Lord that He is the I Am. There may be times when we have a broken heart, and we may not have the energy or the words for complicated prayers. At those moments, I Am is who we need.

CHRIST AS THE GLORY OF JEHOVAH BEING
THE CENTER OF THE GOSPEL FOR THE NEW CREATION

Christ as the glory of Jehovah is the center of the gospel for the new creation (Isa. 40:5; 2 Cor. 4:3-6; 5:17; Gal. 6:15). This wonderful I Am, Jehovah, is our Lord Jesus Christ, and our Christ as the glory of Jehovah is the center of the gospel for the new creation. Isaiah 40:5 says, "The glory of Jehovah will be revealed."

In the Bible, Glory Signifying the Expression of God

In the Bible, glory signifies the expression of God (John 1:1, 14). Jesus, as the glory of Jehovah, is coming to shine Himself into our being. He is the effulgence of God's glory. His birth was the sun shining, and He will come again as the Sun of righteousness. This wonderful Jesus, the Savior, the great I Am, is the center of the gospel, and this gospel is the gospel of glory.

Christ as the Image of God
Being the Effulgence of God's Glory,
and This Effulgence Being like the Shining of the Sun

Christ as the image of God is the effulgence of God's glory, and this effulgence is like the shining of the sun (Heb. 1:3). He wants to come and visit you by shining on you. When you call on Him in a personal way, He answers by shining. He will say, "Here I am. I would like to radiate Myself into you. Please open to Me. Don't try to be different. Don't look at yourself and turn inward. Just behold My face. Turn your heart to Me." Second Corinthians 3:16 and 18 say, "Whenever their heart turns to the Lord, the veil is taken away...We all with unveiled face, beholding and reflecting like a mirror the glory of the Lord, are being transformed into the same image from glory to glory, even as from the Lord Spirit." The words *we all* refer not only to the strong or victorious. *The glory of the Lord* is the glory of Jehovah in the face of Jesus Christ (cf. 4:6). When we behold Him, He shines into us, and a metabolic reaction takes places within us so that the image that we behold is reproduced in our being. The light shining into us does a lot—it heals us, swallows up our death, infuses us with God, and gives us faith.

Christ's First Coming Being the Rising of the Sun

Christ's first coming was the rising of the sun (Luke 1:78).

When Christ Appeared, the Glory of Jehovah Appearing to Be Seen by the God-seekers and Christ-believers

When Christ appeared, the glory of Jehovah appeared to be seen by the God-seekers and Christ-believers (Isa. 40:5, 9).

The Gospel Being the Gospel of the Glory of Christ, Which Illuminates, Radiates, and Shines into the Heart of Man

The gospel is the gospel of the glory of Christ, which illuminates, radiates, and shines into the heart of man (2 Cor. 4:4). When we go out to speak the gospel on the campuses, we should pray, "Lord, shine out through us. Our going is Your shining." Whenever we contact Jehovah, He will shine. Paul says, "Even if our gospel is veiled, it is veiled in those who are perishing, in whom the god of this age has blinded the thoughts of the unbelievers that the illumination of the gospel of the glory of Christ, who is the image of God, might not shine on them" (vv. 3-4). The enemy's strategy is to blind the thoughts of the young people. God's strategy is to have us pray in the name of Jesus to bind the god of this age. Those on the gospel teams are not too young to pray with authority in the name of Jesus to bind the blinding work of the god of this age and to loose the minds of the young people to receive God's shining. Whether those we contact agree verbally or not, our coming to them will open their hearts, and God will shine into them through us.

The Illumination, the Enlightenment, That Makes the Glory of Christ's Gospel Known to Us Issuing from the Shining of God in Our Hearts

The illumination, the enlightenment, that makes the glory of Christ's gospel known to us issues from the shining of God in our hearts (v. 6). Verse 6 says, "Because the God who said, Out of darkness light shall shine, is the One who shined in our hearts to illuminate the knowledge of the glory of God in the face of Jesus Christ." We can have this kind of face-to-face fellowship with Jesus Christ. We can say, "Lord, I come to You with an open face, with an unveiled face, and with an open and turned heart." I pray every morning, "Lord, I turn my heart to You. I open my heart to You. I draw near to You with my turned and opened heart. Lord, I do not want anything from You, and

I do not want You to do anything for me. I just want You Yourself. I only want to behold Your glorious, shining, radiant face."

The Old Creation Coming through God's Outward Shining in Darkness, but the New Creation Being Accomplished by God's Inward Shining in Our Hearts

The old creation came through God's outward shining in darkness, but the new creation is accomplished by God's inward shining in our hearts (Gen. 1:3; 2 Cor. 4:6). The Lord is going to make us a new creation by shining in our hearts. We just need to let Him shine. As an adaptation of a simple children's song, we can sing, "This glorious light of Thine, / I'm going to let it shine. / Into this little heart of mine / I'm going to let it shine / Let it shine, Let it shine, Let it shine." When it comes to the truth, we are high and deep, but when it comes to contacting the Lord, we should be the most simple people. Even this very moment, we can turn our heart and open our heart to Him. We can call, "Lord Jesus," and He will answer right away. He comes as God's glory shining into us. Then we can pray, "Lord Jesus, shine in me. Shine into my whole being."

God's Shining in Our Hearts Bringing into Us a Treasure, the Christ of Glory, Who Is the Embodiment of God to Be Our Life and Our Everything

God's shining in our hearts brings into us a treasure, the Christ of glory, who is the embodiment of God to be our life and our everything (2 Cor. 4:7).

Today, the Glory of Jehovah Being the Resurrected Christ as the Life-giving Spirit Dwelling in Our Spirit

Today, the glory of Jehovah is the resurrected Christ as the life-giving Spirit dwelling in our spirit (1 Cor. 15:45b; 2 Cor. 3:17).

If We Would Experience the Lord's Shining, Our Needing to Have Direct, Personal, Affectionate, and Intimate Contact with Him

If we would experience the Lord's shining, we need to have direct, personal, affectionate, and intimate contact with Him (Psa. 27:4; 2 Cor.

3:18). This is the personal part—the part that is direct, affectionate, and intimate. We can say with sweetness, "Dear Lord Jesus, my Jehovah the Savior. Lord Jesus, You are the great I Am. I love You."

Prayer: Lord Jesus, we love You. With sweetness in our heart we say that we delight to look You in the face. The glory of God is shining from Your face right now. We open to Your shining. Make us a new creation by Your shining. O Lord, thank You for becoming a man in the flesh, for passing through death and resurrection to become the Spirit. Now the Spirit is the extract of Your Being, and You are dwelling in our spirit. We turn to You to behold You, delight in You, enjoy You, and experience You all the time. Bless all the trainees with countless hours of gazing into Your face. May everyone know by direct and personal experience what it is to look at You and to behold Your face in glory. We consecrate ourselves, Lord, to turn to You and to look at You. Praise You, Lord!—R. K.

THE DIVINE ECONOMY IN THE BOOK OF ISAIAH

The Revelation of the Lord Jehovah—
the Manifestation of the Lord Jesus Christ
(Message 19)

Scripture Reading: Isa. 40:5-11; John 1:1, 14; 1 Tim. 3:16; Col. 2:9

I. The last twenty-seven chapters of Isaiah can be considered the extract of the real significance of the New Testament; this extract concerns a person—the Lord Jehovah, the One whom we call the Lord Jesus Christ—Isa. 40:10; Phil. 2:11; Rom. 13:14.

II. What is covered in Isaiah 40 is the revealing of the Lord Jehovah—v. 9:

   A. *Revealing* means "manifesting"; the revealing is the manifestation.

   B. The revealing of the Lord Jehovah is the appearing of the very God, and this Lord Jehovah, the very God, is the Lord Jesus Christ:

      1. Jesus, who is Jehovah, is our God—John 1:1, 14; 8:24, 28, 58.

      2. The revealing of Jehovah is the appearing of Jesus—Matt. 1:21.

      3. Jehovah is revealed through His speaking; the more we listen to the speaking of the Lord Jesus, the more we see Jehovah—Isa. 40:5; John 1:1.

   C. Christ is the complete God manifested in the flesh—1 Tim. 3:16:

      1. The Word, who is God, became flesh—John 1:1, 14:

         a. God, who is the Word, is not a partial God but the entire God—God the Son, God the Father, and God the Spirit.

         b. The Word is God's definition, explanation, and expression; hence, the Word who became flesh is God's definition, explanation, and expression in the flesh.

    2. In incarnation Christ is God manifested in the flesh—
1 Tim. 3:16:

      a. He was manifested in the flesh not only as the Son but
as the entire God—the Father, the Son, and the Spirit.

      b. The entire God was incarnated; thus, Christ in incarnation is the entire God manifested in the flesh.

    3. In Christ dwells all the fullness of the Godhead bodily—
Col. 2:9:

      a. *All the fullness of the Godhead* refers to the entire Godhead, the complete God.

      b. Christ is the embodiment of the Triune God; the Father, the Son, and the Spirit are all embodied in Him.

D. Christ as the glory of Jehovah is the center of the gospel for the new creation—Isa. 40:5; 2 Cor. 4:3-6; 5:17:

    1. Since glory signifies the expression of God, to say that God is glorified means that He is expressed—John 17:4.

    2. Christ as the image of God is the effulgence of God's glory—Heb. 1:3.

    3. The gospel is the gospel of the glory of Christ, which illuminates, radiates, and shines into the heart of man—
2 Cor. 4:3-6.

    4. Today the glory of Jehovah is the resurrected Christ as the life-giving Spirit dwelling in our spirit—1 Cor. 15:45b;
2 Cor. 3:17; 2 Tim. 4:22.

III. God's desire in His economy is to have a corporate expression of Himself for His glory; God wants such a corporate expression so that He may be glorified—1 Tim. 3:15-16; Eph. 3:21; Rev. 21:10-11:

A. God's good pleasure, the desire of His heart, is to have many sons for the expression of His Son so that He may be expressed in the Son through the Spirit—Eph. 1:5, 9; Rom. 8:29.

B. First Timothy 3:15-16 indicates not only that Christ Himself as the Head is the manifestation of God in the flesh but also that the church as the Body is the manifestation of God in the flesh—the mystery of godliness:

    1. God has manifested Himself in Christ as an individual expression in the flesh—v. 16; John 1:1, 14; Col. 2:9.

2. Now God is manifested in the church, the Body of Christ, as the enlarged corporate expression in the flesh—Eph. 1:22-23; 1 Tim. 3:15-16:

   a. *Godliness* in verse 16 refers to God as life lived out in the church to be expressed.

   b. The manifestation of God in the flesh began with Christ when He was on earth.

   c. The manifestation of God in the flesh continues with the church, which is the increase, enlargement, and multiplication of the manifestation of God in the flesh.

C. God is glorified, expressed, in the church—Eph. 3:21:

  1. This glory comes to us with God and, after being worked into us, will return to God with us.

  2. God's glory is wrought into the church, and He is expressed in the church:

   a. The dispensing of the Triune God issues in glory—Rom. 8:18, 21.

   b. We are being transformed into the same image from glory to glory—2 Cor. 3:18.

   c. In the oneness in the divine glory, the believers, their self having been fully denied, enjoy the glory of the Father as the factor of their perfected oneness and thus express God in a corporate, built-up way—John 17:22; cf. 7:18.

D. An outstanding feature of the New Jerusalem is that it has the glory of God, His expression—Rev. 21:10-11:

  1. The entire New Jerusalem will bear the glory of God, which is God Himself shining out through the city.

  2. The glory of God—God Himself being manifested—will be the content of the New Jerusalem, for the city will be completely filled with His glory.

THE REVELATION OF THE LORD JEHOVAH—
THE MANIFESTATION OF THE LORD JESUS CHRIST

In this message we will continue our fellowship on Isaiah 40. In the previous message we saw that Christ, as the glory of Jehovah, is the center of the gospel for the new creation. The particular burden of that message was that we would see, realize, and experience Jesus as Jehovah. The Lord Jesus is the I Am; He is Jehovah God come in the flesh. He is the only One who can declare, "Before Abraham came into being, I am" (John 8:58). He is the very "I AM WHO I AM" manifested to Moses in Exodus 3:14. The name *Jehovah* is first used in Genesis 2, but the meaning of this name is revealed only in Exodus 3. Moreover, in Message 1 we presented the matter of the glory of Jehovah shining into us to make us a new creation. Now we will consider Isaiah 40 again from a very similar angle but with a different emphasis.

The title of this message is "The Revelation of the Lord Jehovah— the Manifestation of the Lord Jesus Christ." Isaiah 40 is concerned with God's manifestation. Verse 9 says, "Behold your God!" To behold God, He must be revealed, expressed, and manifested. The Lord Jehovah revealed in Isaiah 40 is the Lord Jesus Christ manifested in the New Testament. During the time for prophesying after the previous message, one of the brothers spoke an enlightening word. He said that a veil had been removed and that he had received the shining of the light to realize that he no longer has an Old Testament God and a New Testament God; he realized that the Old Testament Jehovah is the New Testament Jesus. We do not have two Gods, nor do we have a God who is drastically different in the New Testament from what He was in the Old Testament. The Old Testament reveals the Lord Jehovah, and the New Testament manifests the Lord Jesus Christ. Eventually, every knee, whether in heaven, on earth, or under the earth, will bow, and every tongue will confess that Jesus Christ is the Lord—the very Jehovah.

Now we need to dwell on this matter of the Lord's manifestation, revelation, and expression. God's expression is a matter of His glory. Actually, God's entire economy is wrapped up with His glory. Genesis 2:7 reveals that we are vessels, and according to Romans 9:23, we are vessels of mercy, which God has before prepared unto glory. We were created to contain and express the Triune God, who is the God of glory. The Father is called the Father of glory (Eph. 1:17), the Lord is the Lord of glory (1 Cor. 2:8), and the Spirit is called the Spirit of glory (1 Pet. 4:14). According to Romans 3:23, to sin is to fall short of the glory of God. Thus, sin is the expression of something other than God. Even if it is an expression of our good, natural virtues, it is at best an expression of our good self, which falls short of God's glory. God measures us by His glory. Actually, sin is the negation of Genesis 1:26. This verse reveals that we were created in God's image in order to express God in glory and that we were charged to represent God with His authority for His dominion. Since sin is related to our falling short of God's glory (Rom. 3:23) and since sin is lawlessness (1 John 3:4), which is the total rebellion against God's authority, for man to sin is to fall short of God's intention in creating us in His image and for His dominion.

Nevertheless, the gospel, the good news, is the gospel of the glory of Christ. The Christ, who is the effulgence of God's glory (Heb. 1:3), became the Lamb of God (John 1:29), and He died on the cross as the fulfillment of the type of the bronze serpent (3:14). He was made sin for us (2 Cor. 5:21). Through His redemptive death He fulfilled all the requirements of God's righteousness, holiness, and glory. Hence, we can be redeemed, forgiven, cleansed, justified, and reconciled to God so that the very Christ of glory, the pneumatic Christ, can enter into our spirit as our hope of glory. Colossians 1:27 says, "To whom God willed to make known what are the riches of the glory of this mystery among the Gentiles, which is Christ in you, the hope of glory." After being regenerated, we begin the long process of transformation from one degree of glory to another degree of glory (2 Cor. 3:18), that is, from no glory to a little glory, from a little glory to more glory, from more glory to much glory, from much glory to mostly glory, and eventually from mostly glory to complete glory. Thus, God's full salvation leads to our glorification. The issue of the glorification of all believers will be the universal, corporate expression of the Triune God of glory—the New Jerusalem.

In Ephesians 3, after he utters such a marvelous prayer for us to experience Christ wrought into our being, Paul exclaims, "To Him be the glory in the church" (v. 21). Before the Lord Jesus died, He prayed for His glorification in John 17. He prayed that He would be glorified in resurrection and that this glorification in resurrection would cause all of His redeemed and regenerated people to be incorporated into Himself to become, together with Him, the corporate expression of the Triune God. As He prayed for His glorification, He also prayed for our oneness, that we would be one in the Father's name, which is to be one in the Father's divine life, and that we would be one in the sanctifying word, which is the divine reality, or truth. Then He prayed for the highest level of oneness, that we would be one in the divine glory. To be one in the divine glory, there cannot be any divisive factor of self-expression; rather, the self of every believer must be fully denied so that corporately we will shine forth the glory of God. The Lord's prayer in John 17 has yet to be fully answered; nevertheless, since the Lord Himself prayed for this, it will surely happen.

Second Corinthians 3:18 says that we are being transformed into the Lord's image from glory to glory. This glory is not merely an individual radiance but the glory for which the Lord prayed in John 17:22, saying, "The glory which You have given Me I have given to them, that they may be one, even as We are one." The self is inherently divisive, and the expression of the self causes division. Therefore, whenever we are in the self and express the self, we rob God of glory and bring division into the Body.

However, we are now in a process of transformation, and eventually we will become the very glory of God. *Hymns,* #501 says, "Thy Spirit will me saturate, / Every part will God permeate, / Deliv'ring me from the old man, / With all saints building for His plan." The Triune God of glory is permeating our every part. Day by day He is permeating the parts of our inner being a little more. We will have more glory after reading this message than we had when we began, for we are under the constant infusion of the God of glory. The ultimate consummation of this process will be the city of glory, the New Jerusalem. Revelation 21:9-11 says, "One of the seven angels who had the seven bowls full of the seven last plagues came and spoke with me, saying, Come here; I will show you the bride, the wife of the Lamb. And he carried me away in spirit onto a great and high mountain and showed me the holy city, Jerusalem, coming down out of heaven from God, having the glory of God." The God who is manifested in Isaiah 40 is the same God manifested in Revelation 21 and 22. When He is fully manifested, we will be included in that corporate manifestation of the God of glory. Hallelujah!

In brief, this is God's economy as it relates to God's glory. The God of glory wants a glorious corporate expression, and in order to gain this expression, we were created, redeemed, regenerated, and are being transformed and built up into the Body of Christ to become the New Jerusalem. The day is coming when God will be able to boast to the enemy's shame and point to the overcomers in the churches and say, "Satan, you made them sin. You caused them to live a life of self-glorification, a life of lawlessness, and a life that expresses you through the self. But now look at what I have built up in My recovery on the earth. At least in miniature, they are the glory of God, and this miniature will be enlarged and expanded until it becomes the New Jerusalem. But before that time, you, devil, will be cast into the lake of fire, and My overcomers will become the city of glory." The Bible has such a glorious conclusion!

THE LAST TWENTY-SEVEN CHAPTERS OF ISAIAH BEING CONSIDERED THE EXTRACT OF THE REAL SIGNIFICANCE OF THE NEW TESTAMENT; THIS EXTRACT CONCERNING A PERSON—THE LORD JEHOVAH THE ONE WHOM WE CALL THE LORD JESUS CHRIST

The last twenty-seven chapters of Isaiah can be considered the extract of the real significance of the New Testament; this extract concerns a person—the Lord Jehovah, the One whom we call the Lord Jesus Christ (Isa. 40:10; Phil. 2:11; Rom. 13:14). Isaiah 1—39 corresponds to the Old Testament with its thirty-nine books, and Isaiah 40—66 corresponds to the twenty-seven chapters of the New Testament. In essence Isaiah 40—66 is a revelation of the gospel, that is, the revelation of Christ as the Servant of Jehovah. The extract, essence, distillation, and spirit of these twenty-seven chapters reflects the real significance of the New Testament and concerns a person—the Lord Jehovah, which is the Old Testament designation of our Lord Jesus Christ. If we read the book of Revelation in a proper way, we will realize that it is not a book about locusts, beasts, or a woman riding on a beast; rather, it is the revelation of Jesus Christ. This is why the book is introduced, "The revelation of Jesus Christ..." (1:1). The center of the book of Revelation is a person—the Lord Jesus Christ.

WHAT IS COVERED IN ISAIAH 40
BEING THE REVEALING OF THE LORD JEHOVAH

What is covered in Isaiah 40 is the revealing of the Lord Jehovah (v. 9). The Lord Jehovah is the Old Testament Lord Jesus Christ, and the Lord Jesus Christ is the New Testament Lord Jehovah. When the Lord Jehovah was incarnated and thereby became a man, a God-man, He was manifested as the Lord Jesus Christ. The angel told Joseph, "You shall call His name Jesus" (Matt. 1:21). The name *Jesus* means "Jehovah the Savior" or "the salvation of Jehovah." When we speak of the revelation of the Lord Jehovah in Isaiah 40, we are simultaneously speaking of the manifestation of the Lord Jesus Christ, for the revelation of the Lord Jehovah is the manifestation of the Lord Jesus Christ.

Revealing Meaning "Manifesting";
the Revealing Being the Manifestation

Revealing means "manifesting"; the revealing is the manifestation. In the context of this message, *revealing* equals *manifesting*. Isaiah 40:5-11 says,

> Then the glory of Jehovah will be revealed, / And all flesh will see it together, / Because the mouth of Jehovah has spoken. / A voice said, Cry out. / And he said, What shall I cry? / All flesh is grass / And all its glory is like the flower of the field; / The grass withers, the flower fades, / Because the breath of Jehovah blows upon it. / Surely the people are grass. / The grass withers and the flower fades, / But the word of our God will stand forever. / Go up to a high mountain, / O Zion, who brings glad tidings; / Lift up your voice with power, / O Jerusalem, who brings glad tidings; / Lift it up, Do not be afraid. / Say to the cities of Judah, / Behold your God! / Behold, the Lord Jehovah will come as a mighty One, / And His arm will rule for Him. / Behold, His reward is with Him, / And His recompense before Him. / He will feed His flock as a Shepherd; / In His arm He will gather the lambs; / In His bosom He will carry them. / He will lead those who are nursing the young.

What a manifestation! With His might, with His reward, and ultimately with His shepherding heart, He will gather the lambs in His bosom. How sweet it is to meet in a home with many lambs and to sense that the manifested Lord Jesus Christ, the revealed Lord Jehovah, is there as a Shepherd gathering His lambs into His bosom. Hence, these verses speak of the revelation of the Lord Jehovah, which revelation is the manifestation of the Lord Jesus Christ.

The Revealing of the Lord Jehovah Being the Appearing of the Very God, and This Lord Jehovah, the Very God, Being the Lord Jesus Christ

The revealing of the Lord Jehovah is the appearing of the very God, and this Lord Jehovah, the very God, is the Lord Jesus Christ. In 6:1 Isaiah saw the Lord, which in Hebrew is *Adonai,* sitting on a high and lofty throne. According to verse 3, "the Lord" is "Jehovah of hosts." Then in verse 5 Isaiah says, "My eyes have seen the King, Jehovah of hosts." In John 12:41, after John quotes from the Old Testament, he says, "These things said Isaiah because he saw His glory and spoke concerning Him." Isaiah saw the glory of the Lord Jesus and spoke concerning Him. This indicates that the Jesus revealed in the Gospels, especially in the Gospel of John, is the glorious Jehovah concerning whom Isaiah prophesies in chapter 40.

Jesus, Who Is Jehovah, Being Our God

Jesus, who is Jehovah, is our God (John 1:1, 14; 8:24, 28, 58). John 1:1 says, "In the beginning was the Word, and the Word was with God, and the Word was God." This eternal Word, who was the complete God, became flesh (v. 14). Then in chapter 8 this Word who became flesh, who is both the Son of God and the Son of Man, is the I Am (vv. 24, 28, 58). In verse 24 the Lord says, "Therefore I said to you that you will die in your sins; for unless you believe that I am, you will die in your sins." We will not die in our sins, for we have died in our organic union with the I Am; we are one with Christ in His crucifixion (Rom. 6:5; Gal. 2:20). Then in John 8:28 Jesus says, "When you lift up the Son of Man, then you will know that I am." The Son of Man being lifted up refers to His death on the cross. Therefore, in principle, whenever He is lifted up, exalted, and magnified, the unbelievers will know that He is the I Am.

The Lord Jesus is the only person who can say "I Am" in an absolute sense. But in Isaiah 47, in Jehovah's indictment of Babylon, we see something frightening, horrifying, and despicable. Verse 8 says, "Now hear this, O lover of pleasure, / Who dwells securely / And says in your heart, / I am, and there is none besides me." Here Babylon is personified as a woman, a lover of pleasure, who says in her heart, "I am." What an insult it is for this evil woman, Babylon, a lover of pleasure and the mother of the harlots and the abominations of the earth, to declare, "I am." She thinks that she dwells securely in her Babylonian capital, carrying out in her heart the rebellion revealed in Isaiah 14. Surely she deserves to be annihilated, and the time of her destruction is at hand. Only God can say absolutely, "I Am."

The Revealing of Jehovah Being the Appearing of Jesus

The revealing of Jehovah is the appearing of Jesus (Matt. 1:21). Let us consider how the appearing of Jesus is the revealing of Jehovah. We see this in His being called *Jesus,* which means "Jehovah the Savior" (footnote 1 on v. 21). We also see this in the Lord's speaking something that He alone could say: "I do not seek My glory" (John 8:50). Every other person who has ever lived has sought glory for himself. Every fallen man seeks his own glory. Thus, by saying, "I do not seek My glory," the Lord Jesus is saying, "I do not seek to express Myself." In verse 54 He went on to say, "If I glorify Myself, My glory is nothing; it is My Father who glorifies Me." Jesus is the only person who ever lived who did not seek His own glory.

This matter of seeking God's glory is intrinsically related to our speaking. Isaiah 40:5 says, "The glory of Jehovah will be revealed, / And all flesh will see it together, / Because the mouth of Jehovah has spoken." It is the mouth of Jehovah that manifests the glory of Jehovah. John 1:14 says, "The Word became flesh and tabernacled among us (and we beheld His glory)." *His glory* here is the glory of the Word that speaks God. Speaking is related to glory, the very expression of God.

Many programs on the radio or in other forms of media contain the vain speakings of people who are exhibiting themselves to obtain glory. In 7:18 the Lord spoke a word that every aspiring minister of the new covenant should consider: "He who speaks from himself seeks his own glory; but He who seeks the glory of Him who sent Him, this One is true, and unrighteousness is not in Him." The Lord Jesus sought the glory of God, the One who sent Him; therefore, He is true, genuine, and real. This is an indictment of the entire religious system, which is full of people who speak from themselves as they seek their own glory.

Many years ago, the Lord as the Spirit manifested Himself to me and exposed all of my so-called preaching prior to that day as being a seeking after self-glory. That preaching was nothing more than a feeding on the emotional response and the appreciation of the congregation. I condemned and renounced that, and I resolved, insofar as a man can resolve while trusting only in the mercy of God, to never speak like that again. At least five years passed in the church life before I could speak publicly, and even today all my speaking is measured and evaluated not by the letter but by the glory of the revealed and manifested God.

My encouragement is that there is a God-man in my spirit who does not seek His own glory but the glory of the One who sent Him. Hence, John 5—8 reveals that the Son can do nothing from Himself. His speaking and His teaching are not His (8:28; 7:16), nor does He seek His own will (5:30; 6:38). Moreover, before His death He told the Father, "I have glorified You on earth, finishing the work which You have given Me to do" (17:4). Furthermore, He did not come in His own name (5:43). What a marvelous person! He is sinless, yet before beginning His ministry, He was baptized by John. That baptism was a declaration that, as a man in the old creation, He was good only for termination and burial and that He would never do anything from Himself. He never prayed or spoke anything from Himself, nor did He ever seek anything for Himself. Everything came out from the Father within Him, and He spoke what He heard the Father speaking. Because of this, God could be expressed in Him. He had the option of merely living in His perfect humanity. If He had, surely everyone would have been impressed with such a good and perfect man, but that is not what impresses us about Him when we read the Gospels. Rather, whenever we contact Him, whenever we hear Him, and whenever we see Him, we contact, hear, and see God Himself. This is the essence of the ministry of the new covenant.

When a new covenant minister speaks God's word, others will see God, be drawn to God, extol God, and glorify God, not the earthen vessel that speaks the word. As a pattern to us, Paul says, "We do not preach ourselves but Christ Jesus as Lord, and ourselves as your slaves for Jesus' sake. Because the God who said, Out of darkness light shall shine, is the One who shined in our hearts to illuminate the knowledge of the glory of God in the face of Jesus Christ" (2 Cor. 4:5-6). There is no shining when people speak from themselves. This is a very severe but blessed lesson that every minister of the Word must learn. How dare anyone stand in the church or stand at the podium and speak from the self! God wants to be expressed, but His expression must be through the Word. In 1 Corinthians 14:24-25 Paul says, "If all prophesy and some unbeliever or unlearned person enters, he is convicted by all, he is examined by all; the secrets of his heart become manifest; and so falling on his face, he will worship God, declaring that indeed God is among you." An unbeliever will be convicted by a group of people expressing God by speaking Him. Hence, we will never give up on recovering the practice of all the saints prophesying. We will present this matter again and again until it becomes prevailing among the churches in the Lord's recovery.

The Lord, who is the very Jehovah, manifested God and revealed God, not simply because He contained God but because He denied Himself so that the God of glory within Him could be expressed. Surely the Lord's disciples did not behold His glory only on the Mount of Transfiguration. They were under the Lord's "full-time training" day by day for three and a half years, living with God in the flesh and beholding His glory.

Jehovah Being Revealed through His Speaking; the More We Listen to the Speaking of the Lord Jesus, the More Our Seeing Jehovah

Jehovah is revealed through His speaking; the more we listen to the speaking of the Lord Jesus, the more we see Jehovah (Isa. 40:5; John 1:1). We need to be filled with the word by reading, pray-reading, memorizing, studying, musing on, and singing the word until we are constituted with the word in order to speak the word so that God may be expressed.

Christ Being the Complete God Manifested in the Flesh

Christ is the complete God manifested in the flesh (1 Tim. 3:16). We use the adjective *complete* to make it clear that we are not tritheists. It was not only one-third of the Godhead that became flesh; rather, the entire Triune God was manifested in the flesh. According to John 14:10, the Son is in the Father, the Father is in the Son, and the Father does His works in the Son. Moreover, the Lord was conceived of the Holy Spirit (Matt. 1:20), who is the very essence of His Being. Thus, the entire Triune God was embodied in Christ. He is the manifestation of the complete God. In the previous message we emphasized that Jesus is

Jehovah God come in the flesh. Here we emphasize that Jesus is the complete Triune God manifested in the flesh.

The Word, Who Is God, Becoming Flesh

The Word, who is God, became flesh (John 1:1, 14). God, who is the Word, is not a partial God but the entire God—God the Son, God the Father, and God the Spirit. The Word is God's definition, explanation, and expression; hence, the Word who became flesh is the definition, explanation, and expression in the flesh.

In Incarnation Christ Being
God Manifested in the Flesh

In incarnation Christ is God manifested in the flesh (1 Tim. 3:16). Verse 16 says, "Confessedly, great is the mystery of godliness: He who was manifested in the flesh, / Justified in the Spirit, / Seen by angels, / Preached among the nations, / Believed on in the world, / Taken up in glory." We are orthodox in that we believe the Son of God was incarnated. However, there is a difference between being orthodox in a historical sense and being orthodox in a biblical sense. We believe that the Son of God was incarnated, but what the Bible actually says is that God was "manifested in the flesh." The entire God, the complete God, the totality of the Godhead, was manifested in the flesh.

His Being Manifested in the Flesh
Not Only as the Son but as the Entire God—
The Father, the Son, and the Spirit

He was manifested in the flesh not only as the Son but as the entire God—the Father, the Son, and the Spirit. If we do not believe that the entire God was manifested in the flesh and insist that only the Son was manifested in the flesh, then we are tritheists. If we believe that while the Son was on the earth by Himself the Father was in the heavens by Himself and the Spirit was somewhere in between, then we have divided the Godhead into three separate parts. On one hand, we should not be tritheists; on the other hand, we should not be modalists, who believe that the three of the Godhead did not co-exist. They teach that God originally existed as the Father, that He then played another role as the Son, and that, after the Son's death and resurrection, He became the Spirit. We reject this heresy. We must understand that through incarnation the entire Triune God was manifested in the flesh as the man Jesus.

The Entire God Being Incarnated; Thus, Christ in Incarnation Being the Entire God Manifested in the Flesh

The entire God was incarnated; thus, Christ in incarnation is the entire God manifested in the flesh. Here I would point out that our way of composing the message outlines is virtually a matter of presenting the Lord's ministry in outline form. This is not a legality; it is simply our organic practice. Our feeling is that, since there are such rich utterances for us to use, which are patently superior to anything that we could produce by ourselves, why would we not use them? All the ministry publications contain utterances from a minister of God who did not speak from himself.

In Christ Dwelling All the Fullness of the Godhead Bodily

In Christ dwells all the fullness of the Godhead bodily (Col. 2:9). Verse 9 says, "For in Him [Christ] dwells all the fullness of the Godhead bodily." *All the fullness of the Godhead* refers to the entire Godhead, the complete God. Christ is the embodiment of the Triune God; the Father, the Son, and the Spirit are all embodied in Him. This truth requires some explanation, but even more, it needs our proclamation.

Christ as the Glory of Jehovah Being the Center of the Gospel for the New Creation

Christ as the glory of Jehovah is the center of the gospel for the new creation (Isa. 40:5; 2 Cor. 4:3-6; 5:17). God wants to have a new creation consisting of redeemed created human beings mingled with Himself. This new creation is actually composed of the sons of God who are the reproduction and multiplication not of the only begotten Son, who cannot be reproduced or multiplied, but of the firstborn Son, the first God-man. The gospel of the glory of God is the gospel in which the glorious Christ shines forth through transparent vessels into open human hearts. When His shining reaches our spirit and we believe into the light, we become sons of light (John 12:36), children of light, and even light itself. Ephesians 5:8 says, "You were once darkness but are now light in the Lord; walk as children of light." Hence, this gospel is the first step in annihilating Satan's evil work and in carrying out God's economy.

First John 3:8 says, "For this purpose the Son of God was manifested, that He might destroy the works of the devil." Whenever the
Son of God is manifested, He undoes, annihilates, deconstructs, disas-
sembles, and destroys the works of the devil. Has not the devil worked
on us and in us? Has he not constituted us such a perversion in our
fallen nature? The one thing that can undo such works of the devil is
our opening our heart to allow the Son of God to be manifested in us.
His manifestation will undo everything the devil has done to us. Satan
is the universal loser; all his works have been brought to naught.

In 2 Thessalonians 2:8 Paul reveals how the Lord, leading the overcoming bridal army, will deal with Antichrist. The man of lawlessness,
the son of perdition, will sit in the rebuilt temple in Jerusalem. He will
oppose and exalt himself above all that is called God, declaring that he
is God and demanding to be worshipped as God (vv. 3-4), whom the
Lord Jesus will slay by the breath of His mouth and bring to nothing
by the manifestation of His coming (v. 8). The Lord will bring him
to nothing by the shining forth, the brightness, of His *parousia*, His
presence. He will come and reveal Himself, yet He will not come
alone but as a corporate person. The overcomers have been hidden in
their descent with Him from the throne to the air, and then they will
descend with Him to the earth as their Commander-in-chief shines in
His glory. His shining will consume the Antichrist, and the whole earth
will see the glory of Jehovah.

Since Glory Signifies the Expression of God, to Say That God Is Glorified Meaning That He Is Expressed

Since glory signifies the expression of God, to say that God is glorified means that He is expressed (John 17:4). Today's religions,
including Christianity, are merely systems of self-glorification. The
clergy-laity system is a system in which gifted professional performers
express themselves, and the more successful one becomes, the bigger
his congregation becomes. If their so-called preaching and singing were
judged by the manifested glory of Jehovah, surely they would all pros-
trate themselves before Him in shame. The Lord must gain something
on this earth that glorifies Him. There are many ways to define the
Lord's recovery, but in the context of this message, the intrinsic definition of the Lord's recovery is the recovery of God's expression.

Christ as the Image of God Being
the Effulgence of God's Glory

Christ as the image of God is the effulgence of God's glory (Heb. 1:3).

The Gospel Being the Gospel of the Glory of Christ,
Which Illuminates, Radiates, and Shines
into the Heart of Man

The gospel is the gospel of the glory of Christ, which illuminates, radiates, and shines into the heart of man (2 Cor. 4:3-6). Christ is God radiating, God shining forth. Whenever we preach the gospel with someone, one should pray while the other one is speaking. The one who speaks should speak from the Spirit, expressing the Lord, while the one who prays should pray to bind the god of this age, who is trying to blind the thoughts of the unbelievers. Some may want to argue or reason; let them argue and just simply shine on them through your speaking. Our father Abraham was saved and justified through the appearing of the God of glory again and again. Eventually, there was a reaction to God's shining into Abraham—faith; he believed God, and God accounted it to him as righteousness (Gen. 15:6). Although we must speak, we should not trust our words. Instead, we need to be one with the shining Christ to shine Him into the hearts of men.

Today the Glory of Jehovah Being the Resurrected Christ
as the Life-giving Spirit Dwelling in Our Spirit

Today the glory of Jehovah is the resurrected Christ as the life-giving Spirit dwelling in our spirit (1 Cor. 15:45b; 2 Cor. 3:17; 2 Tim. 4:22). "The glory of Jehovah" in Isaiah 40:5 is the pneumatic Christ who dwells within us in our spirit. Colossians 1:27 says, "To whom God willed to make known what are the riches of the glory of this mystery among the Gentiles, which is Christ in you, the hope of glory."

GOD'S DESIRE IN HIS ECONOMY
BEING TO HAVE A CORPORATE EXPRESSION
OF HIMSELF FOR HIS GLORY;
GOD WANTING SUCH A CORPORATE EXPRESSION
SO THAT HE MAY BE GLORIFIED

God's desire in His economy is to have a corporate expression of

Himself for His glory; God wants such a corporate expression so that He may be glorified (1 Tim. 3:15-16; Eph. 3:21; Rev. 21:10-11). God's desire is to expand the revelation, the manifestation, the expression, the glory, from one person, God the Son, into many persons, the sons of God. God's desire and goal in His economy is to have a corporate expression of Himself for His glory. Hence, we need to consider the progress of God's manifestation in His economy from one person, Christ, to God's manifestation in a corporate man that includes not only Christ but also all of us. To pray, "Lord, make me part of Your corporate expression," touches the desire of His heart. If we see short-ages in the brothers, we can simply pray, "Lord, fill this brother with Your glory. I believe that You are in him." We can boldly proclaim and fully believe that God will back up our word, for He desires to gain a corporate expression so that He can be glorified.

As lovers of God, what God wants and desires should matter to us. Eventually, there must be a shift in our inner being from what we want and desire to what God wants and desires. I know a brother who was in the full-time training some years ago. His desire, his goal, was to become a pilot and fly jets. Then a gradual shift took place in his being, and eventually he no longer had that desire to fly jets; instead, his desire was to be one with God for His glorification. We should never try to change what we want; we should simply be open to the Lord and let the God of glory shine in us. His shining will touch our wants and desires. Eventually, He will shine in us to such a degree that we will be able to say in simplicity, "Lord, I only want what You want. I only desire what You desire." Then matters such as whom we should marry, what we should do, and where we should go will all become matters of how God can gain us the most for His glory. Then we would marry, serve, or move for the glory of God, the expression of God. The Bible says, "Do all to the glory of God" (1 Cor. 10:31). Therefore, what God wants and desires needs to be worked into us to become what we want and desire. May we all pray, "Father, may the desire of Your heart become the desire of my heart. Because You desire a corporate expres-sion, my desire is that You would gain a corporate expression." We should never try to reform or change ourselves, nor should we hide from ourselves or from the God of glory. Rather, we need to be open and transparent with the Lord and allow Him to shine within us. His shining will do a wonderful work in us.

God's Good Pleasure, the Desire of His Heart, Being to Have Many Sons for the Expression of His Son So That He May Be Expressed in the Son through the Spirit

God's good pleasure, the desire of His heart, is to have many sons for the expression of His Son so that He may be expressed in the Son through the Spirit (Eph. 1:5, 9; Rom. 8:29).

First Timothy 3:15-16 Indicating Not Only That Christ Himself as the Head Is the Manifestation of God in the Flesh but Also That the Church as the Body Is the Manifestation of God in the Flesh— the Mystery of Godliness

God Having Manifested Himself in Christ as an Individual Expression in the Flesh

First Timothy 3:15-16 indicates not only that Christ Himself as the Head is the manifestation of God in the flesh but also that the church as the Body is the manifestation of God in the flesh—the mystery of godliness. God has manifested Himself in Christ as an individual expression in the flesh (v. 16; John 1:1, 14; Col. 2:9). When the Lord was glorified on the Mount of Transfiguration, a voice from heaven said, "This is My Son, the Beloved, in whom I have found My delight" (Matt. 17:5). God wants to reproduce and multiply His Son, the One in whom He is manifested, into many sons, those in whom His manifestation can be magnified.

Now God Being Manifested in the Church, the Body of Christ, as the Enlarged Corporate Expression in the Flesh

Now God is manifested in the church, the Body of Christ, as the enlarged corporate expression in the flesh (Eph. 1:22-23; 1 Tim. 3:15-16). *Godliness* in verse 16 refers to God as life lived out in the church to be expressed. The manifestation of God in the flesh began with Christ when He was on earth. The manifestation of God in the flesh continues with the church, which is the increase, enlargement, and multiplication of the manifestation of God in the flesh. The church is the enlarged corporate expression, the enlarged manifestation of God in the flesh.

This is why we must eventually be brought to learn the fundamental lesson of denying the self, which is to not express the self. This does not imply that we should not prophesy out of a fear of expressing the self. Actually, to not prophesy is to protect the self. To know when to prophesy is simply a matter of following the prompting of the Spirit. Before we stand to speak, we need to make a decision in our will, not trusting our feelings. If we make the decision to speak, we will have more faith, our spirit will be stronger, our speaking will come from our mingled spirit, and the Lord will be expressed through us. But then after we speak, we may be flooded with self-consciousness. We may examine, perhaps for days, what we said. After giving a message in which I poured out my being, I became very self-conscious for days. Eventually, I went to Brother Lee and told him about it, thinking that he would give me profound help, which he did, but not according to my concept. He said, "Brother, forget about it." How can we forget about our speaking? We need to hide under the blood of Jesus. We need to pray, "Lord, cover me with Your precious blood." We are in the life-long process of being transformed from glory to glory. To be sure, we cannot remain silent until we are fully glorified. If this were the case, no one would speak until the rapture. Rather, we must realize that we have Christ as glory in our spirit; therefore, whenever we speak from our spirit in faith, God will be manifested.

God Being Glorified, Expressed, in the Church

This Glory Coming to Us with God and, after Being Worked into Us, Returning to God with Us

God is glorified, expressed, in the church (Eph. 3:21). This glory comes to us with God and, after being worked into us, will return to God with us. Hence, verse 21 says, "To Him be the glory in the church." This glory comes to us not merely from God but with God and, after being worked into us, will return to God with us. A two-way traffic of glory is being established between God and us. Glory comes to us with God whether or not we are aware of it. The God of glory is being worked into us. He is permeating and saturating our every part. Eventually, there will be some return traffic; the glory in us will begin to emerge. Even now some degree of glory is being expressed; otherwise, there could not be glory in the church. Ultimately, this glory returns to God with us. We are being constituted with the Triune God of glory to be His expression.

God's Glory Being Wrought into the Church, and His Being Expressed in the Church

The Dispensing of the Triune God Issuing in Glory

God's glory is wrought into the church, and He is expressed in the church. The dispensing of the Triune God issues in glory (Rom. 8:18, 21). In Message 5 of the 2003 Memorial Day weekend conference on "Living an Overcoming Life by the Law of the Spirit of Life," there is a section entitled "The Dispensing of the Triune God as Life into Our Tripartite Being according to His Righteousness, through His Holiness, and unto His Glory" (*The Ministry*, vol. 7, no. 7, pp. 112-116). If we want to become the glory of God, we must be open to receive His dispensing. In our personal times with Him, the Lord first cleanses us and forgives us, and then He wants us to open to receive His dispensing. His dispensing is based upon His righteousness shown in redemption and through His holiness in resurrection, but the goal is His glory. The more we let Him fill us, the more we will be able to express Him as glory.

On one hand, those who are extroverts are quite busy and active in their times with the Lord. In their prayers, they have intense one-way conversations with the Lord, talking to Him all the time and praying desperately concerning their situation and even concerning their need to enter into the kingdom. It is very difficult for them to let the Lord dispense Himself into them because they are so active. They need to calm themselves down and call on the Lord's name, saying, "Lord Jesus, I just open to you." On the other hand, those who are introverts are quite subjective and introspective. They have no problem coming to the Lord and opening to Him, yet when the Spirit prompts them, saying, "I want to come out of you. I want to be expressed," they become entangled in their subjective considerations and feelings. They may question whether this prompting is really of the Lord or is it simply their own feeling.

Whether you are one of the extroverts who has trouble opening to let God in or one of the introverts, the majority, who would rather not stand in front of thousands of people and let the Lord flow out, both need to let Him come in and let Him flow out for His glory. We need to let Him in by speaking to Him and opening to Him. We may say, "Lord, I love You. I open my whole being to You right now. Work Yourself into me today. Lord, strengthen me with power into my inner man today." Then we need to let Him flow out by speaking from our spirit. Such speaking need not to be with spiritual terminology. We may sense that a person is down and simply say with a heart of love, "Sister, how are you?" If we would shout, "Praise the Lord!" the sister may be inwardly trampled. At that moment she may not be able to bear such a greeting. Instead, she may need something incarnated, something human. For example, if one is grieving the loss of a family member, we may simply ask, "How are you? How is your mother taking the loss of your grandmother? Is she okay?" In this way we let the Lord flow out. Such a dispensing of Christ is unto His glory.

Being Transformed into the Same Image from Glory to Glory

We are being transformed into the same image from glory to glory (2 Cor. 3:18). Once we had nothing, but now we have the Christ of glory within us and are progressing from glory to glory. Those who attended the recent full-time training graduation can testify that glory was expressed through those trainees. Honestly speaking, I did not see that amount of glory in those trainees when they entered the training just two years earlier. This is just one illustration of how we are being transformed from glory to glory.

In the Oneness in the Divine Glory, the Believers, Their Self Having Been Fully Denied, Enjoying the Glory of the Father as the Factor of Their Perfected Oneness and Thus Expressing God in a Corporate, Built-up Way

In the oneness in the divine glory, the believers, their self having been fully denied, enjoy the glory of the Father as the factor of their perfected oneness and thus express God in a corporate, built-up way (John 17:22; cf. 7:18). The Lord must gain a group of blended co-workers as the intrinsic center of His work on earth today. These being-blended co-workers are not limited to those in Southern California but include whoever would give himself to the blending for the sake of the Body. What the Lord's recovery needs to see among the elders and even more among the co-workers is a group of brothers who are one in the Father's glory, where there is no envy, no rivalry, no self-expression, no competition, and no self-exaltation. The Lord has to have as a model such a group of co-workers. The Lord's prayer in John 17 must be fulfilled in the overcomers in the church age.

The Lord must gain some who are willing to fully deny their self.

We may not know what it means to fully deny our self, but we are in the process. If the Lord can gain a group of brothers and then expand that into a large number of saints that are one in the divine glory, the church will be built up and the bride will be prepared. This is the building of God for the corporate expression of the Triune God. We thank the Lord that we are one in the Father's name and thereby one in His life. His life makes us one. We also thank the Lord that we are one in the sanctifying word. Nevertheless, we need to humble ourselves, realizing that we cannot truly say that we are one in the divine glory, that among us there is no self-expression whatsoever. Yet we need to have faith in the Lord that we are on the way.

Recently, a number of brothers gathered together for a few days, and I can testify before the Lord and before the enemy that there was more oneness in that coordination than I have ever known in my whole life. Please pray for all the co-workers for the sake of the Lord's recovery. We must have one recovery doing one work in one flow with one ministry to express the glory of our one God. Individually, the co-workers have different measures, different functions, and different areas of service, but if we are all governed by the vision of God's eternal economy, we will renounce and repudiate the self, especially the self that longs to speak its own words, and give ourselves to be trained to seek only the glory of God. The Lord must have some who are willing to pay the price for God's glorification, who are willing to lose and deny the self, and who are willing to learn to speak from and through a pure and single heart so that God can be glorified. Ultimately, this will consummate in the New Jerusalem.

An Outstanding Feature of the New Jerusalem
Being That It Has the Glory of God, His Expression

An outstanding feature of the New Jerusalem is that it has the glory of God, His expression (Rev. 21:10-11). The entire New Jerusalem will bear the glory of God, which is God Himself shining out through the city. The glory of God—God Himself being manifested—will be the content of the New Jerusalem, for the city will be completely filled with His glory. The New Jerusalem is the city of glory. The chorus of *Hymns*, #976 says, "Lo, the holy city, / Full of God's bright glory! / It is God's complete expression / In humanity."—R. K.

THE DIVINE ECONOMY IN THE BOOK OF ISAIAH

Christ as the Servant of Jehovah
Typified by Cyrus the King of Persia
and by Israel
(Message 20)

Scripture Reading: Isa. 41:2, 8-16, 25; 42:1a; 43:7, 10; 44:1-5, 21, 28; 45:1, 4, 13; 46:11, 13; 48:14; 49:3

I. Three parties are used by Isaiah to typify Christ as the Servant of Jehovah: Cyrus the king of Persia, Israel, and Isaiah the prophet:

    A. They all did the same thing to please God by serving to release God's people, to build up God's house, the temple, and to build up God's kingdom, signified by the city of Jerusalem; thus, they all typify Christ as God's Servant—Luke 4:18-21; Matt. 16:18-19.

    B. All who are in Christ (1 Cor. 1:30) and who are thus one with Christ to release God's people and to build up His house and His kingdom are servants of God; those who are one with Christ have become a great corporate Christ (12:12; Col. 3:10-11), the same as the individual Christ in being the testimony and servant of God:

        1. We need to be one with Christ to release God's people from the captivity of Satan back to the enjoyment of God as their possession—Isa. 61:1-2; Luke 4:18-21:

            a. In eternity past God chose millions of people, but they were all captured by Satan, typified by Nebuchadnezzar the king of Babylon—Eph. 1:4; Isa. 14:12-23; 1 John 5:19; Rom. 7:14.

            b. Our preaching of the gospel is to release these captives to make them the sons of God, the members of Christ, and the constituents of the new man—Matt. 12:28-29; Gal. 3:26; Rom.12:4-5; Col. 3:10-11.

        2. We need to be one with Christ to release God's people

from Babylon (apostate Christendom) and the principle of Babylon; anything that is Babylonian gives Satan the ground to defeat the people of God—Isa. 48:20; 41:21-29; Rev. 17:3-5; Josh. 7:21:

a. The principle of Babylon is man's endeavor to build up something from earth to heaven by human ability—Gen. 11:1-9; 1 Cor. 3:12.

b. The principle of Babylon is hypocrisy—Rev. 17:4, 6; Matt. 23:25-32; Josh. 7:21; Acts 5:1-11; Matt. 15:7-8; 6:1-6.

c. The principle of Babylon is that of not considering herself a widow but of glorifying herself and living luxuriously—Isa. 47:8b; Rev. 18:7; Luke 18:3; Matt. 9:14-15.

d. The principle of Babylon is for man to make a name for himself and deny God's name—Gen. 11:4; Rev. 3:8; 2 Cor. 11:2; 1 Cor. 1:10.

e. The principle of Babylon is confusion—Gen. 11:6-7; cf. Rom. 15:5-6; 1 Cor. 1:10; Phil. 2:2; 1 Tim. 1:3-4.

f. The principle of Babylon is scattering, with each one going his own way and his own direction—Gen. 11:8; cf. Deut. 16:16; Psa. 133; 1 Kings 12:26-32.

g. The principle of Babylon is mixture; anything which is halfway and not absolute is called Babylon—2 Chron. 36:6-7; Ezra 1:11; cf. 2 Kings 17:8.

h. The Lord's call in the book of Revelation is for His people to come out of Babylon—Isa. 52:11-12; Rev. 18:4-5.

3. We need to be one with Christ to build up the church as God's temple—Eph. 2:21-22; Matt. 16:18; 1 Cor. 14:4b.

4. We need to be one with Christ to build up the church as God's kingdom—Matt. 16:18-19, 24; Rom. 14:17-18.

II. Christ as the Servant of Jehovah is typified by Cyrus in the following aspects:

A. He was raised up by Jehovah (Isa. 41:2a, 25a; 45:13a; Acts 3:26a), anointed by Jehovah (Isa. 45:1a; Luke 4:18a), and loved by Jehovah (Isa. 48:14b; Matt. 3:17).

B. He did God's pleasure on Babylon (Isa. 48:14; 46:11), symbolizing the Roman Catholic Church (Rev. 17:3-5).

C. He was God's counselor (Isa. 46:11b) to subdue the nations and have dominion over the kings (41:2b, 25; 45:1b; Ezra 1:2a; Acts 5:31; Rev. 1:5a).

D. He was Jehovah's shepherd (Isa. 45:1) for the fulfilling of His desire in building up the city (symbolizing the kingdom) and the temple of God and in releasing God's captives (44:28; 45:13; Ezra 1:2-3; John 2:19; Luke 4:18b).

III. Christ as the Servant of Jehovah is typified by Israel in the following aspects:

A. Israel was chosen by Jehovah and upheld with the right hand of His righteousness—Isa. 41:10.

B. Israel overcame the enemies by Jehovah and rejoiced and gloried in Him, the Holy One of Israel—vv. 8-16; 42:1a; Rom. 8:37; 1 Thes. 2:19-20.

C. Israel was the witness of Jehovah—Isa. 43:10; Rev. 1:5a; 3:14; Acts 1:8.

D. The Spirit of Jehovah was poured out on Israel for the blessing of his offspring—Isa. 44:1-5, 21; Matt. 3:16; Luke 4:18-19.

E. Jehovah was glorified in Israel—Isa. 43:7; 49:3; 46:13b; John 17:1; 12:28:

1. Israel is God's servant in the sense of fulfilling God's desire in His economy to have a corporate expression of Himself for His glory; in this sense Israel was one with Christ as God's servant—Isa. 41:8; 45:4; 49:3; Hosea 11:1; cf. Matt. 2:15.

2. In the present age the church as the testimony of God serves God for the expression of God, the glory of God—Rev. 1:2; Eph. 3:21; Gal. 6:16.

3. The glorification of God is the purpose of our service; the highest service we can render to God is to express Him in His glory—Eph. 1:23; 1 Cor. 10:31.

CHRIST AS THE SERVANT OF JEHOVAH
TYPIFIED BY CYRUS THE KING OF PERSIA AND BY ISRAEL

Prayer: Lord, we open up our whole being to You. We praise You again for another time together. We turn our hearts to You. We love You, Lord Jesus. We give You the preeminence. We pray for one another that You would grant us all a spirit of wisdom and revelation. Unveil us to see more of Your preciousness and peerless worth. We look to You to speak to us. We pray that You would give each of us an ear to hear what You are speaking to the churches.

The first two messages were based on Isaiah 40. We have seen that Christ is the glory of Jehovah and the revealing of Jehovah. In the remaining twenty-six chapters Christ is revealed as the Servant of Jehovah. The title of this message is "Christ as the Servant of Jehovah typified by Cyrus the King of Persia and by Israel." There are many types and figures of Christ in the Old Testament. It is easy to see that Israel is a type of Christ, but it is quite striking to realize that Christ is also typified by Cyrus the king of Persia. In this message we want to see more of Christ. We all need to experience more of Christ as the Servant of Jehovah so that we can be one with Him to carry out His eternal economy. When we come to Message 24, we will see in more detail how Christ as the Servant of Jehovah is also typified by Isaiah the prophet.

In this message we will see that all three—Cyrus, Israel, and Isaiah—typify Christ as the Servant of Jehovah, serving God to carry out His economy in three particular ways. First, Christ is the Servant of Jehovah in our spirit. If we touch Him, enjoy Him, are filled with Him, and allow Him to flow out of us, we will be one with Him to release God's chosen people from any kind of captivity. We all need to be released. I hope that this message will result in a further release of any who are under some kind of oppression, burden, suppression, or bondage. The Lord is the releasing One; He releases all the captives of Satan. He releases God's chosen people from Satan, sin, death, and

Babylon. In particular, we need to see what Babylon is, and we need to be released from every vestige of Babylon. Second, Christ as the Servant of Jehovah, as typified by these three persons, also labors to build up God's house, the temple, which signifies the church as the house of the living God. Third, Christ as the Servant of Jehovah builds up God's kingdom, which is signified by the city of Jerusalem.

THREE PARTIES BEING USED BY ISAIAH
TO TYPIFY CHRIST AS THE SERVANT OF JEHOVAH:
CYRUS THE KING OF PERSIA, ISRAEL, AND ISAIAH THE PROPHET

Their All Doing the Same Thing to Please God by Serving to Release God's People, to Build Up God's House, the Temple, and to Build Up God's Kingdom, Signified by the City of Jerusalem; Thus, Their All Typifying Christ as God's Servant

Three parties are used by Isaiah to typify Christ as the Servant of Jehovah: Cyrus the king of Persia, Israel, and Isaiah the prophet. They all did the same thing to please God by serving to release God's people, to build up God's house, the temple, and to build up God's kingdom, signified by the city of Jerusalem; thus, they all typify Christ as God's Servant (Luke 4:18-21; Matt. 16:18-19).

The Lord's recovery is for the carrying out of God's good pleasure (Eph 1:5). The Lord has a recovery, and He has put us in it. There is something that makes God happy, and we are here to make Him happy, to please Him. Paul says, "Therefore also we are determined, whether at home or abroad, to gain the honor of being well pleasing to Him" (2 Cor. 5:9). If God is happy within us, we also will be happy. We are determined to gain the honor of being well pleasing to Him. Enoch was a person who pleased God. According to Genesis 5, Enoch walked with God for three hundred years, and then God took him through rapture (vv. 22-24). Hebrews 11:5 says, "By faith Enoch was translated so that he should not see death; and he was not found, because God had translated him. For before his translation he obtained the testimony that he had been well pleasing to God." This indicates that before Enoch was translated, his whole being was permeated to the extent that he obtained the testimony that he was well pleasing to God. We also want to obtain such a testimony personally, as members of His Body, and corporately, as churches in the Lord's recovery.

The three persons in the book of Isaiah who typify Christ also pleased God by serving Him. They served by releasing God's people, by building up God's house, the temple, and by building up God's kingdom, signified by the city of Jerusalem. God's people, the Old Testament Israel, were in Babylonian captivity. Nebuchadnezzar, the king of Babylon, invaded Israel and Jerusalem, destroyed the temple and the city, took God's people captive, and carried away all the vessels of God's house to Babylon and put them in his temple of idols. Apparently, God's testimony was utterly destroyed. Nevertheless, the Lord raised up another king, Cyrus the king of Persia, who destroyed the Babylonian Empire and established the Medo-Persian Empire. God raised up Cyrus, a Gentile king, in a particular way. According to Ezra 1, God stirred up his spirit to make a decree and a proclamation to release God's people Israel so that they could go back to Jerusalem and rebuild the temple (vv. 1-4). This was a great thing.

Why would a Gentile king do such a thing? This was surely God's sovereign working—to raise up a Gentile king and to stir up his spirit to make a proclamation that in effect said, "Hear this, all who are under my reign. I have conquered the king of Babylon. Now the Medo-Persian Empire is the ruling authority on this earth. My spirit is stirred up, and I want to release these particular people to go back to their city, Jerusalem, to rebuild the temple and the city." This is why we can say that Cyrus typifies Christ. Christ is doing the same thing. He is releasing us from every kind of bondage, including Satan, sin, and death. He is releasing us for a particular purpose—to build up the church as the house of God and the Body of Christ and to build up the kingdom of God for His expression and His dominion over all the earth.

All Who Are in Christ and Who Are Thus One with Christ to Release God's People and to Build Up His House and His Kingdom Being Servants of God; Those Who Are One with Christ Having Become a Great Corporate Christ, the Same as the Individual Christ in Being the Testimony and Servant of God

All who are in Christ (1 Cor. 1:30) and who are thus one with Christ to release God's people and to build up His house and His kingdom are servants of God; those who are one with Christ have become a great corporate Christ (12:12; Col. 3:10-11), the same as the individual Christ in being the testimony and servant of God. It is a fact that we are in Christ. First Corinthians 1:30 says, "Of Him you are in Christ Jesus."

We were born in Adam, but we have been transferred out of Adam into Christ. All who are in Christ and are one with Christ are servants of God to release God's people and to build up His house and His kingdom. I hope that all of us, especially the young people, would realize that to serve God makes us the wisest people on the earth. There is no calling more noble. The highest job and the most glorious destiny is to serve God by being one with Him as the indwelling Servant of Jehovah in our spirit to release God's people and to build up His house and His kingdom. We are now one with Christ and have become a great corporate Christ. First Corinthians 12:12 says, "Even as the body is one and has many members, yet all the members of the body, being many, are one body, so also is the Christ." Here the Body of Christ is called "the Christ." We with Christ are the corporate Christ, the new man. Christ is in all the members of the new man, and He *is* all the members of the new man (Col. 3:11). As the corporate Christ, we are a corporate servant of God, serving Him in these three ways.

Our Needing to Be One with Christ
to Release God's People from the Captivity of Satan
Back to the Enjoyment of God as Their Possession

We need to be one with Christ to release God's people from the captivity of Satan back to the enjoyment of God as their possession (Isa. 61:1-2; Luke 4:18-21). According to Isaiah 14, Nebuchadnezzar the king of Babylon is a figure of Satan (vv. 4, 12-15). We need to be one with Christ to release God's people from the captivity of Satan back to the enjoyment of God as their possession. Isaiah 61:1-2 says, "The Spirit of the Lord Jehovah is upon Me, / Because Jehovah has anointed Me / To bring good news to the afflicted; / He has sent Me to bind up the wounds of the brokenhearted, / To proclaim liberty to the captives, / And the opening of the eyes to those who are bound; / To proclaim the acceptable year of Jehovah." The Lord Jesus quoted these verses in Luke 4:18-19 and applied them to Himself. It was as if He were saying, "The Spirit of the Lord God is upon Me and has anointed Me because He chose Me to do some particular things. He chose Me to announce the gospel to the poor, to proclaim release to the captives, to give sight to the blind, and to proclaim the year of jubilee." When we are one with Christ in our spirit, His commission becomes our job and career. The first thing He is doing through us is announcing the gospel to the poor. He is also proclaiming release to the captives, recovery of sight to the blind, sending away in release all those who are oppressed, and proclaiming the acceptable year of the Lord, which is the year of jubilee.

When the Lord began His ministry, His custom was to go into the synagogue and read from the Scriptures. Luke 4 says that He went into the synagogue in Nazareth, and when the scroll of Isaiah was handed to Him, He unrolled it and found a particular place. He read Isaiah 61:1-2 and then said, "Today this Scripture has been fulfilled in your hearing." (Luke 4:21). This is a great thing. Verses 17-22 say,

> The scroll of the prophet Isaiah was handed to Him. And He unrolled the scroll and found the place where it was written, "The Spirit of the Lord is upon Me, because He has anointed Me to announce the gospel to the poor; He has sent Me to proclaim release to the captives, and recovery of sight to the blind, to send away in release those who are oppressed, to proclaim the acceptable year of the Lord, the year of jubilee." And when He rolled up the scroll and gave it back to the attendant, He sat down. And the eyes of all in the synagogue were fixed on Him. And He began to say to them, Today this Scripture has been fulfilled in your hearing. And all bore witness to Him and marveled at the words of grace proceeding out of His mouth.

That surely was an awesome day. The words that had been written seven hundred years earlier by the prophet Isaiah were fulfilled right before those who were in that synagogue.

Announcing the Gospel to the Poor

Christ was anointed to announce the gospel to the poor. If we are one with Christ as the Servant of Jehovah, we need to be those who announce the gospel to the poor. The gospel is the first thing. *The poor* here does not necessarily refer to those who are poor in material things but to those who do not have God's presence. Anyone who does not have God's presence is poor. Anyone who does not have the unsearchably rich Christ in them is poor in God's sight. There are many who are very wealthy in material things, but they are still suffering oppression, captivity, and binding. To be poor is to be devoid of God's presence. The Spirit as the reality of Christ who is the embodiment of God the Father is the very presence of the Triune God in our spirit.

If we are going to announce the gospel to the poor, we must be rich. We need to be "rich toward God" (12:21). This phrase is from the Lord's concluding word in the following parable:

> The land of a certain rich man brought forth abundantly. And he reasoned in himself, saying, What shall I do, for I have no place where I may gather my crops? And he said, I will do this: I will tear down my barns and build larger ones, and I will gather there all my wheat and my goods. And I will say to my soul, Soul, you have many goods laid up for many years; rest, eat, drink, be merry. But God said to him, Foolish one, this night they are requiring your soul from you; and the things which you have prepared, whose will they be? So is he who stores up treasure for himself and is not rich toward God. (vv. 16-21)

This rich man was very wealthy with so much produce that his barns could not contain it. Therefore, he said in his heart, "I will hoard my wealth and enjoy it. I don't have to worry about a thing. My soul can indulge itself in all my riches." However, God said to him, "Foolish one, this night they are requiring your soul from you" (v. 20).

We do not know how long we have on this earth. We can spend our time trying to become rich in this world, but eventually we will be taken. The rich man was indulging himself in luxury and the riches of this world because he had so much wealth, and the Lord said, "So is he who is not rich toward God" (v. 21). It is a real blessing to be rich toward God. Surely, we desire that God would look at us and say, "This brother is rich in My sight. That sister is rich toward Me." To be rich is to be filled with the true riches, which are the riches of Christ. Christ is so many rich items. He is our peace, our joy, our light, our life, our dwelling place, our air, our sunshine, and our soil. He is whatever we need. He is whatever any man needs. We all need to be rich with Christ.

It is possible, even as a believer, to be poor. The Lord said to the church in Laodicea, "Because you say, I am wealthy and have become rich and have need of nothing, and do not know that you are wretched and miserable and poor and blind and naked" (Rev. 3:17). Those in Laodicea had the attitude that they were rich and had need of nothing. We should all beware of having such an attitude. We should never have the thought that we are rich and have need of nothing no matter how old we are, how long we have been a believer, how much we have learned and experienced, or how long we have been in the Lord's recovery. We should not have the thought, "I know that. I've done that. I've heard that. I've seen this already." To have such thoughts is to say, "I am rich and have need of nothing." Those with such an attitude are lukewarm, and God is not pleased with them. To be lukewarm is the most terrible condition. The Lord said, "Because you are lukewarm and neither hot nor cold, I am about to spew you out of My mouth" (v. 16). The Lord seemed to be saying to the church in Laodicea, "You say that you are wealthy, but you do not realize that you are poor. You are poor in the riches of Christ, in the experience of Christ, and in the enjoyment of Christ. 'You are wretched and miserable and poor and blind and naked.'" The Lord then said, "I counsel you to buy from Me gold refined by fire that you may be rich, and white garments that you may be clothed and that the shame of your nakedness may not be manifested, and eyesalve to anoint your eyes that you may see" (v. 18). The Lord counsels them to buy. We must pay the price to enjoy God as the real gold every day in order to be filled with the divine riches so that we can announce Him to the poor. Without God man is poor, destitute. Who is going to preach the gospel if we do not? We must go and preach the gospel of the unsearchable riches of God in Christ.

Proclaiming Release to the Captives

Christ was commissioned to proclaim release to the captives. Luke 4:18 says, "He has sent Me to proclaim release to the captives." Fallen man, every unbeliever, is under Satan's domination. Isaiah 42:7 says, "To open the eyes of the blind, / To bring the prisoner out from the prison, / Those who dwell in darkness from the prison house." People under Satan's domination are captives in his prison house, and we were all the same. We were under Satan's usurpation, manipulation, and bondage. Satan was reigning over us. The book of Romans shows us that Satan dwells in and works through the flesh of fallen man as the law of sin and of death (7:21, 23-25; 8:2).

Man is in bondage; man suffers so many different kinds of addictions. For example, gambling is a terrible addiction. Recently, my wife and I went to visit her parents in Colorado. As we were driving there, our route took us through the city of Las Vegas. We could see a pyramid on one side of the highway and a sphinx on the other; it was as if we were in Egypt, which in the Bible typifies the world system that holds every man in slavery. We praise the Lord that today there is a church in Las Vegas; that is the only real treasure in that city.

Otherwise, it is an evil place; it is commonly referred to as "sin city." It is hard to believe that all those buildings were constructed in the middle of the desert just so that people could go there and indulge their lusts twenty-four hours a day. The law of sin and of death is prevailing there. People go there to gamble and lose all their money; this can become a terrible addiction. They cannot help themselves because they are under the bondage of Satan. How can they be released? The Lord must send some there to announce the good news and proclaim release from Satan's captivity and domination. As believers in Christ, we should pray over Luke 4:18-19.

We need to pray, "Lord, make me truly rich. I want to be rich in the enjoyment of Christ." Paul says that he announced the unsearchable riches of Christ as the gospel (Eph. 3:8). This helps us to understand that being poor has nothing to do with material things. We are poor if we are not filled with the riches of Christ. In 2 Corinthians 6:10 Paul speaks concerning himself and those with him, saying, "As made sorrowful yet always rejoicing; as poor yet enriching many; as having nothing and yet possessing all things." This verse describes the paradox of the Christian life. Paul says, "As sorrowful yet always rejoicing." It seems that because of our outward sufferings, we should be sorrowful, but within we are rejoicing. "As poor yet enriching many" is our experience in our service. We are those who are poor outwardly, yet we make people rich. If someone were to ask us what kind of work we do, we should say, "My job is to make people rich. I can tell you how to be rich." Surely this would be an excellent opening for the gospel. Our career is to make people rich.

We need the real wealth; we need to be rich toward God. If we are to proclaim release to the captives, first, we ourselves must be released. Not only are the unbelievers captives of Satan, but thousands of believers are also in captivity. We should pray, "Lord, I want to be released from everything of Satan's captivity. Release me from every kind of bondage and every kind of addiction. I would like to enjoy You in my spirit as the law of the Spirit of life, freeing me moment by moment from the law of sin and of death in my flesh. I would like to remain in touch with You, Lord. Right now I would contact You, touch You, and switch You on in my being. I want to enjoy You as the automatic God installed within me as an automatic law. I want to enjoy You as the spontaneous principle, the innate and automatic function of the Spirit within me, freeing me spontaneously, effortlessly, and unconsciously from the law of sin and of death. Lord, I want to be freed from every kind of bondage and addiction so that I can announce You to others and bring them to touch You, to enjoy You, and to be freed from all satanic bondage." This is our gospel.

Recovery of Sight to the Blind

Christ announced the recovery of sight to the blind. The gospel announcement that we are making is not only the release of the captives but also the recovery of sight to the blind. Many of us can recall the blindness that we were under before we were saved or before we came into the Lord's recovery. It is terrible to be blind. If we do not know God, we are blind. To know God is to have our eyes opened. If we do not know God, the origin of the universe, and the destiny of man, we are blind. To know God, to know the origin of the universe, to know the destiny of man, and to know the snares of the devil is to have our eyes opened.

If we are going to open the eyes of others, first our eyes need to be fully opened. We need to pay the price every day. We need to pray, "Lord, I would like to see more and more of You today. Grant me a spirit of wisdom and revelation. I want to pay the price to have a time with You in the morning where I can buy the Spirit as the eyesalve to anoint my eyes that I might see You more." When our eyes have been enlightened, we can go forth and open the eyes of the unbelievers and of the many believers who remain in darkness, but first we need to see.

Sending Away in Release Those Who Are Oppressed

In Luke 4:18 the Lord went on to say, "To send away in release those who are oppressed." The word translated *oppressed* comes from a verb meaning "to break in pieces." People who are under Satan's oppression are broken people. If we do not go to speak to them, who will release them from this satanic oppression? We must preach the gospel of God's economy all over the earth to release so many oppressed people. People may be oppressed outwardly by their family, by their business, by their school, by their sickness, and by their sins. The satanic oppression is prevailing in this dark world. People may also be oppressed psychologically. They may live in a nice house on a nice street. They may drive a nice car and have a great family, but in their soul, in their psychological being, they sense oppression and dissatisfaction. Inside they are depressed, restless, unhappy, and uneasy. They may also have a spirit of fear. They may be full of fears. All of these come from Satan and his satanic oppression. We, therefore, need to go and preach the gospel so that Christ can fill them and release them from the captivity, bondage, and oppression of Satan.

Personally and individually, we need to pray over these verses. We can say, "Lord, release me from any kind of satanic oppression in my being. I don't want to be oppressed, depressed, or uneasy. I want to enjoy You as my jubilee." Adam's fall was the beginning of the age of misery. Christ's coming was the beginning of the New Testament age, which is the age of joy, ecstasy, and jubilee.

In Eternity Past God Choosing Millions of People, but Their Being All Captured by Satan, Typified by Nebuchadnezzar the King of Babylon

In eternity past God chose millions of people, but they were all captured by Satan, typified by Nebuchadnezzar the king of Babylon (Eph. 1:4; Isa. 14:12-23; 1 John 5:19; Rom. 7:14). First John 5:19 says, "The whole world lies in the evil one." The word *lies* here conveys the thought of remaining "passively in the sphere of the evil one's influence, under the evil one's usurpation and manipulation. While the believers are living and moving actively by the life of God, the whole world (and especially the people of the world) is lying passively under the usurping and manipulating hand of Satan, the evil one" (footnote 3). This is why we need to preach the gospel. I hope we would have a burden to preach the gospel. I worked for an oil company in Houston after I graduated from college. Outwardly, I looked great, wore a nice suit, and had a good job with a somewhat promising future. If you had seen me on the elevator on the way to the twentieth floor, you might have thought, "Here is a young man who is going places." However, deep within I was miserable, and an enlightened believer surely would have had some realization of my inward condition. An enlightened believer is one who has experienced being released from satanic bondage, who has had his eyes opened, and who is burdened to build up the temple and the city. Such a believer knows God, knows the origin of the universe, knows the destiny of man, and knows God's economy. If such a one had seen me on that elevator, surely he would have realized, "This guy is totally miserable!" I was inwardly miserable because I did not know the meaning of my life. I remember riding on that elevator and thinking, "Is this the end of my life? Will I ride this elevator to the twentieth floor until I am sixty-five years old, collect my retirement check, and eventually end up in a coffin? Is this all there is to life?" These were my thoughts in those days. I am so glad that someone left a gospel tract in a laundromat. I do not know who it was; I hope that I will be able to welcome him into the kingdom in the coming age. Someone simply put a gospel tract at the back of a laundromat in Houston. Perhaps they said to themselves, "Maybe someone will read this tract. I'll put it right here." That person has no idea what that tract did. I went to that particular laundromat to do my laundry, and the Lord had prepared me. I read the tract, I prayed the prayer at the end, and I received Christ into me right there in that laundromat. The person who left that tract has no idea what they did. Then the Lord brought me into His recovery. What a mercy! What if someone had not put that tract there? What if someone had not spoken to me about the recovery? Where would I be today? I shudder to think about it. Brothers and sisters, it is not a small thing to distribute tracts or to send books to people you know. Consider Luke 4 again. The Lord said that He was anointed, which means that He was commissioned. He is now within us as the anointed and commissioned One. We have the ministry of the age, and we can proclaim this ministry as the gospel. This ministry proclaims the year of jubilee, that is, the year of ecstasy and joy of God's economy. The jubilee begins with preaching the gospel to unbelievers.

These points are not only the gospel for unbelievers. They also should be the content of our shepherding one another. It is not a small thing when we pray for one another. We need to pray for the saints because the Lord never gives up on anyone. When we are down, when we are backslidden, or when we are "out of it," those are all signs of Satan attacking us, oppressing us, and bringing us into bondage, darkness, and imprisonment. When we shepherd the saints, we dispense Christ into them, which helps them to contact Christ so that they can be released from all of Satan's oppression.

Our Preaching of the Gospel Being to Release These Captives to Make Them the Sons of God, the Members of Christ, and the Constituents of the New Man

Our preaching of the gospel is to release these captives to make them the sons of God, the members of Christ, and the constituents of the new man (Matt. 12:28-29; Gal. 3:26; Rom. 12:4-5; Col. 3:10-11).

This is our gospel. Matthew 12:28-29 says, "If I, by the Spirit of God, cast out the demons, then the kingdom of God has come upon you. Or how can anyone enter into the house of the strong man and plunder his goods unless he first binds the strong man? And then he will thoroughly plunder his house." We need to consider the whole context of these verses. The Pharisees were jealous of the Lord. The religionists are always jealous of the lovers of Jesus and want to kill them. The Lord healed one who was blind and dumb by casting out the demon that possessed him (v. 22). Verse 24 says, "But the Pharisees, hearing this, said, This man does not cast out the demons except by Beelzebul, ruler of the demons." The Lord cast out demons by the Spirit of God, but they said that He was doing it by the ruler of the demons. The footnote on *Beelzebul* in Matthew 10:25 says,

> Beelzebub, meaning "the lord of flies," was the name of the god of the Ekronites (2 Kings 1:2). It was changed contemptuously by the Jews to Beelzebul, which means "the lord of the dunghill," and was used for the ruler of the demons (Matt. 12:24, 27; Mark 3:22; Luke 11:15, 18-19). In Matthew 9:34 the Pharisees, the leading ones of the Jewish religion, reviled the heavenly King by saying that He cast out demons by the ruler of demons. In using this most blasphemous name, they expressed their strongest objection and rejection.

Satan is the "lord of the flies." All men without Christ are "flies," and Satan is their lord. He leads these flies to the dunghill. This was the reason the Jews changed the name of Beelzebub to Beelzebul and used that name for Satan. The lord of the flies becomes the lord of the dunghill. The whole world is a dunghill. It does not matter whether you are at the bottom or the top; it is still a dunghill, and Satan is the lord of the dunghill.

The Lord Jesus responded to those who accused Him by saying in essence that this was not possible or logical. Matthew 12:25-26 says, "Knowing their thoughts, He said to them, Every kingdom divided against itself becomes desolate, and every city or house divided against itself will not stand. And if Satan casts out Satan, he is divided against himself. How then will his kingdom stand?" This was a brilliant answer, given by God Himself. He went on to say, "But if I, by the Spirit of God, cast out the demons, then the kingdom of God has come upon you" (v. 28). The Lord does everything by the Spirit for the kingdom of God the Father. He does everything by another One and for another One.

The Pharisees did everything by themselves and for themselves. In their midst One was standing who was the center and embodiment of the Divine Trinity, and His testimony was, "I do not do anything by Myself and for Myself; I do everything by another One and for another One. I do everything by the Spirit of God for the kingdom of God the Father. I cast out demons by the Spirit of God."

In verse 29 He goes on to say, "How can anyone enter into the house of the strong man and plunder his goods unless he first binds the strong man? And then he will thoroughly plunder his house." We cannot plunder the house of the strong man and take his goods unless we first bind the strong man. We need to pray for our relatives, our friends, our colleagues, and all unbelievers, saying, "Lord, bind the strong man!" We need to pray for so many of the saints whom we love, but who are not in the meetings. Satan has many goods; he has fallen mankind as the goods in his house, but our Lord is stronger than he. Therefore, we need to ask Him to bind the strong man so that we can enter into Satan's kingdom and plunder his goods, making them the Lord's goods. We belong to God; we are His goods. This is the reason that we need to preach the gospel.

Needing to Be One with Christ to Release God's People from Babylon (Apostate Christendom) and the Principle of Babylon; Anything That Is Babylonian Giving Satan the Ground to Defeat the People of God

We need to be one with Christ to release God's people from Babylon (apostate Christendom) and the principle of Babylon; anything that is Babylonian gives Satan the ground to defeat the people of God (Isa. 48:20; 41:21-29; Rev. 17:3-5; Josh. 7:21). Babylon represents apostate Christendom. The word *apostate* refers to a falling away and a degradation. Christendom is utterly degraded; it has fallen away from the pure revelation in the holy Word. We all need to see this clearly, and we need to pray, "Lord, unveil me and open my eyes to see Babylon in the way that You see it. I want to see a vision of Babylon." One of the major unveilings in the book of Revelation is the vision of Babylon. The first vision that John saw was the vision of the golden lampstands, the vision of the churches as the golden lampstands (1:12). John saw this vision in spirit (v. 10). We need to be in spirit to see the golden lampstands. Then in chapter 4 he saw the vision concerning the destiny of the world. We also need to be in spirit to see this vision (v. 2). In 17:3

John says, "He carried me away in spirit into a wilderness; and I saw a woman sitting upon a scarlet beast, full of names of blasphemy, having seven heads and ten horns." This evil woman is called "the great harlot" (v. 1). She is a terrible woman, yet we must be in our spirit to see what she is as Babylon. We must see this woman; otherwise, we will remain in Babylonian captivity to a certain degree. God hates Babylon. He hates anything that is apostate, anything that is not according to His Word, and anything that is an impure mixture. Furthermore, God hates any sympathy for or toleration of evil and worldly things. He hates compromise and lukewarmness. We need to realize this and stand firm against the world and Babylon, which is apostate Christendom.

We need to pray about this. Not long after I came into the church life, we were taking care of a brother, a brand new one, a brilliant person who was in medical school. We brought him to the large meetings of the church, and I sat next to him. Benson shared in that meeting on Babylon, and as he shared, speaking very strongly against Babylon, it seemed like fire was coming out of him. So I was praying for this new one because in one of his first meetings he was hearing point after point about Babylon and apostate Christendom. Although I was clear myself about Babylon, I was praying for this new brother. After the meeting he got up and went to the book room. I was fearful to speak to him because he was really steeped in apostate Christendom, but I asked him, "Brother, what did you think of the meeting?" He said, "Well, I really need to consider before the Lord everything that was shared and pray about it." This brother did pray, and today he is a very dear brother in the Lord's recovery.

If the brothers speak about apostate Christendom as Babylon and you feel they are too strong, it means you have not fully seen what Babylon is. Today my wife loves the recovery very much; she also loves me and prays for me all the time. When she first met me, I was an unbeliever, a heathen, and she prayed a long time for my salvation. Later, I received the Lord and came into the church life. When I first told her about the church life and the Lord's recovery, she thought I was crazy, but she was willing to come and see. She was quite involved with Christianity, so when the brothers spoke about Babylon, it was hard for her to receive it, but then the Lord showed her a vision of Babylon.

We need to be released from Babylon and the principle of Babylon.

Anything that is Babylonian gives Satan the ground to defeat God's people. We should never tolerate anything in us that is Babylonian. We love all God's children. We love all our brothers and sisters in Christ. If they are born again, we love them. Regardless of where they may be, we love all the brothers. That is our standing. However, we do not love Babylon; rather, we hate Babylon. We love all the brothers, but we hate Babylon. In Revelation 18:4 John "heard another voice out of heaven, saying, Come out of her, My people, that you do not participate in her sins and that you do not receive her plagues."

It is quite striking that at the end of the Bible there are two women. Of one it says, "On her forehead there was a name written, MYSTERY, BABYLON THE GREAT, THE MOTHER OF THE HARLOTS AND THE ABOMINATIONS OF THE EARTH" (17:5). Babylon the great is a mystery, and we need revelation from God to unveil this mystery. Chapters 17 and 18 expose this woman as the consummate harlot. The other woman is unveiled in chapters 19 through 22. She is the bride of Christ (19:7; 21:9). Do you want to be involved with this evil harlot, or do you want to be part of Christ's bride? The Lord's recovery is here to call all God's people out of Babylon so that they may be built up as His pure, spotless, unadulterated bride. The prepared bride cares only for Christ, is constituted purely of Him, takes only His way, and serves only by His means. The material for building up the church is nothing other than Christ and His riches.

In Revelation there are these two women—the harlot and the bride. We in the Lord's recovery desire to practice the pure church life in each locality without any of the evil teachings, evil practices, and evil traditions that have their source in the harlot, Babylon. The pure teaching of the Bible is the teaching of God's economy, and this is what we teach in the Lord's recovery. This is our "major"; this is our unique teaching. We do not want to teach "different things" (1 Tim. 1:3-4). We need to practice the church life according to the divine revelation of the Bible. We do not want any leaven (Matt. 13:33 and footnotes). Leaven is used to make bread easier to eat; spiritually speaking, leaven typifies teachings that bring the truth in God's Word down to a lower, even fallen, standard. It is easy to lower the standard, but it is difficult to raise it. To bring things up from a fallen standard to God's divine standard is not so easy; but this is the way that we are taking in His recovery. We aspire to do everything according to the divine standard revealed in the Holy Bible, that is, according to the way of God's economy, which is

God's plan to dispense Himself in Christ as the Spirit with all His riches into His chosen people in order to "Christify" them and build them up as the Body of Christ to become His bride and His wife—the New Jerusalem, a corporate woman fully united, mingled, saturated, and incorporated with Christ to display and express Him to the entire universe forever and ever. We are here for this. We desire that all God's chosen people would be released from everything Babylonian and be built up as the Body to be the New Jerusalem as God's temple and God's kingdom to bring Christ back so that we can marry Him and enjoy Him on our wedding day of a thousand years. When Babylon, the great harlot, is judged, there is great rejoicing in heaven (Rev. 18:20).

The Principle of Babylon Being
Man's Endeavor to Build Up Something
from Earth to Heaven by Human Ability

The principle of Babylon is man's endeavor to build up something from earth to heaven by human ability (Gen. 11:1-9; 1 Cor. 3:12). The source of Babylon in the Old Testament was Babel, which eventually became the capital of Babylon (Gen. 10:10; Dan 1:1-2). In Genesis 11 the people wanted to build up something from earth to heaven in order to make a name for themselves (vv. 3-4). Footnote 1 on verse 4 says,

> The city built by man's labor signifies that man had forsaken God and replaced Him with a man-made and godless culture (see footnote 2 on Gen. 4:17).

In building the tower of Babel, the people used brick, not stone (11:3-4). Footnote 1 on verse 3 says,

> God's building is of stones (1 Kings 6:7; Matt. 16:18; John 1:42; 1 Cor. 3:12a; 1 Pet. 2:5; Rev. 21:18-20), which are produced by God's divine work through creation and transformation, whereas the building of the city and tower of Babel was of bricks (cf. Exo. 1:11, 14a), which are the result of human labor through the burning of the God-created earth.
>
> The earth is for growing life (Gen. 1:11). To make bricks is to kill, to burn, the element of the earth that grows life. In figure, the earth signifies humanity (2:7; 3:19; Matt. 13:3-8 and footnotes; 1 Cor. 15:47a). Thus, the rebellion instigated by Satan kills the element within man that grows

the divine life, by burning it out, and it misuses man to build up a man-made and godless life.

Babylon burns all the life out of people. I know a young man who went to a seminary. Before he went to the seminary, he had a heart for the Lord, but now it seems that he barely believes in God. The life within him and his love for the Lord were almost completely burned out. This shows how evil Babylon is.

We all must beware of our human ability. In the Lord's recovery we do not want to do anything by our human ability, and we never want to treasure or uplift anyone's human ability. Apostate Christendom uplifts and treasures human ability. If a person is especially gifted or a great star in the world, Christendom will exalt him. However, we all need to realize that our human ability is dung; we should not treasure it. God is the One who has given us our human ability, but He wants us to do everything by Christ as our strength and in Christ as our ability. In serving the Lord we must reject everything of our "wood-grass-stubble being." This means that we must reject everything of our natural man, everything of the fallen flesh, and everything of our natural, lifeless, earthen source. We want everything that we are and do to come out of God as our source, to be by God as our power, strength, and ability, and unto God for His glory. This is the essence of the pure church life, not treasuring or building up anything by human ability.

The Principle of Babylon Being Hypocrisy

The principle of Babylon is hypocrisy (Rev. 17:4, 6; Matt. 23:25-32; Josh. 7:21; Acts 5:1-11; Matt. 15:7-8; 6:1-6). The woman in Revelation 17:4 was gilded with gold, precious stone, and pearls. The things of apostate Christendom, especially the things of the Roman Catholic Church, have been transmitted into all the denominations and free groups so that there are vestiges of Babylon in all of them. Thus, they are the many daughters of the great harlot (v. 5). Hypocrisy is the principle of Babylon. The New Jerusalem is pure gold; in contrast, the woman, Babylon the Great, is *gilded* with gold. Pure gold, pearls, and precious stone are the materials that comprise the New Jerusalem, but Babylon is merely gilded with these materials; beneath this gilded surface lies something that is utterly evil and rotten. This is hypocrisy. Outwardly, there is some gold, some pearls, and some precious stones, signifying something of God's nature, Christ's redemption, and the Spirit's transformation, but this is merely an outward display, a gilding.

We need to pray, not only concerning outsiders but concerning ourselves, "Lord, I don't want merely to be gilded with You. Save me from hypocrisy." If a cup is merely gilded, a small scratch will expose the true nature that lies beneath the surface. However, if a cup is pure gold, no matter how deeply it is scratched, all you can see is gold. We do not want to be merely gilded with the Triune God; we want to be those who are thoroughly constituted with Him.

The evil woman holds "a golden cup full of abominations and the unclean things of her fornication" (v. 4). Outwardly, it looks very nice, having the appearance of godliness, but within there are many terrible things. For example, some may compromise a little by taking worldly ways or using worldly means to preach the gospel. They may say that it is too difficult to gain the increase in the recovery if we are too pure; therefore, they put a little leaven in to make it easier to take. White bread is so easy to chew and eat, but unleavened bread is harder to eat. Nevertheless, unleavened bread is pure. Leaven signifies evil things and worldly doctrines. Anything that is not in the Bible as our content, our way, and our means to carry out God's economy is leaven. We must preach the gospel in a pure way, not using worldly means. When Paul went to Macedonia, he did not put on a dramatic performance or show a movie to attract the unbelievers. He did not say, "It is too hard for unbelievers to understand the gospel, so let me show them a religious film." If it is not in the Holy Bible, we should not do it; otherwise, what kind of fruit will be produced? When we preach that kind of gospel, we will produce a mixed people. We will produce worldly Christians because we took a worldly way. The Lord's recovery is here to produce the overcomers. Every young person on a college campus longs to be absolute for something real. They do not want to be lukewarm people, living a lukewarm existence. God is absolute, and man was created in the image of the absolute God. Man, in His created nature, longs to be pure and absolute. This is what every man is seeking, especially the young people. They all are searching; therefore, they are asking themselves, "Should I be absolute for music? Should I be absolute for sinful things? Should I be absolute for the world or for money?" This is why, when we show them the meaning of the universe, the destiny of man, God's economy, and God's heart's desire by means of prayer, the Word, and the Spirit, their hearts are captured. They realize that to be an overcomer and part of the bride of Christ to bring

Him back is the noblest endeavor in the universe. Surely, we cannot compromise in this.

In Matthew 23 the Lord rebuked the religious Pharisees, especially with regard to their hypocrisy. In verse 25 He says, "Woe to you, scribes and Pharisees, hypocrites! For you cleanse the outside of the cup and the dish, but inwardly they are full of extortion and self-indulgence." Surely we do not want to be like this. In our natural man we may want to compromise, but we should stand against our flesh and our stinking, rotten self and stand with the Spirit in our spirit. The Lord told those religionists, "Woe to you, scribes and Pharisees, hypocrites! For you resemble whitewashed graves, which outwardly appear beautiful but inwardly are full of dead men's bones and all uncleanness. So you also outwardly appear righteous to men, but inwardly you are full of hypocrisy and lawlessness" (vv. 27-28).

Anything that is Babylonian gives Satan the ground to defeat the people of God. In Joshua 6 the children of Israel had a glorious victory in defeating Jericho. However, in chapter 7 God's people were defeated by the much smaller city of Ai. To gain the victory over Ai should have been easy (vv. 3-4), yet they were defeated. When Joshua went to the Lord concerning this defeat, he discovered that one of the Israelites, Achan, had taken things from Jericho—a mantle of Shinar (a Babylonian garment), some silver, and some gold—and had hidden them in his tent (vv. 20-21). A garment is for outward appearance. We all need to be saved from any kind of pretense, which is hypocrisy. If we mean business with the Lord to pursue Him, to gain Him, to live Him, and to come together and minister Him to one another, we need to ask Him to save us from all hypocrisy.

In Matthew 15:7-8 the Lord says, "Hypocrites! Well has Isaiah prophesied concerning you, saying, 'This people honors Me with their lips, but their heart stays far away from Me.'" It is not a small thing to turn our heart to the Lord. We do not want merely to render Him lip service. We would turn our heart to Him and give Him our heart, saying, "Lord Jesus, I give my heart to You. I want You to make Your home in my heart." In Matthew 6:1-6 the Lord speaks concerning our giving alms, our praying, and our fasting. In this portion the Lord seems to be saying, "Do not do any of these things for a public show." Of course, we need to pray, and we need to pray publicly in the meetings, but we need to be saved from hypocrisy. Having a secret time with the Lord every day is the best way to be saved from hypocrisy. We need to have some personal experiences of Him, including times of secret, hidden prayer with Him that no one else knows about. The Lord was saying, "Don't be like the hypocrites who pray on the street corners so that everyone will say, 'Look at that!' Don't be like those who when they give alms they sound a trumpet and when they give an offering everyone knows about it." I am so grateful that in the churches in the Lord's recovery, it is sometimes even difficult to find the offering box.

In a denomination in the neighborhood where I grew up, they published a list of everyone who made donations. Those at the top of the list—the honor roll—were those who gave the most, and those at the bottom were those who gave the least. In Luke 21 the Lord praises an utterly poor widow who put two lepta (the smallest Roman coin) in the temple treasury, saying, "Truly I tell you that this poor widow has cast in more than all of them, for all these out of their surplus have cast in something into the gifts, but she out of her lack has cast in all the living that she had" (vv. 3-4). I doubt that this widow would even "make the list" in today's Christianity. Since our Father sees in secret and rewards us in secret, we need to do everything, as much as possible, in secret. We need to pray in secret, give in secret, and fast in secret. When we pray, we should enter into our private room, shut the door, and pray to our Father who is in secret. We should treasure our time with the Lord in the morning. It is our secret time with Him when we really receive His substance into us, for it is He Himself that makes us real.

The Principle of Babylon Being
That of Not Considering Herself a Widow
but of Glorifying Herself and Living Luxuriously

The principle of Babylon is that of not considering herself a widow but of glorifying herself and living luxuriously (Isa. 47:8b; Rev. 18:7; Luke 18:3; Matt. 9:14-15). Isaiah 47:8 also speaks of Babylon as a woman, saying, "Now hear this, O lover of pleasure, / Who dwells securely / And says in your heart, / I am, and there is none besides me; / I will not dwell as a widow." In one sense, we are the Lord's bride, but in another sense, we need to realize that we are a widow in this world. Even though the Lord lives within us, our Husband is not here. He is no longer in the world, but we are in this world; therefore, we are like a widow. We long for Him to come back. How can we be fully happy if He is not here? To bring Him back is our career. In this sense we are a widow.

This evil woman lives luxuriously. As believers we should not have anything in excess. Paul says, "Godliness with contentment is great gain; for we have brought nothing into the world, because neither can we carry anything out. But having food and covering, with these we will be content. But those who intend to be rich fall into temptation and a snare and many foolish and harmful desires, which plunge men into destruction and ruin. For the love of money is a root of all evils, because of which some, aspiring after money, have been led away from the faith and pierced themselves through with many pains" (1 Tim. 6:6-10). If we have the intention or aspiration to be rich, we will eventually fall into destruction and ruin, piercing ourselves through with many pains. We are not here to glorify ourselves or to live luxuriously; we are here to deny ourselves, to give what we have for the Lord's interest, and to be rich toward God.

The Principle of Babylon Being
for Man to Make a Name for Himself
and Deny God's Name

The principle of Babylon is for man to make a name for himself and deny God's name (Gen. 11:4; Rev. 3:8; 2 Cor. 11:2; 1 Cor. 1:10). The tower of Babel was built because men wanted to make a name for themselves, forsaking God and replacing Him with a man-made and godless culture. To take any name other than Christ is spiritual fornication. A man would not be happy if his wife were to take another name, a name different from her husband's. The Lord is our Husband. We should never take any name other than His name. The church is "Mrs. Christ." We should not take any other name.

Some may ask us, "To what denomination do you belong?" The Bible utterly condemns the practice of having denominations. We have no other name than that of Christ. In 1 Corinthians 1:11-13 Paul seems to be saying, "Why do you claim to be of me, Paul, and others of Apollos or Cephas? Were you baptized into any of our names? Was Paul crucified for you? Why do you then take my name and denominate yourselves, saying, 'We are of Paul. We are the Pauline denomination," and others, "We are the Petrine denomination?'" We should not take any name other than that of Christ. We have been betrothed to Christ; He is our Husband (2 Cor. 11:2). When others ask us, "What church do you belong to?" we should say, "I belong to the same church that you belong to, and that church is the Body of Christ." There is only one church.

The Principle of Babylon Being Confusion

The principle of Babylon is confusion (Gen. 11:6-7; cf. Rom. 15:5-6; 1 Cor. 1:10; Phil. 2:2; 1 Tim. 1:3-4). At Babel man's language was confounded so that they did not understand one another. The many languages that resulted at Babel led to confusion and division. Confusion equals division. We need to be saved from all kinds of confusion. If someone takes another husband or takes the name of another, that causes confusion. However, in the New Testament Paul says that we need to have the same mind, be in one accord, have one mouth, speak the same thing, have the same opinion, and have the same love (1 Cor. 1:10; Rom. 15:6; Phil. 2:2). What a glory that we all can speak the same in the Lord's recovery. We should not teach different things; we should simply teach God's economy, having one mouth and one ministry to build up the one Body.

The Principle of Babylon Being That of Scattering, with Each One Going His Own Way and His Own Direction

The principle of Babylon is scattering, with each one going his own way and his own direction (Gen. 11:8; cf. Deut. 16:16; Psa. 133; 1 Kings 12:26-32). The situation among Christians today is one of being scattered through confusion and division. If Paul were here today to write a letter to the saints in Anaheim, to whom would he send it? It was very simple in his day. There was only one church in Corinth and only one church in Ephesus. There was only one church in every city. All the believers in Corinth, all the "called saints," were the church in Corinth (1 Cor. 1:2). The clear pattern in the New Testament is that of one church for one city and of one city with one church (Rev. 1:11). It is very simple. All the believers in a particular city are the church in that city. However, this is not their name but simply a description of what they are. We are the church, and we happen to live and meet in Anaheim. We are the believers, the called saints, in Anaheim, so we are simply the church in Anaheim. It is so simple. Regrettably, this is not the practice among Christians today. There is the Taiwan Church in America. A brother once told me that his denominational background was the African Methodist Episcopal Church.

African denotes division based on something racial and cultural, *Methodist* denotes division based on something related to practice, and *Episcopal* denotes division based on something related to organization. What confusion! We are all believers in Christ; thus, we are the church, the one Body of Christ. The situation today is one of much scattering.

At the end of Brother Lee's life, he charged a few of us to continue to gather the saints in the recovery together seven times a year. He said, "I want you to consider this as my will." For this reason, we have endeavored to come together for these seven "annual feasts"—two semi-annual trainings (summer and winter), two international trainings for elders and responsible ones (spring and fall), and three international conferences (Chinese-speaking, Thanksgiving, and Memorial Day). Brother Lee said that we should consider this as his will. We should not think that he said this in a light way. Consider where would the recovery be today if we had not held these seven feasts for all these years since our brother's departure. This has been a great source of blending for the entire recovery. We also need to blend locally and with the churches in our area. It is so good that we can come together to blend in this way. When we come together and open to have fellowship with the saints and the churches, our biased and warped characteristics are being blended out of us. We are one Body, standing on the ground of locality; we are also one Body with one teaching, speaking the same thing. We do not agree with any kind of scattering. Instead, we meet as the church on the ground of oneness in our locality, which includes all the believers. We also exercise to gather together as much as possible. At the end of the Bible, there is only one church and one city—the New Jerusalem; there is no longer any scattering. I encourage you all to make at least one of these feasts every year. Pray about this.

First Kings 12:26-33 records the sin of Jeroboam. Ten of the tribes of the children of Israel rebelled and caused Israel to be divided. Two tribes remained with Rehoboam the king of Judah, and the rest followed Jeroboam, as the king of Israel. Jeroboam was very concerned that the people would go up to worship at Jerusalem. In verse 27 he says, "If this people go up to make sacrifices in the house of Jehovah at Jerusalem, the heart of this people will return to their lord, to Rehoboam the king of Judah; and they will slay me and return to Rehoboam the king of Judah." To prevent this, Jeroboam set up two idols, two golden calves—one in Bethel and one in Dan—and caused the people to worship them. This and other acts of Jeroboam's apostasy are repeatedly referred to as "the sins of Jeroboam" (12:30; 13:34; 15:26, 30, 34; 16:19, 26). He was a person who was ambitious to have his own kingdom to fulfill his selfish desires; he did not want God's people to gather together in oneness. Our coming together in oneness kills all our ambition. It is wonderful to come together in this way.

The Principle of Babylon Being Mixture;
Anything Which Is Halfway and Not Absolute
Being Called Babylon

The principle of Babylon is mixture; anything which is halfway and not absolute is called Babylon (2 Chron. 36:6-7; Ezra 1:11; cf. 2 Kings 17:8).

The Lord's Call in the Book of Revelation Being
for His People to Come out of Babylon

The Lord's call in the book of Revelation is for His people to come out of Babylon (Isa. 52:11-12; Rev. 18:4-5). Isaiah 52:11 and 12 say, "Depart! Depart! Go out from there! / Do not touch any unclean thing! / Go out from the midst of her! Cleanse yourselves, / You who bear the vessels of Jehovah! / For you will not go out in haste, / And you will not go in flight; / For Jehovah will go before you, / And the God of Israel will be your rear guard." Revelation 18:4 and 5 say, "I heard another voice out of heaven, saying, Come out of her, My people, that you do not participate in her sins and that you do not receive her plagues; for her sins have accumulated up to heaven, and God has remembered her unrighteousnesses." We do not take the way of the world, nor do we compromise with Babylon. Our way to carry out God's work and to preach the gospel is by prayer, the Word, and the Spirit. We hate what God hates. We hate the clergy-laity system because that is what God hates. He commended the church in Ephesus saying, "This you have, that you hate the works of the Nicolaitans, which I also hate" (2:6). However, due to a further degradation of the church in Pergamos, the *work* of the Nicolaitans had become the *teaching* of the Nicolaitans (v. 15). It would be terrible if, in our church meetings, we went back to the practice of one man speaking and the rest listening. While there is a time and place for ministry meetings, the church meetings should be characterized by mutuality in which each one speaks, all prophesy, and each one has something to minister to others. It would be terrible if some would say, "This is too hard. Let's just have one brother speak." Brother Lee labored intensely for years in order to pull us out of our own practice of the clergy-laity system so that all of us would function and speak for the Lord. It is a glory to have a church meeting on the Lord's Day morning in which all the saints prophesy. This is a glory to God, and it builds up the church.

Needing to Be One with Christ
to Build Up the Church as God's Temple

We need to be one with Christ to build up the church as God's temple (Eph. 2:21-22; Matt. 16:18; 1 Cor. 14:4b). To build up the church as God's temple, we need to give ourselves to grow in life, to exercise our spirit daily, and to prophesy, to speak for the Lord. Such practices build up the church as God's temple.

Needing to Be One with Christ
to Build Up the Church as God's Kingdom

We need to be one with Christ to build up the church as God's kingdom (Matt. 16:18-19, 24; Rom. 14:17-18). We build up the church as God's kingdom by denying ourselves, by not loving ourselves, and by loving the Lord in our spirit. We deny ourselves by living by the Spirit in our spirit. The kingdom of God is righteousness, peace, and joy in the Holy Spirit.

CHRIST AS THE SERVANT OF JEHOVAH
BEING TYPIFIED BY CYRUS

His Being Raised Up by Jehovah,
Anointed by Jehovah, and Loved by Jehovah

Christ as the Servant of Jehovah is typified by Cyrus in the following aspects. He was raised up by Jehovah (Isa. 41:2a, 25a; 45:13a; Acts 3:26a), anointed by Jehovah (Isa. 45:1a; Luke 4:18a), and loved by Jehovah (Isa. 48:14b; Matt. 3:17). These characteristics not only refer to Cyrus; they also refer to Christ. Cyrus was raised up by Jehovah, and Christ was raised up by Jehovah (Acts 3:26a). Cyrus was anointed by Jehovah, and Christ was anointed by Jehovah (Luke 4:18a). Cyrus was loved by Jehovah, and Christ is God's Son, the Beloved (Matt. 3:17).

His Doing God's Pleasure on Babylon,
Symbolizing the Roman Catholic Church

He did God's pleasure on Babylon (Isa. 48:14; 46:11), symbolizing the Roman Catholic Church (Rev. 17:3-5).

His Being God's Counselor to Subdue the Nations
and Have Dominion over the Kings

He was God's counselor (Isa. 46:11b) to subdue the nations and have dominion over the kings (41:2b, 25; 45:1b; Ezra 1:2a; Acts 5:31; Rev. 1:5a). This is fulfilled in Christ.

His Being Jehovah's Shepherd for the Fulfilling
of His Desire in Building Up the City
(Symbolizing the Kingdom) and the Temple of God
and in Releasing God's Captives

He was Jehovah's shepherd (Isa. 45:1) for the fulfilling of His desire in building up the city (symbolizing the kingdom) and the temple of God and in releasing God's captives (44:28; 45:13; Ezra 1:2-3; John 2:19; Luke 4:18b).

CHRIST AS THE SERVANT OF JEHOVAH
BEING TYPIFIED BY ISRAEL

Israel Being Chosen by Jehovah and Upheld
with the Right Hand of His Righteousness

Christ as the Servant of Jehovah is typified by Israel in the following aspects. Israel was chosen by Jehovah and upheld with the right hand of His righteousness (Isa. 41:10). Israel typifies the corporate Christ.

Israel Overcoming the Enemies by Jehovah
and Rejoicing and Glorying in Him,
the Holy One of Israel

Israel overcame the enemies by Jehovah and rejoiced and gloried in Him, the Holy One of Israel (vv. 8-16; 42:1a; Rom. 8:37; 1 Thes. 2:19-20). Christ does the same.

Israel Being the Witness of Jehovah

Israel was the witness of Jehovah (Isa. 43:10; Rev. 1:5a; 3:14; Acts 1:8). Christ is God's faithful Witness. He is the testimony of God and the expression of God. We also are His witnesses as a part of the corporate Christ.

The Spirit of Jehovah Being Poured Out on Israel for the Blessing of His Offspring

The Spirit of Jehovah was poured out on Israel for the blessing of His offspring (Isa. 44:1-5, 21; Matt. 3:16; Luke 4:18-19). The Spirit of Jehovah was also poured out on Christ.

Jehovah Being Glorified in Israel

Jehovah was glorified in Israel (Isa. 43:7; 49:3; 46:13b; John 17:1; 12:28). In the New Testament, God is gloried in Christ and in the church, the Body of Christ. God is glorified in the corporate Christ.

Israel Being God's Servant in the Sense of Fulfilling God's Desire in His Economy to Have a Corporate Expression of Himself for His Glory; in This Sense Israel Being One with Christ as God's Servant

Israel is God's servant in the sense of fulfilling God's desire in His economy to have a corporate expression of Himself for His glory; in this sense Israel was one with Christ as God's servant (Isa. 41:8; 45:4; 49:3; Hosea 11:1; cf. Matt. 2:15). Thus, Israel typifies the corporate Christ, the corporate servant of God. In Matthew 2 the angel warned Joseph to flee Israel because Herod was going to seek the child, Jesus, to destroy Him; therefore, Joseph took the child and His mother and fled into Egypt. Later, after Herod's death, they were called out of Egypt and dwelt in Nazareth. Quoting from the Old Testament prophet Hosea, verse 15 says, "Out of Egypt I called My Son" (cf. Hosea 11:1). In Hosea it refers to Israel, but in the fulfillment of the prophecy, it refers to Christ's coming out of Egypt as a child. This shows that Israel is a type of Christ.

In the Present Age the Church as the Testimony of God Serving God for the Expression of God, the Glory of God

In the present age the church as the testimony of God serves God for the expression of God, the glory of God (Rev. 1:2; Eph. 3:21; Gal. 6:16). According to Galatians 6:16, the church is the Israel of God.

The Glorification of God Being the Purpose of Our Service; the Highest Service We Can Render to God Being to Express Him in His Glory

The glorification of God is the purpose of our service; the highest service we can render to God is to express Him in His glory (Eph. 1:23; 1 Cor. 10:31). This is our highest service. We want God to be expressed; this is to glorify Him in the purest way.

Let us be those who are one with Christ as God's Servant to release God's chosen people from all kinds of captivity and to build up the church as God's temple and as God's kingdom. This will bring the Lord back.—E. M.

THE DIVINE ECONOMY IN THE BOOK OF ISAIAH

The Revelation and Experience of Christ
as the New Covenant
(Message 21)

Scripture Reading: Isa. 42:6; 49:8; Jer. 31:31-34; Heb. 8:8-12

I. In Greek the same word is used for both *covenant* and *testament:*
   A. A covenant and a testament are the same, but when the maker of the covenant is living, it is a covenant, and when he has died, it is a testament; a testament in today's terms is a will.
   B. A covenant is an agreement containing some promises to accomplish certain things for the covenanted people, while a testament is a will containing certain accomplished things that are bequeathed to the inheritor—Heb. 9:16-17; cf. Deut. 11:29; 28:1, 15; Jer. 31:31-32.

II. The old covenant, the law, is the testimony of God, the portrait of God, showing us who God is and exposing man, subduing man, and conducting God's chosen ones to Christ—Psa. 78:5; 119:88b; Gen. 1:26; Rom. 3:19-20; Gal. 3:23-25; John 10:9-10.

III. The old covenant of the law is a portrait of God, but the new covenant of grace is the person of God—1:16-17:
   A. The law makes demands upon man according to what God is; grace supplies man with what God is to meet what God demands—1 Cor. 15:10.
   B. When we believe into Christ, the person of this portrait comes into us and He fulfills in us the righteous requirements of the law as we walk according to the spirit and set our mind on the spirit—Ezek. 36:26-27; Rom. 8:2, 4, 6, 10.
   C. In the new covenant God puts Himself into His chosen people as their life, and this life is a law, a spontaneous, automatic principle—Heb. 8:10; Rom. 8:2.
   D. In essence this law is God in Christ as the Spirit, and in function it has the capacity to deify us and to constitute us the

members of the Body of Christ with all kinds of functions—vv. 10, 6, 11, 28-29.

IV. Christ Himself is the new covenant, the new testament, given to us by God—Isa. 42:6; 49:8; Jer. 31:31-34; Heb. 8:8-12:

    A. Through His death Christ fulfilled the demands of God's righteousness according to His law and enacted the new covenant (Rom. 6:23; 3:21; 10:3-4; Luke 22:20; Heb. 9:16-17), and in His resurrection He became the new covenant with all of its bequests (1 Cor. 15:45b; Isa. 42:6; Phil. 1:19).

    B. In His ascension Christ opened the scroll of the new covenant concerning God's economy, and in His heavenly ministry He is carrying out its contents—Rev. 5:1-5.

    C. As the Lion of the tribe of Judah, Christ overcame and defeated Satan, as the redeeming Lamb, Christ took away the sin of fallen man, and as the seven Spirits, Christ infuses us with Himself as the contents of the scroll of the new covenant—vv. 5-6.

    D. God's salvation, God's blessings, and all of God's riches have been covenanted to us, and this covenant is Christ:

        1. The reality of all the hundreds of bequests in the New Testament is Christ—Gen. 22:18a; Gal. 3:14; 1 Cor. 1:30; 15:45b; Eph. 1:3.

        2. Christ is the reality of the new testament, the reality of all that God is and of all that God has given to us; therefore, Christ is the new testament.

        3. The bequests are many, but all these many bequests are actually one person—the pneumatic Christ; God has willed Himself in Christ as the Spirit to us—John 20:22; Eph. 3:8.

        4. The bequests bequeathed to us by the Lord in the new testament are inexhaustible, and they are for us to experience and enjoy through the Spirit for eternity—Heb. 9:15.

V. Our spirit is the "bank account" of all the bequests of the new covenant; by the law of the Spirit of life, all of these bequests are dispensed into us and made real to us—Rom. 8:2, 10, 6, 11, 16; Heb. 8:10; John 16:13:

    A. In our spirit we have the presence of God, the speaking of God, the meeting with God, and the dispensing of God through His operation as the law of the divine life to impart and inscribe Himself into all our inward parts—Heb. 8:10.

B. The Lord makes His covenant known to those who fear Him, and He dispenses Himself as the unsearchable reality of His covenant to those who love Him—Psa. 25:14; Isa. 11:2-3a; 1 Cor. 2:9.

C. Christ as the new covenant is our portion, our cup of salvation and our cup of blessing; we can drink Him as our salvation and blessing by calling upon His precious name— Luke 22:20; Psa. 16:5; 23:5; 116:13; 1 Cor. 10:16a.

D. Christ is the pneumatic Executor, Mediator, of the new covenant in our spirit; as the Executor He makes every bequest of His will available and real as we receive the word of His will by means of all prayer—Heb. 8:6; 1 John 5:6.

E. As the surety of the new covenant, Christ is the pledge that everything in the new covenant will be fulfilled; He guarantees and ensures the effectiveness of the new testament— Heb. 7:22.

F. As the divine High Priest, Christ is executing the new covenant by interceding for us, praying that we would be brought into the reality of the new covenant—v. 25; Rom. 8:34, 26.

G. As the Minister of the holy places, Christ is serving us with the bequests, the blessings, of the new testament, making the facts of the new covenant effective in our experience—Heb. 8:2.

H. In order to receive the application of all the blessings in the new covenant, we need to be those who respond to Christ's heavenly ministry by entering into His intercession for the churches and His ministering God into others—Gen. 14:18-20; Heb. 7:25; 8:2; Acts 6:4.

THE REVELATION AND EXPERIENCE OF CHRIST
AS THE NEW COVENANT

Prayer: Lord Jesus, we love You. Thank You for all that You have done and are doing in us. Thank You that we can take the cup of salvation and call upon Your name. Lord Jesus, we call upon Your name for this meeting, and we consecrate ourselves to You. Lord, open Your heart to us and show us more of Your glorious person. Lord, bring us into a deeper and richer experience of You. Use this message to prepare us more to be Your bride. Amen.

The title of this message is "The Revelation and Experience of Christ as the New Covenant." In this message we will consider a great revelation in the Holy Scriptures. I am concerned that many of us, especially the young ones and new ones, do not know or see what the new covenant is intrinsically. Some may not even know what the words *covenant* and *testament* mean. It is critical that we see this matter because the new covenant is actually God's New Testament economy. God's economy is God's testament, God's will, to us. Moreover, we need to see that the new covenant is a person—Christ Himself. Isaiah 42:6 says, "I am Jehovah; I have called You in righteousness; / I have held You by the hand; / I have kept You and I have given You / As a covenant for the people, as a light for the nations." This verse, as a prophecy concerning Christ, indicates that God would give Himself in Christ as a covenant for His people. This shows that Christ Himself is the covenant. Then 49:8 says, "Thus says Jehovah, / In an acceptable time I have answered You, / And in a day of salvation I have helped You; / And I will preserve You and give You for a covenant of the people, / To restore the land, to apportion the desolate inheritances." This verse also reveals that Christ Himself is the new covenant that God has made with us. In Jeremiah 31:31-34 God spoke a promise to Israel, which was then quoted by Paul in Hebrews 8:8-12. In so doing, Paul reveals that the believers in Christ are under this new covenant with its particular blessings and bequests. Now as we consider the message outline, may the Lord unfold a fresh revelation in our being and enlighten our understanding to see and know who He is and what He wants to do in us.

IN GREEK THE SAME WORD BEING USED
FOR BOTH *COVENANT* AND *TESTAMENT*

In Greek the same word is used for both *covenant* and *testament.* The words *covenant* and *testament* are synonyms. Therefore, the new covenant is the new testament, and the ministers of the new covenant are the ministers of the new testament. Although these words are synonymous, there is still a distinction between a covenant and a testament.

A Covenant and a Testament Being the Same, but When the Maker of the Covenant Is Living, It Being a Covenant, and When He Has Died, It Being a Testament; a Testament in Today's Terms Being a Will

A covenant and a testament are the same, but when the maker of the covenant is living, it is a covenant, and when he has died, it is a testament; a testament in today's terms is a will. If a rich man promises to bequeath all his riches to us, he is making a covenant with us. There are many promises in the Bible, including promises in the old covenant concerning the new covenant. A covenant is full of promises. Hebrews 8:6 speaks of a better covenant enacted upon better promises; this is the new covenant. A covenant becomes a testament when the maker of the covenant dies. Only then does the covenant become a will, fulfilling the promises to those to whom the riches have been bequeathed. Thus, a testament is a will.

We need to see what God has willed to us. We are not speaking of earthly riches, which are vanity and will eventually be consumed by fire. God has bequeathed to us in His will the unsearchable riches of Christ. The Bible is God's will to us. Moreover, God made a covenant with us. He came in Christ through incarnation, passed through human living, died an all-inclusive death, and resurrected to become the life-giving Spirit. He died to satisfy all the righteous requirements of God's law, and in resurrection He became the life-giving Spirit as the reality of the new covenant. Now He has bequeathed all that He is to us in His will. We all are in God's will! All the riches of the person of Christ have been willed to us. The Bible is our written will. If we want to know what has been willed to us, we need to know the Bible. If we do not read the will, we will not know what has been bequeathed to us. Furthermore, whatever is written in the Bible as a will is now a reality in our spirit. In the United States there is a large amount of gold deposited at Fort Knox. In the same principle our spirit is the "Fort Knox" of the riches of Christ. Our spirit contains all the unsearchable riches of Christ. Nevertheless, we need to read the Bible in order to fully realize what is in this will.

A Covenant Being an Agreement Containing Some Promises to Accomplish Certain Things for the Covenanted People, While a Testament Being a Will Containing Certain Accomplished Things That Are Bequeathed to the Inheritor

A covenant is an agreement containing some promises to accomplish certain things for the covenanted people, while a testament is a will containing certain accomplished things that are bequeathed to the inheritor (Heb. 9:16-17; cf. Deut. 11:29; 28:1, 15; Jer. 31:31-32). In His covenant God promised to accomplish certain things for us, but His testament is a will that contains all the accomplished things that are now bequeathed to us, the inheritors. We are all inheritors of the Triune God. God has willed Himself in Christ as the Spirit to us with all His unsearchable riches. Humanly speaking, to bequeath is to leave property and riches to another upon one's death. In the spiritual realm, after Christ died on the cross and became the life-giving Spirit in resurrection, He became the reality of the new covenant. In His covenant He has bequeathed Himself to us with all His unsearchable riches. Christ as the unsearchable riches of the Triune God, typified by the all-inclusive good land, has been willed to us.

It would be ridiculous if a person had a billion dollars in his bank account yet worried about how he would pay his bills. If he had a billion dollars but had no knowledge of his wealth, it would be as if he were still poor. Without a clear realization of his wealth, he may even behave as a poor beggar. Many times in our Christian life we behave as if we are poor beggars, without realizing that we are glorious inheritors of all that God is. God is whatever we need. Without a realization of our glorious wealth, we will be forced to pray like beggars instead of glorious inheritors. We need to realize how rich we are. Furthermore, we need to be those who make others rich also, making them glorious inheritors of the wealth of God.

Hebrews 9:16 and 17 say, "Where there is a testament, the death of him who made the testament must of necessity be established. For a testament is confirmed in the case of the dead, since it never has force when he who made the testament is living." Hence, Christ died so that He could become the Spirit and bequeath Himself to us.

Deuteronomy 28:1 and 15 say, "If you listen diligently to the voice of Jehovah your God and are certain to do all His commandments, which I am commanding you today, Jehovah your God will set you high above all the nations of the earth...But if you do not listen to the voice of Jehovah your God and are not certain to do all His commandments and His statutes, which I am commanding you today, all these curses will come upon you and overtake you." God made the old covenant with the people of Israel; that covenant was the law. He covenanted with His people according to the law. It is as if He were saying, "If you obey the law, you will be blessed, but if you do not obey the law, you will be cursed." The condition of the covenant for blessing was obedience to the law, to God's voice. If Israel obeyed the law, they would be blessed in every way.

Deuteronomy 11:29 says, "When Jehovah your God brings you into the land which you are entering to possess, you shall put the blessing upon Mount Gerizim and the curse upon Mount Ebal." According to God's ordination, when the children of Israel were entering into the good land, Moses commanded that six tribes go to Mount Gerizim and the other six to Mount Ebal (27:12-13). The tribes at Mount Gerizim were to declare to the children of Israel that if they obeyed the voice of Jehovah, they would be blessed to the uttermost in the good land. However, the tribes at Mount Ebal were to declare a curse to those who would not obey Jehovah's commandments. Thus, the old covenant consists of a blessing and a curse. According to the old covenant, the condition for blessing was to obey the law, and the issue of not obeying the law was that one would be cursed. In the old covenant one is blessed if he keeps the law and cursed if he does not keep the law.

Praise the Lord that God became a man who, on the cross, was made a curse for all men. By His death Christ redeemed us out of the curse of the law (Gal. 3:13). It was impossible for man to satisfy the demands of the law. Hence, God made a new covenant with man. Jeremiah 31:31-32 says,

> Indeed, days are coming, declares Jehovah, when I will make a new covenant with the house of Israel and with the

> house of Judah, not like the covenant which I made with
> their fathers in the day I took them by their hand to bring
> them out from the land of Egypt, My covenant which they
> broke, although I was their Husband, declares Jehovah.

Then verses 33 and 34 speak concerning the contents of the new covenant:

> This is the covenant which I will make with the house of
> Israel after those days, declares Jehovah: I will put My law
> in their inward parts and write it upon their hearts; and I
> will be their God, and they will be My people. And they will
> no longer teach, each man his neighbor and each man his
> brother, saying, Know Jehovah; for all of them will know
> Me, from the little one among them even to the great one
> among them, declares Jehovah, for I will forgive their iniq-
> uity, and their sin I will remember no more.

This is the new covenant that Jehovah promised to His people and that Paul referred to in Hebrews 8:8-12.

How are we blessed in the new covenant? First Corinthians 2:9 and 10 say, "As it is written, 'Things which eye has not seen and ear has not heard and which have not come up in man's heart; things which God has prepared for those who love Him.' But to us God has revealed them through the Spirit, for the Spirit searches all things, even the depths of God." We need to pray that the Lord would reveal the awesome significance of this verse in relation to the new covenant. We have seen that under the old covenant Mount Gerizim represented blessing and Mount Ebal represented cursing—that if we keep the law, we will be blessed, but if we do not keep the law, we will be cursed. However, under the new covenant Christ's death fulfilled all the righteous requirements of the law. Then He entered into resurrection to become the life-giving Spirit, and now He is able to indwell us. These verses reveal that we are blessed simply by loving the Lord. In the new covenant we need only to love Christ in order to enjoy Him as all the riches in the divine and mystical realm. To love the Lord is the unique commandment in the New Testament. Hence, it is a great thing to say, "Lord Jesus, I love You." We must never graduate from this. Otherwise, we will be cursed, not because we have disobeyed the law but because we do not love the Lord. As lovers of the Lord, we should frequently ask ourselves, "How is my romance with the Lord?" We need to pray, "Lord, I want my love for You to be fresh and new. Infuse me with Your love. Lord, I want to love You more today than I have ever loved You in my entire life." If we love the Lord in this way, we will be blessed with things that eye has not seen, ear has not heard, and which have not come up in man's heart.

Conversely, 16:22 says, "If anyone does not love the Lord, let him be accursed!" In the New Testament God's blessing or curse is not a matter of whether or not we keep the law; it is a matter of whether or not we love the Lord. To not love the Lord is a great curse, but whenever our love for the Lord is fresh and new, we are blessed and happy because we are enjoying His dispensing. Whenever our heart is turned away from Him, we feel terrible. Surely it is a terrible experience to not love the Lord.

This is why when we minister the Word, especially to the young people, we try to help them to love the Lord. This is why many may regard us as being "crazy." For example, the world may consider it "crazy" for young people to sacrifice their personal freedom and the comfort of living at home to attend the full-time training. At home they have their own room and enjoy their mother's cooking. Moreover, they are able to do whatever they want and go wherever they please, but in the training they are "imprisoned" and required to follow a strict schedule. Nevertheless, the full-time training is a "prison" of divine enjoyment. Few people, even believers, understand the way that we have chosen to take in the Lord's recovery. Many think that we are crazy. Indeed, love causes one to be "crazy." We all need to be the crazy lovers of Jesus.

THE OLD COVENANT, THE LAW, BEING THE TESTIMONY OF GOD, THE PORTRAIT OF GOD, SHOWING US WHO GOD IS AND EXPOSING MAN, SUBDUING MAN, AND CONDUCTING GOD'S CHOSEN ONES TO CHRIST

The old covenant, the law, is the testimony of God, the portrait of God, showing us who God is and exposing man, subduing man, and conducting God's chosen ones to Christ (Psa. 78:5; 119:88b; Gen. 1:26; Rom. 3:19-20; Gal. 3:23-25; John 10:9-10). The law is a portrait, a picture, of God. When man looks at the law and sees God's portrait, he realizes that he could never be like God. God is holy and righteous, but man is common, sinful, and lawless. Thus, one of the functions of the law as a portrait of God is to expose man. We need to see that God's intention in creating us in His image and according to His likeness is

His desire that we will become Him in life and nature. He wants us to contain Him and be filled, saturated, and soaked with Him to express Him. But man became utterly fallen; therefore, God gave man the law to show man that He is righteousness, holiness, glory, life, love, and light. As fallen men we are unrighteous, unholy, dead, hateful, and darkness. We are not at all like God. Thus, the law exposes our sinful conduct and our evil nature and subdues us under God's righteous condemnation.

We were created to be like God but without the life and nature of God; thus, for man to try to express God is like a monkey trying to imitate a man. Through the fall man became exactly the opposite of God. Thus, the law as the testimony, the portrait, of God reveals who God is, exposing man, subduing man, and conducting man to Christ. According to Galatians 3:23-25, the law functions as a child-conductor. The word for *child-conductor* in Greek may also be rendered *escort, guardian,* or *custodian,* one who cares for a child who is under age and conducts him to the schoolmaster. Similarly, the law as a portrait of God exposes, subdues, and convicts us, causing us to realize our need of God and thereby bringing us to Christ. Hallelujah!

Today we no longer need the law, for we have been brought to Christ. Once we receive Christ into us, we no longer need the law. Since we have the person, we no longer need the portrait. Surely we prefer the person to the portrait. For example, it would be terrible if a man became enamored with a picture of his wife but ignored her person. In the same principle the law is merely the picture of God, but Christ is the person of God. Under the old covenant the law, the picture of God, portrays His attributes of love, light, holiness, and righteousness, but in the new covenant Christ, the person of God, *is* love, light, holiness, and righteousness. Moreover, He wants to dispense Himself with all that He is in His divine attributes into us to fill and uplift our human virtues. In this way we can be filled with Him as love, light, holiness, and righteousness to become Him in life and nature but not in the Godhead and to express Him. How marvelous!

THE OLD COVENANT OF THE LAW BEING A PORTRAIT OF GOD, BUT THE NEW COVENANT OF GRACE BEING THE PERSON OF GOD

The old covenant of the law is a portrait of God, but the new covenant of grace is the person of God (John 1:16-17). Verses 16 and 17 say, "For of His fullness we have all received, and grace upon grace. For the law was given through Moses; grace and reality came through Jesus Christ." The law as the photograph, or portrait of God, was given through Moses to the children of Israel. In other words, this verse is saying, "This is the portrait of God. You could never be like that in your fallen condition. What you need is Someone to redeem you by dying for you to satisfy the righteous requirements of the law, which you could never fulfill, and then in resurrection dispense Himself into you as grace. Thus, He will become your enjoyment, your person, your life, and your everything, and you will become the testimony of Jesus in actuality. By enjoying and being filled with Him you will become not a portrait but the very expression of God."

We are those who are receiving grace upon grace. Our Christian life should be a life not of sigh upon sigh, moan upon moan, or complaint upon complaint but of grace upon grace. Grace is God enjoyed by us. Hence, under the old covenant we receive the law as the portrait of God, but in the new covenant we receive grace as the enjoyment of God. The law exposes our condition to the uttermost so that we would realize that we are not like God. If we try to keep the law by our natural strength, our natural man, we will be condemned and cursed. Instead of endeavoring to keep the law, we should enjoy Christ in order to be filled with Him. He has come to be enjoyment upon enjoyment to us. As we enjoy Him as grace, we become Him, and thus, we become His testimony, His expression. This is God's purpose.

The Law Making Demands upon Man according to What God Is; Grace Supplying Man with What God Is to Meet What God Demands

The law makes demands upon man according to what God is; grace supplies man with what God is to meet what God demands (1 Cor. 15:10). Recently, I have been touched by the characteristics of a normal daily Christian life. In John 1:16 we see the phrase *grace upon grace.* When we wake up in the morning, we should pray, "Lord, I want today to be a day of receiving grace upon grace, a day of experiencing You as enjoyment upon enjoyment." Proverbs 4:18 says, "The path of the righteous is like the light of dawn, / Which shines brighter and brighter until the full day." Two characteristics of our daily Christian life should be "grace upon grace" and "brighter and brighter." If we sense that we are in darkness, we need to pray, "Lord, I repent. I want to be full of light. Fill me with Your presence. Lord, I want the rest of my life to become brighter and brighter." The path of a Christian shines brighter and brighter day by day. Recently, we published a book by Brother Lee entitled *A Blessed Human Life*. A blessed human life is a life of enjoying grace upon grace and of shining brighter and brighter.

In 2 Corinthians 3:18 Paul says, "We all with unveiled face, beholding and reflecting like a mirror the glory of the Lord, are being transformed into the same image from glory to glory, even as from the Lord Spirit." This verse indicates that our Christian life should be a life of being transformed from glory to glory.

Psalm 84:5-7 says, "Blessed is the man whose strength is in You, / In whose heart are the highways to Zion. / Passing through the valley of Baca, / They make it a spring; / Indeed the early rain covers it with blessings. / They go from strength to strength; / Each appears before God in Zion." In the church life, the house of God, which is the church of the living God, we may pass through "the valley of Baca," the valley of weeping, yet by enjoying the Lord we make it a place of springs, causing us to go on from strength to strength.

Finally, 2 Corinthians 4:16 says, "We do not lose heart; but though our outer man is decaying, yet our inner man is being renewed day by day." Praise the Lord that our daily Christian life is a life of enjoying grace upon grace, of shining brighter and brighter, of being transformed from glory to glory, of going from strength to strength, and of being renewed day by day. This should be our daily experience in the Lord's recovery. We are not here seeking to go to heaven when we die; we are here to enjoy the Lord day by day in order to become His testimony, His expression.

When We Believe into Christ, the Person of This Portrait Coming into Us and His Fulfilling in Us the Righteous Requirements of the Law as We Walk according to the Spirit and Set Our Mind on the Spirit

When we believe into Christ, the person of this portrait comes into us and He fulfills in us the righteous requirements of the law as we walk according to the spirit and set our mind on the spirit (Ezek. 36:26-27; Rom. 8:2, 4, 6, 10). The old covenant, the law, is the portrait of God that reveals who God is. God is life, love, light, holiness, righteousness, and glory. The new covenant is the very person of God—

Christ—who is the life-giving Spirit in our spirit. Christ is living, real, and available for us to experience; therefore, we can contact Him, see Him, and touch Him at any given moment. Moreover, He is dispensing Himself into us so that we would become Him in life and nature. Ezekiel 36:25-27 is a prophecy in which the Lord reveals some of the promises of the new covenant:

> I will sprinkle clean water upon you, and you will be clean; from all your filthiness and from all your idols I will cleanse you. I will also give you a new heart, and a new spirit I will put within you; and I will take away the heart of stone out of your flesh, and I will give you a heart of flesh. And I will put My Spirit within you and cause you to walk in My statutes, and My ordinances you shall keep and do.

The Lord will cleanse us from all our filthiness and from all our idols with His precious blood shed on the cross. Moreover, He will give us a new heart. God Himself is the new covenant. This covenant is new because God is new, and He has willed Himself to us. In the entire universe only God is new; everything else is old. Hence, when God enters into our heart, our heart becomes a new heart. When He enters into our spirit, our spirit becomes a new spirit. When God indwells us, we have a new heart to love Him and a new spirit to contact Him. This is the essence of the new covenant. When we were saved, we began to love the Lord with our new heart. Perhaps we came into a meeting and heard people saying, "Lord Jesus, I love You." This may have infused a love for the Lord into us. Through that, the Lord put Himself into our heart. He put Himself as the *new* nature into our heart. The function of our new heart is to love Him, and the function of our new spirit is to contact Him. We can hear Him and see Him by exercising our new spirit. Moreover, by His Spirit within, He causes us to walk in His statutes, to walk according to the inner law of life. By walking according to our spirit, we spontaneously fulfill the righteous requirements of the law.

In the New Covenant God Putting Himself into His Chosen People as Their Life, and This Life Being a Law, a Spontaneous, Automatic Principle

In the new covenant God puts Himself into His chosen people as their life, and this life is a law, a spontaneous, automatic principle

(Heb. 8:10; Rom. 8:2). The old covenant, the law, is a written code of conduct, which is a portrait of God. When fallen man looks at that portrait, he is exposed, convicted, and subdued. However, when fallen man is exposed, convicted, and subdued, he can repent and be conducted to Christ so that when he turns to Christ and opens to Him, Christ as the Spirit will enter into his spirit. As the Spirit, Christ is not merely a written code but a life-law, a spontaneous and automatic principle that operates within us. As the Spirit in our spirit, He is the automatic, installed God. Whenever we contact Him, whenever we call on Him, saying, "Lord Jesus, I love You," He, as the life-law, is switched on in our being, causing us to spontaneously, automatically, effortlessly, and unconsciously live the Christian life. Thus, we live God by touching Him in our spirit, for whenever we touch Him, He imparts Himself as the law of life into all the parts of our soul—into our mind, emotion, and will. It is in this way that He inscribes Himself on our hearts (2 Cor. 3:2-3), causing us to gradually become a living letter of Christ so that when people look at us, they can read and know Christ in us.

In Essence This Law Being God in Christ as the Spirit, and in Function Its Having the Capacity to Deify Us and to Constitute Us the Members of the Body of Christ with All Kinds of Functions

In essence this law is God in Christ as the Spirit, and in function it has the capacity to deify us and to constitute us the members of the Body of Christ with all kinds of functions (Rom. 8:10, 6, 11, 28-29). When we contact God in our spirit, when we switch Him on, He automatically dispenses Himself into us to deify us by renewing us with the new nature of God, by transforming us with the rich person of God, and by conforming us to the wonderful image of Christ. In short, whenever we are enjoying Christ as the law of life, He is deifying us.

Moreover, as we enjoy Him, contact Him, love Him, and have personal time with Him, we, as members of His Body, spontaneously begin to manifest certain functions. When our children are babies, we surely do not expect them to be able to do those things that we can do. For example, it would be ridiculous for a father to expect his infant son to be able to play baseball, yet this is often our attitude with new believers. Therefore, the newly saved ones among us should not be expected to do that much but should simply be encouraged to enjoy the Lord in the church life. When they are enjoying the Lord, He is switched on within them and is dispensing Himself into them, causing them to grow in life. In the churches in the Lord's recovery, we need to pray for the growth in life. We all need to pray, "Lord, grow in me." It is a tragedy when a Christian does not grow in life. We need to pray, "Lord, do not let me stop growing in life." According to *The Experience of Life*, our Christian life should be a progressing life, yet it is possible for us to stop progressing, to stop growing. It would be terrible for a child to stop growing at the age of ten and have to live his whole life as a small boy. That is not normal. Hence, we need to pray, "O Lord, grow in me today. Grant me this day's growth in life." Therefore, in our caring for people, we do not want to minister the law, the portrait of God, telling them that they need to behave in this and that way. Rather, we need to encourage them to simply enjoy the person of Christ.

As the new ones enjoy the Lord, they will spontaneously begin to function as members of the Body. Our functions issue out of our growth in life. I received the Lord at a laundromat in downtown Houston by reading a tract and then praying the prayer that was printed there. At the time, I had no idea what it meant to be a Christian. For instance, no one told me that I needed to read the Bible; nevertheless, I spontaneously began to love the Bible, and I read it all the time. I did not know that a person had come into me or that I had a spirit, but by the Lord's mercy something had been switched on within me, causing me to love the Lord and to read the Bible. Thus, He began to grow in me. At work, I told one of my colleagues, "I want to let you know that I met Jesus." He replied, "You met who? Are you crazy?" No one told me to preach the gospel, but out of my love for the Lord, the gospel- preaching function spontaneously came forth in me. No crazy lover of Jesus can keep himself from speaking of Him.

Therefore, we need to grow in life by enjoying the Lord, and then our enjoyment will spontaneously issue in various functions. When I first began to meet with the church in Houston, I wondered why they would wake up so early on Saturday mornings to mow a lawn that was not their own. To people in the world that may seem crazy. Not only so, but as one brother was pushing the lawn mower, another was reading the Bible to him. Nevertheless, I eventually found that I myself could scarcely wait for Saturday morning to come so that I could go to the meeting hall to be with the brothers, pray-read the Word, enjoy the Lord, be "electrified" with God, and function in carrying out the practical service of the church. This is just one illustration of a spontaneous function that comes out of our growth in life. When we switch Him on, we will grow in life, and as we grow in life, we cannot help but to function as a member of His Body.

CHRIST HIMSELF BEING THE NEW COVENANT, THE NEW TESTAMENT, GIVEN TO US BY GOD

Through His Death Christ Having Fulfilled the Demands of God's Righteousness according to His Law and Enacting the New Covenant, and in His Resurrection His Becoming the New Covenant with All of Its Bequests

Christ Himself is the new covenant, the new testament, given to us by God (Isa. 42:6; 49:8; Jer. 31:31-34; Heb. 8:8-12). Through His death Christ fulfilled the demands of God's righteousness according to His law and enacted the new covenant (Rom. 6:23; 3:21; 10:3-4; Luke 22:20; Heb. 9:16-17), and in His resurrection He became the new covenant with all of its bequests (1 Cor. 15:45b; Isa. 42:6; Phil. 1:19). God's law reveals that He is righteous, and because He is righteous and we are sinful, we must die. God is pure righteousness and therefore cannot tolerate sin. If there is any sin, the sentence for the sinner is death. Thus, Romans 6:23 says, "The wages of sin is death." According to God's righteousness, we should have died, but God Himself became a man to be our Substitute; He died for our sins, having paid the debt for all our sins. The wages of our sin was death, but Christ received those wages for all men. Based on this, God must forgive us of our debt; otherwise, He would not be righteous. We can say to God, "You must forgive me because You are righteous." Because Christ paid the price for man's sins on the cross, according to God's righteousness, He must forgive us. Righteousness is so very powerful that God Himself is bound by it to forgive us; He has no choice.

By His death Christ fulfilled all the demands of God's righteousness according to His law, and He enacted the new covenant. When the Lord established His table, He said, "This cup is the new covenant established in My blood, which is being poured out for you" (Luke 22:20). The Lord paid the price for man's sins by shedding His pure, sinless blood, and today the new covenant has become "this cup" from which we may drink. This implies that the Lord Himself has become "this cup" so that we can drink of, enjoy, be soaked in, and saturated with Him as the Spirit. Christ is the very new covenant cup of blessing.

He died to enact the new covenant, but in His resurrection He became the new covenant itself. Just as a person's last will and testament becomes in force when he dies, the Lord's death enacted the new covenant. But in His resurrection, Christ became the new covenant, for the last Adam became a *zoe*-giving Spirit (1 Cor. 15:45b). Thus, the life-giving Spirit is the new covenant. He is not giving us money or property but something that no one else in this universe is able to give—*zoe*, which is the Greek word for the eternal, uncreated, divine, indissoluble, unbreakable, wonderful life of God. The Greek word *bios* refers to the physical life, and the word *psuche* to the psychological life. If we merely had our *bios* and our *psuche*, we would be miserable. What makes us truly rich is *zoe*, which is a person—Christ Himself as the life-giving Spirit. He is the *zoe*, and He gives us *zoe*. Therefore, in resurrection Christ became the new covenant, which is simply the *zoe*-giving Spirit in our spirit.

In His Ascension Christ Opening the Scroll of the New Covenant concerning God's Economy, and in His Heavenly Ministry His Carrying Out Its Contents

In His ascension Christ opened the scroll of the new covenant concerning God's economy, and in His heavenly ministry He is carrying out its contents (Rev. 5:1-5). In His death He enacted the new covenant, in His resurrection He became the new covenant, in His ascension He opened the scroll of the new covenant, and in His heavenly ministry He is carrying out the new covenant. Revelation 4—5 depicts the scene immediately after Christ's ascension, for verse 6 says, "I saw in the midst of the throne...a Lamb standing as having just been slain." This throne is also the throne of God. Verses 1 through 5 say,

> I saw on the right hand of Him who sits upon the throne a scroll written within and on the back, sealed up with seven seals. And I saw a strong angel proclaiming with a loud voice, Who is worthy to open the scroll and to break its seals? And no one in heaven nor on the earth nor under the earth was able to open the scroll or look into it. And I wept much because no one was found worthy to open the scroll or look into it. And one of the elders said to me, Do not weep; behold, the Lion of the tribe of Judah, the Root of David, has overcome so that He may open the scroll and its seven seals.

The scroll here must be the new covenant, the grand title deed in the universe, enacted with the blood of the Lamb for God's redemption of the church, Israel, the world, and the universe. This scroll is a record of God's thought concerning the church, Israel, the world, and the universe. The content of this scroll is the entire will of God—His heart's desire, including His thought concerning the church, Israel, the world, and the universe.

This scroll needed to be opened, unveiled, and dispensed; however, no one was found who could open the scroll and unlock its seals. This caused John to weep. We must realize that if there were no one to open the scroll of God's new covenant and if its contents, which are Christ Himself, were not released, unveiled, and dispensed into people, the whole universe would be vanity, empty, for we would not know the secret of the universe. There must be someone to open the scroll of the new covenant, to unveil its secrets, and to dispense its riches into us. Then one of the angelic elders said to John, "Do not weep; behold, the Lion of the tribe of Judah, the Root of David, has overcome so that He may open the scroll and its seven seals" (v. 5). The Lion of the tribe of Judah is worthy to open the scroll of God's new covenant. He is worthy to release all its contents. Then when John turned, he saw a Lamb standing as having just been slain, having seven horns and seven eyes, which are the seven Spirits of God sent forth into all the earth (v. 6). The Lamb who accomplished redemption for us is worthy to open the scroll of the new covenant.

In His resurrection Christ became the new covenant, the contents of the scroll, in His ascension He opened the scroll to unveil its contents, and in His heavenly ministry He is carrying out the new covenant with regard to the church, Israel, the world, and the entire universe. He is ministering Himself as every bequest of the new covenant to all His chosen people throughout the earth. How marvelous!

As the Lion of the Tribe of Judah, Christ Overcoming and Defeating Satan, as the Redeeming Lamb, Christ Taking Away the Sin of Fallen Man, and as the Seven Spirits, Christ Infusing Us with Himself as the Contents of the Scroll of the New Covenant

As the Lion of the tribe of Judah, Christ overcame and defeated

Satan, as the redeeming Lamb, Christ took away the sin of fallen man, and as the seven Spirits, Christ infuses us with Himself as the contents of the scroll of the new covenant (vv. 5-6). He is the Lion of the tribe of Judah, but when John turned to look, He saw a Lamb. As the Lion of the tribe of Judah, He defeated Satan. The name *Judah* means "praise." This indicates that in His ascension Christ is of the tribe of praise. Thus, in Christ we also are of the tribe of praise. Praise the Lord! Satan hates for us to praise the Lord. One thing that Satan cannot do is to praise the Lord.

As the Lion Christ overcame and defeated Satan, as the redeeming Lamb He took away the sin of fallen man, and as the seven Spirits, signified by the seven eyes of the Lamb, He infuses us with Himself as the contents of the new covenant. In the divine and mystical realm Christ as the Lamb has seven eyes, which are the seven Spirits of God. When we look at and contact Him in our spirit, He infuses us with His seven eyes, transfusing us with Himself as all the riches and all the bequests of the new covenant. He is opening the scroll and dispensing the contents of the scroll into us in an intensified way. Thus, He intensifies us to become the overcomers so that He may consummate the New Jerusalem.

God's Salvation, God's Blessings, and All of God's Riches Having Been Covenanted to Us, and This Covenant Being Christ

The Reality of All the Hundreds of Bequests in the New Testament Being Christ

God's salvation, God's blessings, and all of God's riches have been covenanted to us, and this covenant is Christ. The reality of all the hundreds of bequests in the New Testament is Christ (Gen. 22:18a; Gal. 3:14; 1 Cor. 1:30; 15:45b; Eph. 1:3). In Genesis 22:18 God promised Abraham, saying, "In your seed all the nations of the earth shall be blessed." Then in Galatians 3:14 Paul says, "In order that the blessing of Abraham might come to the Gentiles in Christ Jesus, that we might receive the promise of the Spirit through faith." God promised Abraham the physical good land, but the real blessing of Abraham is the Spirit.

Christ Being the Reality of the New Testament, the Reality of All That God Is and of All That God Has Given to Us; Therefore, Christ Being the New Testament

Christ is the reality of the New Testament, the reality of all that God is and of all that God has given to us; therefore, Christ is the new testament. The New Testament reality of the good land is Christ, and the reality of Christ is the all-inclusive Spirit. He is the reality of all the bequests in the new testament. First Corinthians 1:30 says, "Christ Jesus, who became wisdom to us from God: both righteousness and sanctification and redemption." Christ is wisdom to us from God. He is our righteousness, our sanctification, and our redemption. He is everything to us. He is the life-giving Spirit in whom we have been blessed with every spiritual blessing (Eph. 1:3). We are indeed blessed! Hence, we should never be discouraged but praise the Lord, realizing that we are richly blessed with every spiritual blessing. In the old covenant all of God's blessings were physical and thus not eternal. In the new testament all of God's blessings are spiritual and are just the Spirit, who is Christ Himself.

The Bequests Being Many, but All These Many Bequests Being Actually One Person—the Pneumatic Christ; God Having Willed Himself in Christ as the Spirit to Us

The bequests are many, but all these many bequests are actually one person—the pneumatic Christ; God has willed Himself in Christ as the Spirit to us (John 20:22; Eph. 3:8). If we want to enjoy the bequests of the new testament, we simply need to breathe in the pneumatic Christ. He is the holy *Pneuma*, the Holy Spirit, the holy Breath. He has made it so simple for us to enjoy Him. This matter is deeply profound and worthy of many years of study and consideration, for this comprises the entire contents of God's entire New Testament economy, His new covenant. Although it is utterly profound, it is utterly simple; to enjoy all the bequests of the new covenant, we simply need to call on the name of the Lord Jesus. He has become breath to us.

In Lamentations 3:55-56 Jeremiah says, "I called upon Your name, O Jehovah, / From the lowest pit. / You have heard my voice; do not hide / Your ear at my breathing, at my cry." Perhaps we feel that our own biography could be entitled *Lamentations*. Our environment may be one of sufferings and lamentations, yet we can turn to our spirit and know that we are blessed with the holy Breath, the One whom we can breathe in. When we are in the lowest pit, we should not hold our breath; rather, we should breathe Him in, calling, "O Lord Jesus." We should not lament, saying, "I am in the pit" but instead call, "O Lord Jesus, I am in a pit." When we call, we contact the Lord, and we are inwardly lifted out of the pit.

One of David's mighty men, Benaiah, "went down and struck a lion in the midst of a pit on a snowy day" (2 Sam. 23:20). There may be days when we feel like we are in a pit with a lion on a snowy day. This implies a situation that we cannot get out of by ourselves. It is very difficult to climb up the sides of a pit when it is snowing. Furthermore, this pit has a lion in it. Have you ever had such a day? At such times, what should we do? To kill the lion in that pit on a snowy day, we need to praise the Lord, call on His name, gather with the saints, and read the Bible. By enjoying the Lord we are brought into ascension.

The Bequests Bequeathed to Us by the Lord in the New Testament Being Inexhaustible, and Their Being for Us to Experience and Enjoy through the Spirit for Eternity

The bequests bequeathed to us by the Lord in the new testament are inexhaustible, and they are for us to experience and enjoy through the Spirit for eternity (Heb. 9:15). We will be enjoying Him as all the new covenant bequests for eternity.

OUR SPIRIT BEING THE "BANK ACCOUNT" OF ALL THE BEQUESTS OF THE NEW COVENANT; BY THE LAW OF THE SPIRIT OF LIFE, ALL OF THESE BEQUESTS ARE DISPENSED INTO US AND MADE REAL TO US

Our spirit is the "bank account" of all the bequests of the new covenant; by the law of the Spirit of life, all of these bequests are dispensed into us and made real to us (Rom. 8:2, 10, 6, 11, 16; Heb. 8:10; John 16:13). I love my spirit. I am so happy that I am not an animal. A dog has a body and a soul (mind, emotion, and will). I am happy when my dog greets me and wags its tail whenever I come home. But as much as my dog loves me, it does not have a spirit. It does not ponder the meaning of the universe, nor does it have a conscience. Once when I was working with the brothers on a construction project, I set my lunch on the hood of a truck. When we came out to eat lunch, a dog had eaten my lunch, yet that dog was not bothered in the least about what it had done. This shows that it did not have a spirit because it did not have a conscience. If a brother had eaten my lunch, surely he would have been bothered by his conscience, because he has a spirit. Our spirit is what separates us from the beasts.

Our spirit is not only our God-contacting organ; it is the very dwelling place of God (Eph. 2:22). The house of God, the dwelling place of God, is in our spirit. Furthermore, our spirit may be regarded as a bank account containing the untold billions of bequests that comprise the new covenant. Our spirit is an "account" containing the unlimited, unsearchable Christ and from which we can write a "check" anytime for whatever we need. If we need peace, we can write a check from the bank account in our spirit for Christ as peace. If we need love, we can write a check for love. Our spirit is the divine bank account with all the bequests of the new covenant. Through the inner working of the law of the Spirit of life, all the new covenant bequests are dispensed into us and made real to us.

Romans 8:10 says, "If Christ is in you, though the body is dead because of sin, the spirit is life because of righteousness." No matter how discouraged or tired we may feel, the good news is that our spirit is *zoe*. At least one part of our being, our spirit, is eternal life. Thus, our spirit is the "bank account," in which we have an unlimited supply of life, and this life is God Himself. God in Christ as the Spirit and as all the bequests of the new testament are in my spirit! Thus, we simply need to contact Him in order to enjoy Him as life. By contacting Him, life is dispensed from our spirit into our soul and even into our body.

In Our Spirit Our Having the Presence of God,
the Speaking of God, the Meeting with God,
and the Dispensing of God through His Operation
as the Law of the Divine Life to Impart
and Inscribe Himself into All Our Inward Parts

In our spirit we have the presence of God, the speaking of God, the meeting with God, and the dispensing of God through His operation as the law of the divine life to impart and inscribe Himself into all our inward parts (Heb. 8:10). If we are in a meeting but not exercising our spirit, we are not in the meeting with God. It is possible to sit in a meeting but not be in the meeting with God. If in a meeting we exercise our spirit and say, "Lord, I turn my heart to You. Keep me in my spirit right now," then we will be in the meeting place of God where we have the speaking of God, the presence of God, and the dispensing of God through His operation as the law of the divine life to impart and inscribe Himself into all our inward parts.

The Lord Making His Covenant Known
to Those Who Fear Him, and His Dispensing Himself
as the Unsearchable Reality of His Covenant
to Those Who Love Him

The Lord makes His covenant known to those who fear Him, and He dispenses Himself as the unsearchable reality of His covenant to those who love Him (Psa. 25:14; Isa. 11:2-3a; 1 Cor. 2:9). Christ as the new testament is the deposit in the bank account of our spirit with all the bequests. One way to contact Him is to fear Him. Psalm 25:14 says, "The intimate counsel of Jehovah is to those who fear Him, / And His covenant will He make known to them." If we desire to have the Lord's intimate counsel and His covenant made known to us, we need to fear Him. To fear the Lord is not to be afraid of Him but to have a reverential awe toward Him.

Whenever we exercise our spirit, we enter into a state of awe. One of my favorite words when I was coming into the church life was *awesome*. The only word I could think of to describe the church meetings was *awesome*. To fear the Lord is to have a reverential awe and respect for Him, to honor Him, and to adore Him. Furthermore, to fear the Lord in this sense is to fear nothing except the loss of His presence. We should not be afraid of what others may think about us or of what they may do to us. The only thing that we should fear is losing the Lord's presence. We have the Lord's person in our spirit, but to have His presence means that we have His eyes, that we have His person, that we are in contact with Him, that He is real to us, that we treasure His presence, that we like to live before His face, and that we do not want to lose His smile. Thus, we should not only fear the Lord but also love Him. First Corinthians 2:9 says, "As it is written, 'Things which eye has not seen and ear has not heard and which have not come up in man's heart; things which God has prepared for those who love Him.'" Let us fear the Lord, having a referential awe, respect, and regard for the Lord, and let us love Him.

Christ as the New Covenant Being Our Portion, Our Cup of Salvation and Our Cup of Blessing; Our Being Able to Drink Him as Our Salvation and Blessing by Calling upon His Precious Name

Christ as the new covenant is our portion, our cup of salvation and our cup of blessing; we can drink Him as our salvation and blessing by calling upon His precious name (Luke 22:20; Psa. 16:5; 23:5; 116:13; 1 Cor. 10:16a). The new covenant is our portion, our cup of salvation. First Corinthians 10:16 says, "The cup of blessing which we bless, is it not the fellowship of the blood of Christ?" The cup that we partake of at the Lord's table is a cup of blessing, which signifies Christ as the new covenant becoming our portion. Psalm 16:5 says, "Jehovah is the portion of my inheritance and of my cup." Thus, Christ being our portion also means that He is our cup. This is why when He established His table, the Lord said, "This cup is the new covenant" (Luke 22:20). This means that the cup is Christ Himself as our portion.

Christ is our cup of salvation and our cup of blessing. Honestly, our cup should have been the cup of God's wrath. We were sinful and evil, but on the cross Christ drank the cup of God's wrath for us. He drank the judgment that we deserved, and in resurrection He became the cup of salvation to us. Now we can drink Him in day by day as our redeeming and saving water of life. He is our salvation and our blessing.

If we read Psalm 116 prayerfully we will gain much appreciation of the Lord. In this psalm David was discouraged, feeling that he was in the lowest pit. But God saved David and dispensed Himself into David, causing him to enjoy the riches of God. We must realize that it is God's mercy that we are still in the church. We owe so much to God that we could never repay Him even if we were to live a thousand lives. Charles Wesley wrote a hymn that says, "O for a thousand tongues to sing / My great Redeemer's praise, / The glories of my God and King, / The triumphs of His grace" (*Hymns*, #163). To Wesley, one tongue is not enough to praise the Lord. This means that we owe God our life and everything. In Psalm 116 David appreciates how much the Lord has done for him and how merciful He has been to him. Like him, we all have much to appreciate the Lord for. He has saved us, brought us into His recovery, brought us under the ministry of the age, and by His mercy, He has kept us in the recovery to this day. This is why David's heart responds, saying, "What shall I return to Jehovah / For all His benefits toward me?" (v. 12). What can we give to God? David continues, "I will take up the cup of salvation / And call upon the name of Jehovah" (v. 13). We can give Him that which He loves and which honors Him the most—our taking the cup of salvation and calling on His name. Our taking the Lord as our cup of salvation pleases Him. Our calling on His name honors Him. David does not say, "I will take up the cup of salvation and drink"; rather, he says, "I will take up the cup of salvation and call." This indicates that our calling is our drinking. By calling upon His name, we are saved. By calling upon His name, we are filled, saturated, and soaked with Him. Then we can express Him, and our expressing Him is the greatest honor to Him.

Christ Being the Pneumatic Executor, Mediator, of the New Covenant in Our Spirit; as the Executor His Making Every Bequest of His Will Available and Real as We Receive the Word of His Will by Means of All Prayer

Christ is the pneumatic Executor, Mediator, of the new covenant in our spirit; as the Executor He makes every bequest of His will available and real as we receive the word of His will by means of all prayer (Heb. 8:6; 1 John 5:6). When there is a will, there is also the need for an executor. The executor ensures that the inheritor receives all the bequests contained in the will. In resurrection Christ became the life-giving Spirit as the Executor, the Mediator, of the new covenant in our spirit. As the Executor, He makes every bequest of His will available and real as we take in the word of His will by means of all prayer.

The Bible is our will, and in order for all the bequests in this will to become real to us, we need to pray-read the will. Humanly speaking, a will must be read in order to ascertain its contents. Spiritually speaking, we should not only read but also pray-read our will. When we pray-read the will, the letter of the will is converted into Spirit, which is the reality of the will. Therefore, what we pray-read becomes Spirit and life to us, and the bequests become our reality. It is a great thing to pray-read the Bible; it is our prayer book, and we should not take it for granted.

As the Surety of the New Covenant, Christ Being the Pledge That Everything in the New Covenant Will Be Fulfilled; His Guaranteeing and Ensuring the Effectiveness of the New Testament

As the surety of the new covenant, Christ is the pledge that everything in the new covenant will be fulfilled; He guarantees and ensures the effectiveness of the new testament (Heb. 7:22). Christ is the surety and guarantee of the new covenant within us. When we contact Him, we have the inner sense that everything in the new covenant will be fulfilled. For example, when we contact the Lord, we should have the assurance that we will be part of the wife of the Lamb for eternity. The Lord is our warranty that will never expire. Once I bought a car with a five-year warranty, but as soon as the warranty expired, the car broke down. Our warranty on the new covenant will never expire; He is eternally effective.

As the Divine High Priest, Christ Executing the New Covenant by Interceding for Us, Praying That We Would Be Brought into the Reality of the New Covenant

As the divine High Priest, Christ is executing the new covenant by interceding for us, praying that we would be brought into the reality of the new covenant (v. 25; Rom. 8:34, 26). As the divine High Priest, Christ is praying for each of us and for all of us so that everything in God's new covenant would be real to us.

As the Minister of the Holy Places, Christ Serving Us with the Bequests, the Blessings, of the New Testament, Making the Facts of the New Covenant Effective in Our Experience

As the Minister of the holy places, Christ is serving us with the bequests, the blessings, of the new testament, making the facts of the new covenant effective in our experience (Heb. 8:2). Even this very moment, Christ in His heavenly ministry is praying for us and ministering God into us.

In Order to Receive the Application
of All the Blessings in the New Covenant,
Our Needing to Be Those Who Respond to Christ's
Heavenly Ministry by Entering into His Intercession
for the Churches and His Ministering God into Others

In order to receive the application of all the blessings in the new covenant, we need to be those who respond to Christ's heavenly ministry by entering into His intercession for the churches and His ministering God into others (Gen. 14:18-20; Heb. 7:25; 8:2; Acts 6:4). As the High Priest, Christ is interceding for the churches. When we contact Him, we join Him in His intercession for the saints, for the churches, and for His recovery. In so doing, we are infused with Him and become one with Him to minister God into people. This should be our response to Christ's heavenly ministry for the carrying out of the new covenant.—E. M.

THE DIVINE ECONOMY IN THE BOOK OF ISAIAH

The Revelation and Experience of Christ
as the Light of the World
(Message 22)

Scripture Reading: Isa. 2:5; 9:2; 42:6-7, 16; 49:6; 50:10-11; 60:1-2

I. Today's world ("this darkness"—Eph. 6:12) is fully under the dark ruling of the devil, who rules through his evil angels and "deceives the whole inhabited earth"—Col. 1:13; Dan. 10:19-20, 11; 9:23; Rev. 12:9-11:

   A. The whole world lies in the evil one, but in Christ, the light of the world, the ruler of the world has nothing (no ground, no chance, no hope, and no possibility in anything); furthermore, this Christ is in our spirit, where we can abide to overcome the world of darkness and where the evil one cannot touch us—John 9:5; 1 John 5:19b; John 14:30; 16:33; 1 John 5:4, 18; John 3:6b.

   B. Darkness is dissipated by light; when light comes, darkness is scattered; "the light shines in the darkness, and the darkness did not overcome it"—1:5; Gen. 1:2-3; Rev. 21:24; 22:5; cf. 1:20; 2:1a; Isa. 42:16.

II. In Isaiah 2:5 the prophet sounded forth a call: "House of Jacob, come and let us walk in the light of Jehovah"—cf. Ezek. 14:3.

III. Christ has been called by Jehovah to be a light for the nations, to open the eyes of the blind, to bring the prisoner out from the prison and those who dwell in darkness from the prison house, to be God's salvation unto the ends of the earth—Isa. 42:6-7; 49:6; 9:2; Matt. 4:16; Col. 1:13; Acts 26:18.

IV. Light is the presence of God—1 John 1:5; John 1:4-5; 8:12; cf. Matt. 25:30.

V. At the time of our conversion, light entered into us and we became sons of light and light in the Lord—Gen. 1:3; 2 Cor. 4:6; John 12:36; Eph. 5:8; 1 Pet. 2:9b.

VI.   "Giving thanks to the Father, who has qualified you for a share of the allotted portion of the saints *in the light*"—Col. 1:12 (our italics):

    A.   The only way to partake of Christ and to enjoy Him is in the light; when we turn to the Lord and come into His presence, we are in the light and spontaneously begin to enjoy Him as our portion, as the new covenant—Psa. 16:5, 11; 116:12-13; 36:8-9.

    B.   Light rules by its enlightening; hence, when the light of life shines and rules, it is a kingdom, the kingdom of the Son of the Father's love, in contrast to the authority of darkness, which is the kingdom of Satan—Col. 1:13; Rev. 22:5; John 14:21, 23.

VII.   The seven Spirits of God are the seven lamps of fire, and our spirit is also the lamp of Jehovah, searching all the rooms of our inner being, all the chambers of our soul—Rev. 4:5; Prov. 20:27:

    A.   These two spirits, ours and God's, have been mingled; within our little lamp, our spirit, there is now also another lamp of greater intensity, the sevenfold intensified Spirit—1 Cor. 6:17.

    B.   As our spirit shines through our prayer, the Spirit of God intensifies the shining sevenfold, and under the intensity of this light, we confess and repent to the Lord—Psa. 139:23-24; 1 John 1:7, 9.

    C.   Where the light shines, the life supply goes, and chamber by chamber we are transformed into the Lord's image; this shining, supplying, and transforming make us the golden lampstand—2 Cor. 3:16, 18; Rev. 1:20.

    D.   The parts of our life and living that are closed off from Christ are in darkness, because Christ, the One who is the very light, has no place—Luke 11:33-36.

    E.   The one who experiences the greatest amount of transformation is the one who is absolutely open to the Lord—Psa. 139:23-24; Matt. 5:3.

    F.   Our spirit is the key to life, and prayer is the key to being able to stay in our spirit; God keeps calling us back to our spirit—Eph. 6:18; 1 Thes. 5:17.

VIII. In order for us to walk in the divine light, the Lord has given us the fellowship of life, the blood of Jesus, the word of God, the children of God, and the church of God:

    A. The divine life, the divine fellowship, the divine light, and the blood of Jesus, the Son of God, constitute a spiritual cycle in our Christian life—1 John 1:3-9.

    B. The word of God is a lamp to our feet and a light to our path—Psa. 119:105, 130; Deut. 17:18-20; John 8:12, 32, 36; 5:39-40; Psa. 42:5; Num. 6:25.

    C. The saints are the light of the world as the duplication of Christ—Matt. 5:14; Phil. 2:15-16; Acts 5:20; 13:47; Isa. 49:6; 60:1-3.

    D. The church is a golden lampstand, shining in this age of darkness—Rev. 1:20; cf. Psa. 73:16-22, 25-26.

    E. We can abide in the light by loving the Lord (Col. 1:13; Rev. 2:4, 7) and loving the brothers (1 John 2:10-11; 3:14-17).

IX. The divine light, the presence of God, functions within us in the following ways:

    A. The divine light enlightens the eyes of our heart to see God and to see as God sees—1 John 1:7; Matt. 5:8; 2 Cor. 3:16; Eph. 1:17-18; Psa. 36:9b.

    B. The divine light exposes and reproves us—Eph. 5:13-14.

    C. The divine light supplies us with life—John 1:4.

    D. The divine light heals us—Luke 1:78-79; Mal. 4:2.

    E. The divine light kills the negative things in our being—Isa. 6:1-8.

X. He who fears Jehovah and hears the voice of His Servant has light while walking in darkness—Isa. 50:10-11; Psa. 139:7-12, 23-24.

XI. As we walk in the light day by day and corporately shine Him out in this dark age as His churches, the golden lampstands, we will hasten the day of His coming when we will be fully prepared to be His bride, the New Jerusalem, the city of light and the kingdom of light for the full expression of God as light—Rev. 21:11, 23; 22:5.

THE REVELATION AND EXPERIENCE OF CHRIST
AS THE LIGHT OF THE WORLD

Prayer: Lord, we open to You. Shine in us. We love You as light and declare by faith that we love the light. We come to the light. You, O God, are light, and in You there is no darkness at all. We consecrate this message to You. We pray that You would scatter all the darkness in our being. Shine in us, shine in all the churches, and shine in Your recovery.

As an introduction, it may be helpful to read the following verses:

Isaiah 2:5—House of Jacob, come and let us walk in the light of Jehovah.

Isaiah 9:2—The people who walked in the darkness / Have seen a great light; / Upon those who dwell in the land of the shadow of death / Light has shined.

Isaiah 42:6-7—I am Jehovah; I have called You in righteousness; / I have held You by the hand; / I have kept You and I have given You / As a covenant for the people, as a light for the nations; / To open the eyes of the blind, / To bring the prisoner out from the prison, / Those who dwell in darkness from the prison house.

These verses are prophecies concerning Christ. We should be convinced that the Bible is the Word of God simply by the fulfillment of the prophecies contained in it. For example, the word in 42:6 was written between 760 and 700 B.C., prophesying that Christ would be a covenant for the people and a light for the nations. The fulfillment is found in Hebrews 7:22, which states that Jesus is "the surety of a better covenant," and in Luke 2:32, when Simeon saw the little child Jesus and declared that He was a "light for revelation to the Gentiles."

In Message 21 we considered the revelation and experience of Christ as the new covenant. I was enthralled to see that Christ is the new covenant. We may say that a covenant and a testament are the same, but in a finer sense there is a distinction between them. A covenant comes into effect when a person formally promises to accomplish and do certain things for or on behalf of another party. The covenant becomes a testament when the person who made the covenant dies. When the person who made the promises dies, the covenant becomes a testament, a will.

Christ Himself is the new testament, and we are the beneficiaries in His will. His will contains unsearchable riches that have been bequeathed to us. We are His inheritors, His heirs (cf. Acts 20:32). We are wealthy because we have "billions of dollars" in our divine "bank account." Our spirit is the bank account. All that Christ is with all His unsearchable riches has been deposited into our spirit as His bequests to us. He is the new covenant. When He died, He enacted the new covenant (Heb 9:15). In the same way that a will is enacted and is enforced when someone dies, Christ enacted the new covenant when He died. Then in resurrection He became the new covenant. When someone we love dies, we are sad, even if he has left us billions of dollars in his will. However, when Christ died, He resurrected. He not only willed Himself to us; He also became the actual will in resurrection. He has become the reality of all the bequests in the new testament. By His death He enacted the new covenant, and by His resurrection He became the new covenant, the new testament. Christ is all the blessings in the new testament. He is life, light, peace, joy, and everything that we need. He is the reality of all the unsearchable riches that are bequeathed to us in His will. In His death He enacted the new covenant. In His resurrection He became the new covenant, and now in His ascension He is executing and carrying out the new covenant.

When a person dies, he leaves a will, and he needs an executor of the will. When Christ died, He also left a will and even became that will. Not only so, He is the Executor of the will to ensure that we receive all that has been promised and covenanted to us. We have a life-giving Executor in our spirit. He wants to make sure that we enjoy all that is in the will. Whether we feel it or not, He is in our spirit this very moment. We should not trust in our feelings. He wants to make sure that we enjoy Him continually in a new and fresh way. He is so rich and wonderful. He is the Executor and the Mediator of the new covenant (8:6).

In our spirit He is also the surety of the new covenant (7:22). He is the guarantee that all of His riches will be dispensed into our being and that we will become Him in life and nature to express Him in the whole universe. He is our surety and our warranty. This warranty never runs out. It is not like today's car warranties that last for only five years. He is an eternal surety. He is not only the surety of the new covenant; He is also the High Priest (9:11). He is praying for us so that He can dispense Himself into us. He is also the Minister of the Holy Places to minister God into us (8:2).

The title of this message is "The Revelation and Experience of Christ as the Light of the World." We will see that He is a light for the nations. We should not take this for granted. It is a great thing that in all of human history, there was a man who declared, "I am the light of the world!" (John 8:12). No founder of any religion has ever said this about himself. Christ Jesus, the man who said this, must be God.

TODAY'S WORLD ("THIS DARKNESS") BEING FULLY UNDER THE DARK RULING OF THE DEVIL, WHO RULES THROUGH HIS EVIL ANGELS AND "DECEIVES THE WHOLE INHABITED EARTH"

Today's world ("this darkness"—Eph. 6:12) is fully under the dark ruling of the devil, who rules through his evil angels and "deceives the whole inhabited earth" (Col. 1:13; Dan. 10:19-20, 11; 9:23; Rev. 12:9-11). To appreciate the light we must study the darkness, but we should not be in the darkness. Instead, we want to remain here in the light. Today's world is "this darkness." Ephesians 6:12 says, "For our wrestling is not against blood and flesh but against the rulers, against the authorities, against the world-rulers of this darkness, against the spiritual forces of evil in the heavenlies." When we pray, our wrestling is not against flesh and blood but against the principalities and the powers, against the spiritual forces of evil in the heavenlies. Paul refers to these spiritual forces of evil in the heavenlies as the "world-rulers of this darkness." Thus, in God's eyes, this darkness is the world. The whole world is darkness, even *this darkness*. The world rulers are the evil angels that followed the fallen Daystar, or Lucifer, in his rebellion against God (Isa. 14:12). Daystar became Satan, God's adversary, God's enemy, and one-third of the angels followed him in his rebellion (Rev. 12:4, 7). Satan is the prince, the ruler, of this world (John 12:31). Thus, the world is this darkness. Satan is the ruler of a kingdom that is called the *authority of darkness* (Col. 1:13), and under him are the world-rulers. These world-rulers are evil angels.

We see an example of this warfare in the book of Daniel. Daniel fought the spiritual warfare by praying (9:23). In chapter 10 he began to pray and prayed for three weeks (twenty-one days) until he received a response. The messenger said that he had been dispatched to come the first day that Daniel began to pray but that he was delayed because of the spiritual warfare in the heavens (vv. 12-13). Verse 20 reveals that there was a prince, an evil angel, over Persia and another prince over Javan, which is Greece. If we look at these verses in Daniel in light of Ephesians 6, we can see that these are the world-rulers of this darkness. May the Lord open our eyes to see this. The Bible mentions the names of two positive angels—Michael and Gabriel, and one fallen angel, Daystar, who became Satan, God's enemy (Rev. 12:10 and footnote 2; Isa. 14:12 and footnote 1). Gabriel is God's messenger, and Michael is assigned to protect and fight for Israel. Daniel was a real overcomer as he prayed for God's interest.

Today's world, this darkness, is fully under the dark ruling of the devil who rules through his evil angels and "deceives the whole inhabited earth" (Rev. 12:9). This is a word of light. We must realize that Satan is he who deceives the whole inhabited earth. The world is anti-God and anti-Christ. This world and the philosophy of this world are anti-Israel and anti-Christian. The devil is anti-God, anti-Christ, anti-Israel, and anti-Christian. As this age draws to an end, it will become even darker and darker. Second Timothy 3:12-13 says, "Indeed all who desire to live godly in Christ Jesus will be persecuted. But evil men and impostors will grow worse and worse, deceiving and being deceived." It is quite strange that those who desire to live godly are rewarded by suffering persecution. If we are defamed, maligned, and evil spoken of, that is a good sign that we desire a God-man living, that we desire to live God. Furthermore, this kind of environment will continue to grow worse and worse.

As this age comes to a close, the Antichrist will be manifested. In addition to being anti-Christ, he will be anti-God, anti-Israel, and anti-Christian. He will try to destroy all the Jews and all the Christians. This is darkness. We need to have this kind of realization as we consider the political situation of the world. Today's world is "this darkness," which is anti-God, anti-Christ, anti-Israel, and anti-Christian. God loves Israel, and He loves the church. Satan hates Israel, and he hates the church.

Revelation 12:9 says that Satan is "he who deceives the whole inhabited earth." The context of this verse is that the man-child, the overcomers, are raptured to the heavens, resulting in war in heaven. Therefore, Satan and his angels no longer have a place in heaven and are cast down out of heaven to the earth (vv. 5, 7-9). Then the kingdom of God, referring to the one-thousand-year kingdom of Christ, is ushered in. Verse 10 says, "I heard a loud voice in heaven saying, Now has come the salvation and the power and the kingdom of our God and the authority of His Christ, for the accuser of our brothers has been cast down, who accuses them before our God day and night." Verse 11 goes on to speak of the overcomers. That the overcomers are mentioned in this same context indicates that those who aspire to be overcomers are not deceived by Satan. They do not overcome the accuser because they are great or perfect; rather, "they overcame him because of the blood of the Lamb and because of the word of their testimony, and they loved not their soul-life even unto death" (v. 11).

Daniel was such an overcomer. When the angelic messenger came to him, he addressed him, saying to him twice, "Daniel, man of preciousness" (Dan. 10:11, 19). The King James Version renders this as "a man greatly beloved." This indicates that all the positive angels and the Triune God loved Daniel. Surely, we all would like the angels to address us in such a way. Instead of their needing to say, "Repent and turn to your spirit," which we all need to do, it would be much better if they would say, "Man of preciousness." We need to aspire to be men of preciousness in the sight of God. On another occasion, the messenger said to Daniel, "You are preciousness itself" (9:23). Peter says, "To you therefore who believe is the preciousness; but to the unbelieving, 'The stone which the builders rejected, this has become the head of the corner'" (1 Pet. 2:7), indicating that Christ is the preciousness to His believers. Christ alone is *the preciousness,* but when we enjoy Him as the preciousness, we become men of preciousness. As we enjoy Him, love Him, fellowship with Him, and intimately contact Him as the preciousness, He is being deposited into our entire being as all the bequests of the new covenant. The result is that we become men of preciousness. We then become people whom the Lord wants to steal when He comes back (Rev. 3:3). He will come as a thief in the night. When a thief comes to a house, he does not come to steal the dirty laundry or the trash; he comes to take what is precious. A thief steals the precious things. We need to be the overcomers, those whom the Lord wants to steal when He comes back. We hope He will say, "I want you as part of the man-child or the firstfruits, as part of My bride. Therefore, I will take you. I will rapture you." We need to be the precious ones in the midst of "this darkness."

The Whole World Lying in the Evil One,
but in Christ, the Light of the World,
the Ruler of the World Having Nothing (No Ground,
No Chance, No Hope, and No Possibility in Anything);
Furthermore, This Christ Being in Our Spirit,
Where We Can Abide to Overcome the World of Darkness
and Where the Evil One Cannot Touch Us

The whole world lies in the evil one, but in Christ, the light of the world, the ruler of the world has nothing (no ground, no chance, no hope, and no possibility in anything); furthermore, this Christ is in our spirit, where we can abide to overcome the world of darkness and where the evil one cannot touch us (John 9:5; 1 John 5:19b; John 14:30; 16:33; 1 John 5:4, 18; John 3:6b). The whole world lies in the evil one. This means that the whole world lies passively under the manipulating and usurping control of the evil one. People are manipulated by the devil. We now realize that before we believed in the Lord, we too were manipulated by Satan. We were under his manipulation and usurpation. The whole world lies in the evil one, but we are now in Christ. We have been transferred out of Adam and out of the world into Christ. We have been called out of darkness into His marvelous light. We are now in Christ, and He is the light of the world. John 14:30 says, "The ruler of the world is coming, and in Me he has nothing." Only one person in human history could say such a thing. The Lord Jesus could say, "In Me, this one who deceives the whole inhabited earth, the prince of darkness, the prince over the world rulers of this darkness, has nothing. Here I am, a man in my thirties, but I am also the very God. In Me this one has nothing." This means that in Christ Satan had no ground, no chance, no hope, and no possibility in anything. Today we are in Him, and in Him Satan has nothing. When we are in Christ subjectively, abiding in Him, living in our spirit, and enjoying the One who is in our spirit, the ruler of the world has no ground, no chance, no hope, and no possibility in anything.

Christ is in our spirit. The Christ in whom the ruler of the world has nothing is in our spirit. We can abide in Him in our spirit to overcome the world of darkness because we are where the evil one cannot touch us. First John 5:4 says, "Everything that has been begotten of

God overcomes the world; and this is the victory which has overcome the world—our faith." This verse does not speak of "everyone that has been begotten of God" but of "everything that has been begotten of God." There is one part of our being that is born of God—our spirit. John 3:6b says, "That which is born of the Spirit is spirit." That which is born of the divine Spirit is our human spirit. Our spirit has been born of God, and our spirit overcomes the world. First John 5:18 says, "We know that everyone who is begotten of God does not sin, but he who has been begotten of God keeps himself, and the evil one does not touch him." We are born of God, and in particular, our spirit has been begotten of God. When we are in our spirit, the evil one cannot touch us. This is a great discovery! We know a place to which we can go where the evil one cannot touch us. That place is Christ. I can be in Christ. Where is Christ? He is in our spirit. When we are in our spirit, the evil one cannot touch us. The evil one cannot touch us when we are in Christ in our spirit. For this reason, we all must treasure our spirit.

Darkness Being Dissipated by Light;
When Light Comes, Darkness Being Scattered;
"the Light Shines in the Darkness,
and the Darkness Did Not Overcome It"

Darkness is dissipated by light; when light comes, darkness is scattered; "the light shines in the darkness, and the darkness did not overcome it" (John 1:5; Gen. 1:2-3; Rev. 21:24; 22:5; cf. 1:20; 2:1a; Isa. 42:16). John 1:5 is a good verse to pray over, saying, "O Lord, shine in my darkness. I open to You. Shine in me." If we want to be overcomers, we need to realize that light is an overcomer. The darkness cannot overcome the light. God is light, Christ is light, and He is the One who lives in our spirit. He is the overcoming light in us. Darkness can never overcome light.

We can also see this in Genesis 1. After God created the heavens and the earth, "the earth became waste and emptiness, and darkness was on the surface of the deep" (v. 2). Then the Spirit of God brooded upon the surface of the waters, "and God said..." (v. 3). Hallelujah, "God said"! We should enjoy the God who speaks. God is merely objective to us if we do not enjoy Him as the God who speaks. When God speaks, He speaks light into our being. Verse 3 says, "God said, Let there be light; and there was light."

God is the light, and we need to be light-bearers (v. 14). Revelation

1:20 says, "The mystery of the seven stars which you saw upon My right hand and the seven golden lampstands: The seven stars are the messengers of the seven churches, and the seven lampstands are the seven churches." We need to be the shining stars in this dark age. The Old Testament prophesies that Christ will come as a Star. Numbers 24:17 says, "I see Him, but not now; / I behold Him, but not near. / There shall come forth a Star out of Jacob, / And a Scepter shall rise out of Israel." Christ is the living Star, and He makes us the shining stars. Thus, we become the messengers. Stars are in a heavenly position and condition. They shine in a sevenfold intensified way in this dark age. We should pray, "Lord, I want to be a shining star. I don't want a formal position. I simply want to be someone who is shining." These stars are the messengers of the churches. To be a messenger means that we have a fresh message for God's people. It means that we know God as the One who speaks to us. This means that we are intimate with Him and that He speaks to us. His word is light to us and causes us to become a star. As a star we have a fresh message in us from God to His people. We all should be like this. Whenever we come together, we should present Christ as a fresh message. Whether we are caring for a young one, attending a group meeting, or going to a meeting on the Lord's Day, we should pray, "Lord, speak to me. O God, speak to us. We want You to be our fresh message." What is the message? As John says, "This is the message which we have heard from Him and announce to you, that God is light and in Him is no darkness at all" (1 John 1:5).

We need to be filled with fresh messages. Without such messengers, the Lord has no way to speak to the churches. The letters to each of the seven churches in Revelation 2 and 3 were not written directly to each church, for each one begins, "To the messenger of the church in..." The Lord asked John to write to the messengers, to those who are the shining stars, who are full of light, who love following Christ as the light of the world, who do not tolerate darkness in their being, and who repent whenever they find themselves in darkness. We should be the same. We aspire to be those who are filled with light, who receive fresh messages from the Lord, and who are open to His speaking. If we are like this, the Lord will have a way. It is through such messengers that the Lord speaks to the churches. Without such messengers, the shining stars, He has no way to speak to the churches.

Consider the Lord's Day prophesying meeting. Suppose we all

come together, but no one has labored in the word; we may only sit there and look at one another. How then could the church be built up? The church is built up through the messengers with fresh messages of light for God's people.

IN ISAIAH 2:5 THE PROPHET SOUNDING FORTH A CALL: "HOUSE OF JACOB, COME AND LET US WALK IN THE LIGHT OF JEHOVAH"

In Isaiah 2:5 the prophet sounded forth a call: "House of Jacob, come and let us walk in the light of Jehovah" (cf. Ezek. 14:3). The call to God's people is, "Come and let us walk in the light of Jehovah." At that time, the prophets were fighting the idolatry that was among God's people. As a result of idolatry, they had slipped into darkness. Ezekiel 14:3 says, "Son of man, these men have set up their idols in their hearts and have put the stumbling block of their iniquity before their faces. Should I be inquired of at all by them?" This is very serious; they had set up idols in their hearts. First John is an Epistle full of the sweet, wonderful, and precious fellowship of the divine life, but the last verse, a concluding word, says, "Little children, guard yourselves from idols" (5:21). This is a word for all of us.

An idol is anything that replaces Christ. Anything that occupies our heart instead of Christ, that replaces Christ, or that has a place that is above Christ in our heart is an idol. Anything in our life can become an idol. If we love someone more than the Lord, that person becomes an idol. If we love our children more than the Lord, making them an idol, we will be filled with darkness. We need to give Christ the first place. Surely, we should love our children and our parents, but we should not love anyone above the Lord. We must love Him supremely and give Him the first place in everything. We should not let anything become an idol.

We all have a testimony concerning how we were saved and how we came into the Lord's recovery. Some who have been among us for a long time have paid a great price to come the way of the recovery. They gave up every idol and everything in this world. The world often refers to certain great athletes as *idols*. They call them idols because they have indeed become idols. People worship them. This is darkness. It is possible for us to make any person or any thing an idol. Even our car or our clothes can become an idol.

I can testify concerning my wife that she chose Christ rather than an idol. I met her when we were in college, and at that time, I was an unbeliever. I played sports but had a major knee injury, and she was the student nurse assigned to take care of me. I do not believe that this was a coincidence. When I saw her, it was love at first sight. I was like Isaac who loved Rebekah the moment she came to him. Isaac did not have any choice, but this girl, who is now my wife, had a choice. I was an unbeliever, and she had to make a choice. Would she choose the unbeliever, or would she choose Christ? She did not choose me; she chose Christ. That was surely the right choice. If she had chosen me, that would have been terrible, for I would have been an idol to her, something that replaced Christ. She chose the Lord; therefore, she went one way, and I went another. She went to California, and I went to Texas. Then in Texas I was saved and came into the church life. I believe that was the result of people praying for me. I know that my wife prayed for me. She had prayed for me to be saved, and then I prayed for her to come into the church life. When I told her about the church life, I was very excited. I think I gave her a whole conference in one phone call. She listened to me, but she thought I was crazy. At that point, I realized that I was the one who needed to make a choice. I really had to deal with the Lord. I did not know whether she would come this way. The Lord touched me, and I felt that He was saying, "What will you do? You care for this person very deeply. What will you do if she doesn't come this way?" With tears I said to the Lord, "I consecrate myself to You for Your recovery. I am going this way. If she doesn't take this way, I will still take this way." Eventually, she did come into the recovery, and we are living happily ever after without any idols. Many among us have similar testimonies. As married couples we can testify that the Lord is supreme. He has the first place in our marriage life and in our family life. I hope that all the young people would remember this. Keep the Lord first. Give Him the first place. Do not let a job, school, or even your own comfort become first in your heart. Otherwise, it will become an idol.

CHRIST HAVING BEEN CALLED BY JEHOVAH
TO BE A LIGHT FOR THE NATIONS, TO OPEN THE EYES
OF THE BLIND, TO BRING THE PRISONER OUT FROM THE PRISON
AND THOSE WHO DWELL IN DARKNESS FROM THE PRISON HOUSE,
TO BE GOD'S SALVATION UNTO THE ENDS OF THE EARTH

Christ has been called by Jehovah to be a light for the nations, to

open the eyes of the blind, to bring the prisoner out from the prison
and those who dwell in darkness from the prison house, to be God's
salvation unto the ends of the earth (Isa. 42:6-7; 49:6; 9:2; Matt. 4:16;
Col. 1:13; Acts 26:18). All fallen human beings are in a prison of darkness. Who will go to announce life to them? Who will be a light to
them? In Acts 13 Paul gave a wonderful message in the synagogue at
Pisidian Antioch (vv. 14-43). The following Sabbath most of the city
gathered together to hear him again, but the Jews were filled with jealousy when they saw the crowd and "contradicted the things being
spoken by Paul and blasphemed" (vv. 44-45). At the rejection of his
preaching, Paul and Barnabas said to the Jews, "It was necessary for
the word of God to be spoken to you first. Since you thrust it away and
do not judge yourselves worthy of eternal life, behold, we turn to the
Gentiles" (v. 46). Then they quoted Isaiah 42:6 saying, "For so the Lord
has commanded us, 'I have set you as a light of the Gentiles, that you
would be for salvation unto the uttermost part of the earth'" (v. 47).
This portion from Isaiah is a prophecy concerning Christ, yet Paul and
Barnabas applied it to themselves. Therefore, they were saying, "God
has set us as a light for the nations. We are God's salvation to the uttermost part of the earth, that is, to the Gentiles. We can say this because
we are absolutely one with Christ. We are one with Him as light and as
salvation." This is marvelous. We can become light and even salvation
to people.

LIGHT BEING THE PRESENCE OF GOD

Light is the presence of God (1 John 1:5; John 1:4-5; 8:12; cf. Matt.
25:30). We should not take these things for granted. This is one of the
most priceless definitions of light. What is light? Light is the presence
of God. If we are in God's presence, we are in the light. If we are not in
God's presence, we are not in the light but in darkness. Darkness is the
absence of the presence of God. God lives in us, Christ lives in us, and
He is in us to stay. We cannot simply say, "I don't like You. I want You
to leave," For He will reply, "I like you, and I am not leaving you." He
will surely stay, but we may not have His presence. Brother Lee illus-
trated this in *The All-inclusive Christ*:

> One time four or five of us who were serving the Lord
> together were going to a certain place. We all traveled
> together. One brother at that time, however, was not happy
> with us, yet he had no choice but to go. We all traveled on

the same train: all but this one brother sat in car number one, and he sat by himself in car number two. He went with us, but his presence did not go with us. He left with us, he traveled with us, and he arrived with us, but his presence was not with us. When the brothers came to welcome us, he was there, and through all of our visit in that place, he was there. He was with us, but his presence was not. It was indeed strange. (p. 120)

Sometimes our experience of the Lord is the same. Christ is in us, but He is in the other car. He is in our spirit, but we may not have His practical presence.

Paul said, "Whom you forgive anything, I also forgive; for also what I have forgiven, if I have forgiven anything, it is for your sake in the person of Christ" (2 Cor. 2:10). This means that he forgave in the index of Christ's eyes. To look at the index of the Lord's eyes indicates that we are in His person, in the presence of Christ. This means that He is real to us. When we have the Lord's presence, we have His smile. Nothing is worth losing the Lord's smile. We do not want to miss the Lord's smile in this age.

John 1:4 says, "In Him was life, and the life was the light of men." The life of Christ is the light. In John 8:12 the Lord says, "I am the light of the world; he who follows Me shall by no means walk in darkness, but shall have the light of life." It is a great thing to give ourselves to follow the Lord for the rest of our lives. We can follow Him and say to Him, "Lord, I like following You inwardly. I want to follow You wherever You go." If we follow Him, we will not walk in darkness but will have the light of life.

Matthew 25:30 says, "Cast out the useless slave into the outer darkness. In that place there will be the weeping and the gnashing of teeth." If the Lord's children are faithful in this age to pursue the Lord, to enjoy the Lord, and to minister Him according to what He has given them, they will enjoy the Lord for a thousand years in the next age. He will say, "Well done, good and faithful slave. You were faithful over a few things; I will set you over many things. Enter into the joy of your master" (vv. 21, 23). Surely we want to hear the Lord say, "Well done, good and faithful slave; since you enjoyed Me in the age of grace, enter into a much greater enjoyment of Me, the full enjoyment of Me, in the millennial kingdom." Verse 30, however, speaks concerning "the useless slave," the one who buried what the Lord had given him (v. 25).

The Lord says concerning this one, "Cast out the useless slave into the outer darkness" (v. 30). To be in outer darkness during the millennial kingdom is to be without the Lord's glorious presence.

If in this age we do not live in the person of Christ as the Spirit in our spirit, there will be weeping and gnashing of teeth in the next age. The Spirit is the presence of God. The Spirit in our spirit is light. When we are in our spirit, we are in the light. When we are not in our spirit, we do not have the Lord's presence. Although He lives in us, we may not have Him practically and subjectively as light, for light is the presence of God. Weeping indicates regret, and gnashing of teeth, self-blame. We may regret and blame ourselves saying, "Why didn't I give myself to the Lord? Why didn't I give myself to the church? Why didn't I follow the Lord when He said, 'Go to Moscow'?" If we follow the Lord, we will never have any regrets. Wherever He goes and wherever He sends us, if we have His subjective presence, there can be no regrets. We do not want any regrets in the coming age, nor do we want any regrets in this life, for we love the presence of the Triune God in our spirit.

AT THE TIME OF OUR CONVERSION, LIGHT ENTERING INTO US AND OUR BECOMING SONS OF LIGHT AND LIGHT IN THE LORD

At the time of our conversion, light entered into us and we became sons of light and light in the Lord (Gen. 1:3; 2 Cor. 4:6; John 12:36; Eph. 5:8; 1 Pet. 2:9b). When we were converted, light entered into us, making us sons of light. Our Father is light; His name is Light. When we were begotten of Him, we became sons of light, children of light. For this reason, Paul says, "You were once darkness but are now light in the Lord; walk as children of light" (Eph. 5:8). When Paul describes his experience of salvation in 2 Corinthians 4, he goes all the way back to Genesis 1, beginning with "the God who said, Out of darkness light shall shine" (v. 6). This refers to God's speaking to restore the old creation in Genesis 1:3. Paul then goes on to speak concerning the new creation, saying that this God "is the One who shined in our hearts to illuminate the knowledge of the glory of God in the face of Jesus Christ." God shined in our hearts to make us the new creation; He shined His very face into our spirit. He shined His presence into our spirit. His presence is light, and light was infused into us at our conversion.

First Peter 2:9 says, "You are a chosen race, a royal priesthood, a holy nation, a people acquired for a possession, so that you may tell out the virtues of Him who has called you out of darkness into His marvelous light." We are a chosen race, a royal priesthood, a holy nation, and a people acquired for a possession for a particular reason and commission—to tell out the virtues of Him who has called us out of darkness into His marvelous light. To tell out the virtues of Him is to live Him, expressing His divine attributes through our human virtues. Thus, as we live Him and speak Him to others, we are calling others out of darkness into His marvelous light.

I had a particular experience of this verse while my wife and I were visiting her sister in Hutchinson, Kansas. I went out into a large field on the farm where we were staying, and I was having a wonderful enjoyment of praying over 1 Peter 2:9. I was saying, "To tell out the virtues of Him, Amen. O Lord, I would like to be one with You to tell out Your virtues." Then the Lord spoke to me, saying, "Since you want to do this, I want you to drive into the city of Wichita and find your old coach. I want you to preach the gospel to him." I could not believe it. I kept saying, "This can't be the Lord." I was saying No, but the Lord kept saying Yes. I had all kinds of excuses not to do it, but eventually the light won. I drove all the way to Wichita and went to my old school. I found out that my old coach was now a bank vice-president, so I went to the bank and preached the gospel to him. He did not receive the Lord, but I still pray for his salvation. The point here is that we need to tell out the virtues of Christ.

"GIVING THANKS TO THE FATHER, WHO HAS QUALIFIED YOU FOR A SHARE OF THE ALLOTTED PORTION OF THE SAINTS *IN THE LIGHT*"

"Giving thanks to the Father, who has qualified you for a share of the allotted portion of the saints *in the light*" (Col. 1:12, our italics). Christ is our portion; He has been allotted to us. He is the good land, and each of us has been allotted a portion of Christ. We possess Christ as our good land in the same way that the land of Canaan was allotted to each of the children of Israel. However, we can only enjoy Him *in the light*. Thus, we italicized this phrase to emphasize it.

The Only Way to Partake of Christ and to Enjoy Him Being in the Light; When We Turn to the Lord and Come into His Presence, Our Being in the Light and Spontaneously Beginning to Enjoy Him as Our Portion, as the New Covenant

The only way to partake of Christ and to enjoy Him is in the light; when we turn to the Lord and come into His presence, we are in the light and spontaneously begin to enjoy Him as our portion, as the new covenant (Psa. 16:5, 11; 116:12-13; 36:8-9). We each have received an allotment of Christ for our enjoyment. If we are not in the light, we cannot enjoy Him. We must be in the light.

Light Ruling by Its Enlightening; Hence, When the Light of Life Shines and Rules, It Being a Kingdom, the Kingdom of the Son of the Father's Love, in Contrast to the Authority of Darkness, Which Is the Kingdom of Satan

Light rules by its enlightening; hence, when the light of life shines and rules, it is a kingdom, the kingdom of the Son of the Father's love, in contrast to the authority of darkness, which is the kingdom of Satan (Col. 1:13; Rev. 22:5; John 14:21, 23). When light shines within you, it rules you. When the Lord is shining in you, He rules you. You do not do certain things because you know that if you do them, you will leave the light. Light is also a kingdom in the same way that darkness is a kingdom. This light, which is a kingdom, is the kingdom of the Son of the Father's love. Christ is the Father's love. He is not only the Father's love; He is also our love. Thus, the best way to enjoy the light is to say, "Lord Jesus, I love You." When you say this, light shines within you, and you are brought into a kingdom of light and under the ruling of light. The next time you go shopping, say, "Lord Jesus, I love You." When you pick up something that is on sale to buy it, just say, "Lord Jesus, I love You." You might then decide not to buy it. When you say, "Lord Jesus, I love You," you are ruled. This is to experience the kingdom of the Son of the Father's love.

When we were saved, we were in the light and in the Lord's presence. Perhaps we did not know about our spirit, but we accidentally turned on the switch. We were in the presence of God, and we were in the light. Everything was very enjoyable and simple. However, sooner or later we were distracted from the enjoyment of Christ and failed to take care of His inner shining. For some of us, certain so-called Christian workers led us away from the enjoyment of Christ. Their teachings, forms, works, observances, and religious rituals and duties took us away from the inner shining. We were thus distracted. Now the Lord is calling us back to our spirit to walk in the light of Jehovah.

THE SEVEN SPIRITS OF GOD BEING THE SEVEN LAMPS OF FIRE, AND OUR SPIRIT BEING ALSO THE LAMP OF JEHOVAH, SEARCHING ALL THE ROOMS OF OUR INNER BEING, ALL THE CHAMBERS OF OUR SOUL

The seven Spirits of God are the seven lamps of fire, and our spirit is also the lamp of Jehovah, searching all the rooms of our inner being, all the chambers of our soul (Rev. 4:5; Prov. 20:27). We may understand this by considering the picture of the lampstand, which has seven lamps. Revelation 4:5 speaks of the seven Spirits of God, yet Ephesians 4:4 says there is one Spirit. Is then God's Spirit seven or one? When viewed from the front, the lampstand appears to have seven lights, but when viewed from the side, it appears as one. There is only one Spirit in essence and in existence, yet in function it is sevenfold. The lampstand is a symbol of the Triune God. The gold of the lampstand typifies the Father in His divine nature; the form of the lampstand typifies Christ the Son as the image of the invisible God; and the seven lamps typify the seven Spirits of God as the sevenfold expression and manifestation of the Triune God. The seven Spirits, which comprise the sevenfold intensified Spirit, are the seven lamps. The lampstand is a wonderful piece of furniture in the tabernacle and in the temple that only God could have designed. He Himself provided the design (Num. 8:4) because this piece of furniture is a symbol of the Triune God and the sevenfold intensified Spirit of God.

The seven lamps of fire are burning before the throne through the seven Spirits of God. Proverbs 20:27 says, "The spirit of man is the lamp of Jehovah." God created man with a lamp. The difference between man and every other creature is that we have a lamp within us. We need to see who we are in our spirit. Our spirit is the lamp of the Triune God. When God entered into us, a sevenfold intensified lamp entered into our lamp. The spirit of man is the lamp of Jehovah, and the seven Spirits of God are the seven lamps of fire that entered into our spirit. Therefore, we also should be intensified. When we get into our spirit, we are burned and become burning.

These Two Spirits, Ours and God's, Having Been Mingled; within Our Little Lamp, Our Spirit, There Being Now Also Another Lamp of Greater Intensity, the Sevenfold Intensified Spirit

These two spirits, ours and God's, have been mingled; within our little lamp, our spirit, there is now also another lamp of greater intensity, the sevenfold intensified Spirit (1 Cor. 6:17). We are one spirit with the Lord. The Triune God is in our spirit.

As Our Spirit Shines through Our Prayer, the Spirit of God Intensifying the Shining Sevenfold, and under the Intensity of This Light, Our Confessing and Repenting to the Lord

As our spirit shines through our prayer, the Spirit of God intensifies the shining sevenfold, and under the intensity of this light, we confess and repent to the Lord (Psa. 139:23-24; 1 John 1:7, 9). This is so simple yet very profound. We need to give ourselves to pray. We need to pray ourselves into our spirit, into God, and into the presence of God. We are those who desire to be in our spirit, to gaze on Him, and to behold His beauty. When we pray in this way, the Spirit of God intensifies His shining sevenfold. Then we begin to see. The spirit of man is the lamp of Jehovah. It searches all the chambers of our soul—our mind, emotion, and will. This sevenfold intensified lamp in our lamp has become one lamp, one entity. This sevenfold intensified lamp searches all the chambers of our soul. As this lamp, this light, searches, it shines into our mind, and we realize, "O Lord, forgive me for thinking those thoughts. I repent. Forgive me for thinking that way. Forgive me for having that kind of philosophy." When we came into the church life, we brought all kinds of things with us. We were like a horse pulling Pharaoh's chariot (S. S. 1:9). As a new one, we were like a horse, very absolute. However, behind us we were pulling Satan, typified by Pharaoh, into the meeting. The light kills Pharaoh. We have many things within us that need to be shined on and irradiated.

The light will also shine on our emotion. We do not love what the Lord loves, and we do not hate what the Lord hates. As He shines, we will confess and repent in the light. As we confess, His blood cleanses us from every sin (1 John 1:9). It is wonderful to be cleansed by the Lord's blood from every sin. As we confess, He is faithful and righteous to forgive us our sins and cleanse us from all unrighteousness. Once we confess a sin that the Lord brings to the light, it is forgiven and can never be brought up again at the judgment seat of Christ. We need to keep short accounts with the Lord, confessing any sins that He brings into the light.

Where the Light Shines, the Life Supply Going, and Chamber by Chamber Our Being Transformed into the Lord's Image; This Shining, Supplying, and Transforming Making Us the Golden Lampstand

Where the light shines, the life supply goes, and chamber by chamber we are transformed into the Lord's image; this shining, supplying, and transforming make us the golden lampstand (2 Cor. 3:16, 18; Rev. 1:20). The light shines within us, and the life supply comes to us because this light is the light of life. Where the light shines, life is supplied. It is so good to be in the light. When we are in the light, we are supplied and transformed.

The Parts of Our Life and Living That Are Closed Off from Christ Being in Darkness, Because Christ, the One Who Is the Very Light, Has No Place

The parts of our life and living that are closed off from Christ are in darkness, because Christ, the One who is the very light, has no place (Luke 11:33-36). We need to pray, "Lord, I don't want to close off any part of my life or my living to You." There may be parts of our life that we close off from the Lord. We have many rooms in our house. In some of the rooms, the lights are on, but in others, the lights are off. What about the "rooms" in our inner being and the chambers of our soul? What about our heart with the mind, emotion, will, and conscience? We should not close off any part of our life and our living to the Lord; otherwise, that part will be in darkness.

We need to have the prayer and aspiration to open to the Lord. We can say to Him, "Lord, I want to open my whole being to You without reservation. I open my whole life, my living, and the details of my life to You. I open everything to You. I open to You concerning whom I should marry, where I should go to school, and where I should live. I am open to You if You want me to move and even if You want me to migrate to another country." It is possible for us to close ourselves off from the Lord. When we fellowship with the Lord, we may have some sense within us that the Lord wants us to go to Moscow or St. Petersburg, to a particular campus, or to a city in the United States. He may want us to go and speak to our neighbor. However, if we close off any area of our being or living, that part will be in darkness. We should not be closed to the Lord. It is not worth it.

Maybe you treasure something and do not want to give that to the Lord. If you treasure something more than the Lord and you do not give that to Him, that thing will become an idol and a burden to you. Isaiah 46:1 says, "Their idols are on beasts and cattle; / The things which you carry are a burden, / A load for a weary beast." The idols of the children of Israel became a burden to them. The same thing happens to us.

The Lord wants to write Himself on us so that we become letters of Christ (2 Cor. 3:3). Our hearts are like a piece of paper on which the Lord wants to write with the Spirit of God as the ink. However, if the piece of paper is wadded up into a ball, it is impossible to write on it because it is closed. The paper has to be opened up for someone to write on it. In the same way, we need to be open so that the Lord can write on us.

If we are closed to the light, we may use the things that we hear in the messages or that we read in the word as a reference to judge others, rather than applying them to ourselves. We may read a verse such as, "O house of Jacob, come and let us walk in the light of Jehovah" (Isa. 2:5), to say, "O Lord, thank You that I am in the light. That other person really needs this word." If we pray in this way, we are the ones in darkness. We are like the Pharisee who prayed, "God, I thank You that I am not like the rest of men—extortioners, unjust, adulterers, or even like this tax collector" (Luke 18:11). We should instead be like the tax collector who "standing at a distance, would not even lift up his eyes to heaven, but beat his breast, saying, God, be propitiated to me, the sinner!" (v. 13). He was the one who went home in the light. The one that justifies himself is in darkness. When we go into a dark room and look out through a window, we can see everything that is outside the room quite clearly. If we are criticizing others, it is an indication that we are in darkness.

We should not close off anything from the Lord. This means that we need to keep our heart single. Luke 11:33-36 says,

No one, after lighting a lamp, puts it in the cellar or under the bushel, but on the lampstand, in order that those who enter in may see the light. The lamp of the body is your eye. When your eye is single, your whole body also is full of light; but when it is evil, your body also is dark. Watch out therefore that the light which is in you is not darkness. If therefore your whole body is full of light and does not have any dark part, the whole will be full of light as when the lamp with its rays illuminates you.

I appreciate the phrase *full of light*. We need to pray over these verses and tell the Lord, "I want to be a person full of light. I do not want to have any dark part. I do not want any part of my being to be in darkness. Lord, I would like for my whole being to be full of light."

The One Who Experiences
the Greatest Amount of Transformation
Being the One Who Is Absolutely Open to the Lord

The one who experiences the greatest amount of transformation is the one who is absolutely open to the Lord (Psa. 139:23-24; Matt. 5:3). This is the reason that we need to keep ourselves open to the Lord. Psalm 139:23-24 says, "Search me, O God, and know my heart; / Try me, and know my anxious thoughts; / And see if there is some harmful way in me, / And lead me on the eternal way." We also should pray, "Lord, search me and know my heart." The word *harmful* may be translated *painful* or *idolatrous*. When we enjoy the Lord, He searches us. It is good to be in the light and be shined on. If we take any way other than the way of the Lord's recovery and the way of God's economy, it will be a way of pain. It will be a painful, idolatrous way; a way that causes us harm. Thus, it is good to be in the light and on the way that leads to life, the way of God's economy, by keeping ourselves open to the Lord.

Our Spirit Being the Key to Life, and Prayer Being
the Key to Being Able to Stay in Our Spirit;
God Continuing to Call Us Back to Our Spirit

Our spirit is the key to life, and prayer is the key to being able to stay in our spirit; God keeps calling us back to our spirit (Eph. 6:18; 1 Thes. 5:17). We should turn to our spirit and remain in our spirit.

The best way to touch Him in our spirit is to pray. Prayer is the key to remaining in our spirit.

IN ORDER FOR US TO WALK IN THE DIVINE LIGHT, THE LORD HAVING GIVEN US THE FELLOWSHIP OF LIFE, THE BLOOD OF JESUS, THE WORD OF GOD, THE CHILDREN OF GOD, AND THE CHURCH OF GOD

The Divine Life, the Divine Fellowship, the Divine Light, and the Blood of Jesus, the Son of God, Constituting a Spiritual Cycle in Our Christian Life

In order for us to walk in the divine light, the Lord has given us the fellowship of life, the blood of Jesus, the word of God, the children of God, and the church of God. The divine life, the divine fellowship, the divine light, and the blood of Jesus, the Son of God, constitute a spiritual cycle in our Christian life (1 John 1:3-9). When we contact Christ as life in our spirit, He begins to flow within us. That flow of life is the fellowship of life. It is like the flow of electricity. When the electricity is flowing, the lights are on. When we are in the fellowship, the light shines. When we are in the light, we see who God is, and we see who we are and where we are. This causes us to pray, "I shouldn't have that thought. I should not have done that or said that. I should not have judged or criticized that person. Lord, forgive me." When we confess in this way, the blood of Jesus cleanses us from every sin. This cleansing brings an increased flow of life. The more we are in the fellowship of life, the more light we receive. The more light we receive, the more we see ourselves. We should not think that we are getting worse; we were always this bad. The difference is that the light is getting brighter. Then in the light we confess and enjoy the cleansing of the blood.

Hallelujah for the blood of Jesus! It cleanses us from every sin. "If we confess our sins, He is faithful and righteous to forgive us our sins and cleanse us from all unrighteousness" (1 John 1:9). God has to forgive us of our sins when we confess them. Otherwise, He would not be righteous. Christ paid the debt of all our sins on the cross, once for all eternally. When we confess our sins, which have been taken away on the cross, we enjoy the fresh application of that eternal accomplishment. When we confess our sins in time, God must forgive us because He is righteous, because the debt of sin has been paid, and because we acknowledge that it is sin. He must forgive us because He is righteous and faithful. He is faithful according to His word; and He is righteous in His blood. He paid the price for our sins with His blood. This is a cycle. We need to stay in this cycle.

The Word of God Being a Lamp to Our Feet and a Light to Our Path

The word of God is a lamp to our feet and a light to our path (Psa. 119:105, 130; Deut. 17:18-20; John 8:12, 32, 36; 5:39-40; Psa. 42:5; Num. 6:25). We have the Word of God, but we should not come to read the Bible with our mind. When we come to the Word, we should come with a seeking and praying spirit. John 5:39-40 says, "You search the Scriptures, because you think that in them you have eternal life; and it is these that testify concerning Me. Yet you are not willing to come to Me that you may have life." Whenever we come to the word, we must also come to Him. We have to seek His countenance and seek His face in the word. We should come in a spirit and atmosphere of prayer. Then the word of God becomes a lamp to our feet and a light to our path.

Praise the Lord that we have the Bible. If we want to be in the light, we must open the Bible. Our way of studying the Bible should be in the way of pray-reading the Word. When we study, we study prayerfully and in an atmosphere of prayer. That will bring light into our being.

The Lord, speaking through Moses in Deuteronomy 17, set forth a requirement for the future kings of the children of Israel. Verses 18 through 20 say,

> When he sits on the throne of his kingdom, he shall write out for himself a copy of this law in a book, out of that which is before the Levitical priests. And it shall be with him, and he shall read in it all the days of his life, in order that he may learn to fear Jehovah his God by keeping all the words of this law and these statutes and doing them, so that his heart may not be lifted up above his brothers and he may not turn aside from the commandment to the right or to the left; that he and his sons may extend their days over their kingdom in the midst of Israel.

Jehovah was saying to the children of Israel, "When you have a king among you, I want him to write out his own personal copy of the law." The law is the Pentateuch. To be a good ruler, the king had to take a quill and ink and write out his own personal copy of the law, which comprised the Scriptures at that time. Just consider, what if I were to instruct you to write down the entire New Testament by hand with pen and paper? If you were to write out the entire New Testament, surely you would get something. As you were writing, you would probably begin to pray. The king of Israel was supposed to write out the Scriptures and read it all the days of his life. This would make him a good king, one who feared God, who was not lifted up among his brothers, and who was not proud. This would make him a king that remained on the way of God's economy. This is the reason we also must read the Bible.

The Saints Being the Light of the World
as the Duplication of Christ

The saints are the light of the world as the duplication of Christ (Matt. 5:14; Phil. 2:15-16; Acts 5:20; 13:47; Isa. 49:6; 60:1-3). To be in the light, we must first exercise our spirit to pray. We need to open to the Lord saying, "Lord, I open absolutely to You. I would like to open my whole being toward the New Jerusalem in the same way that Daniel opened his window to pray toward Jerusalem. My aim, Lord, is the New Jerusalem. Your goal is my goal. I exercise my spirit to pray. I want to remain in fellowship with You, to be in the light, and to enjoy the cleansing. Lord, I also want to be in the word so that I can have more light." Such a simple prayer is the means to walk in the light.

We also need to be with the saints, the other believers, because the saints are the light of the world. When we are with the saints, we are in the light. If we are in darkness and cannot get out, we should call a brother, get with the saints, or come to a meeting. When you do this, you enter into the light. Sometimes we are at home in darkness, and a brother calls us. Right away we may inwardly say, "O Lord, forgive me." We do not say it audibly, but we realize that when that brother called, light called. When we are in the presence of some brothers and sisters, we have the sense that we are in the light. Whenever Brother Lee came in the room, it seemed that I inwardly repented and confessed my sin. He did not know, but I was saying, "O Lord, I am not absolute for You. Forgive me." I had such a response because that brother was full of light. We also need to be full of light. If we want to be in the light, we should get with the saints. The saints are the light of the world, and as the duplication of Christ, we need to shine as luminaries in the world.

The Church Being a Golden Lampstand, Shining in This Age of Darkness

The church is a golden lampstand, shining in this age of darkness (Rev. 1:20; cf. Psa. 73:16-22, 25-26). If you want to be in the light, come to the church. The church is a golden lampstand. When you come into the meetings with the saints, you get clear. Psalm 73 is a marvelous psalm written by Asaph. For the first sixteen verses, Asaph describes being in darkness. He considered the wicked, and he wondered why they prospered in the world, why they had no pains, and why they did not have any troubles. We also may say, "Look at the president of IBM, look at those who have a nice job, and look at that one who is an engineer. Here I am in the full-time training. I am suffering every day. When I wake up in the morning, instead of morning watch, I have suffering watch." The psalmist said, "I have been plagued all day long / And chastened every morning" (v. 14). In verse 16 he says, "When I considered this in order to understand it, / It was a troublesome task in my sight."

Then in verse 17 Asaph says, "Until I went into the sanctuary of God; /Then I perceived their end." He came to the meeting, to the sanctuary of God, to the church. The sanctuary of God is our spirit, and the sanctuary of God is the church. When we come to the meeting and get in our spirit, we become clear. When the psalmist came to the sanctuary of God, he became clear and realized that it was not at all as he thought. The rich are actually "in slippery places" and "are made desolate in a moment!" (vv. 18-19). He also declares, "I was like a beast before You" (v. 22). We may pray the same prayer, "Lord, I was a beast before You. Before I came to the meeting, I was a beast, but now I've been 'de-beastized.'" When we first come to the meeting, we may feel like a beast, but when the light shines, we become clear. We start off in darkness, but then we come to the meeting of the church. The psalmist also had a fresh consecration saying, "Whom do I have in heaven but You? / And besides You there is nothing I desire on earth" (v. 25). This is the issue of light.

Our Being Able to Abide in the Light by Loving the Lord and Loving the Brothers

We can abide in the light by loving the Lord (Col. 1:13; Rev. 2:4, 7) and loving the brothers (1 John 2:10-11; 3:14-17). When we say, "Lord

Jesus, I love You," we are in the light. In Revelation 2 the Lord seems to be telling the church in Ephesus, "You have left your first love. Since you have done this, you are in danger of having the lampstand removed from you." This indicates that if we do not love the Lord preeminently, we lose the light of the lampstand. By loving the Lord we keep ourselves in the light. If we would tell the Lord that we love Him a hundred times a day, we would be full of light.

We need to love the Lord, and we also need to love the brothers. First John 2:10-11 says, "He who loves his brother abides in the light...but he who hates his brother is in the darkness and walks in the darkness." According to 3:14, "We know that we have passed out of death into life because we love the brothers." When we are in the light, we want to be with the brothers. When we are in darkness, we would like to board up our windows, take our phone off the hook, and remain isolated. We know we have passed out of death into life when we love the brothers.

Verse 17 says, "Whoever has the livelihood of the world and sees that his brother has need and shuts up his affections from him, how does the love of God abide in him?" When we see a brother in need and shut our affection toward him, that is not loving the brothers. However, if we are in a spirit of prayer, in the church life, in the word, with the saints, in the fellowship, in God's presence, and loving the brothers, then the Lord will show us many needs in the church. We may realize that a brother does not have a watch, and the Lord may tell us to buy a watch for him. Then we buy that brother a watch, and when he is not looking, we put it in an envelope on his chair. This kind of love is too precious. We love the brothers.

THE DIVINE LIGHT, THE PRESENCE OF GOD, FUNCTIONING WITHIN US IN THE FOLLOWING WAYS

The Divine Light Enlightening the Eyes of Our Heart to See God and to See as God Sees

The divine light, the presence of God, functions within us in the following ways. The divine light enlightens the eyes of our heart to see God and to see as God sees (1 John 1:7; Matt. 5:8; 2 Cor. 3:16; Eph. 1:17-18; Psa. 36:9b). The Lord is not only the light; He is in the light. If we walk in the light as He is in the light, we see Him, and we also see what He sees.

The Divine Light Exposing and Reproving Us

The divine light exposes and reproves us (Eph. 5:13-14). It is actually marvelous to be exposed. It is terrible to remain in darkness without even realizing it. What a tragedy it would be to have idols in our being but not know it. To be in the light is marvelous. In the light we see that we are not okay but neither is anyone else. The only One who is okay is Jesus. When He shines on us, we are exposed, reproved, and awakened.

The Divine Light Supplying Us with Life

The divine light supplies us with life (John 1:4).

The Divine Light Healing Us

The divine light heals us (Luke 1:78-79; Mal. 4:2). When He shines, we confess our sins, and the blood of Jesus cleanses us. Then He shines more into us, and we are healed inwardly. Only He can heal the brokenhearted (cf. Isa. 61:1). As He shines on us as light, He is the Sun of righteousness with healing in His wings.

The Divine Light Killing the Negative Things in Our Being

The divine light kills the negative things in our being (Isa. 6:1-8). When Isaiah saw the light in chapter 6, he said, "Woe is me: I am finished" (v. 5). This means that he was killed. Then he was reconstituted and became sendable. In this way he could be sent by the Triune God.

HE WHO FEARS JEHOVAH AND HEARS THE VOICE OF HIS SERVANT HAVING LIGHT WHILE WALKING IN DARKNESS

He who fears Jehovah and hears the voice of His Servant has light while walking in darkness (Isa. 50:10-11; Psa. 139:7-12, 23-24). Isaiah 50:10 says, "Who among you fears Jehovah; / Who hears the voice of His servant; / Who walks in darkness / And has no light? / Let him trust in the name of Jehovah, / And rely on his God." Sometimes you may feel, "I'm in darkness. I don't have any light." What should you do? According to these verses, you need to trust in Him, rely on Him, lean on Him, and depend on Him in the valley. Verse 11 says, "Indeed, all of you who kindle a fire, / Who surround yourselves with firebrands, / Walk into the light of your fire / And into the firebrands which you have lit. / You will have this from My hand: / You will lie down in torment." This means that you should not try to manufacture light. It is a terrible thing to manufacture your own light. Instead, you should simply rely on God and trust in Him. Then you will have light even while walking in darkness.

Isaiah's word on having light while walking in darkness corresponds to Psalm 139. Verses 7 through 12 say,

> Where shall I go, away from Your Spirit, / And where shall I flee from Your presence? / If I ascend into heaven, You are there; / If I make my bed in Sheol, there You are. / If I take the wings of the dawn / And settle at the limits of the sea, / There also Your hand will lead me, / And Your right hand will take hold of me. / And if I say, Surely darkness will cover me, / And the light around me will be night; / Even the darkness is not dark to You, / And night shines like day; / The darkness is like the light.

This is the same psalm in which the writer says, "Search me, O God, and know my heart" (v. 23). When we are passing through a valley, having some kind of suffering or turmoil, or feeling oppressed and discouraged, we can call on the Lord. In the middle of everything, we can say, "O Lord, I rely on You, I trust in You." Then we will have light even while we are walking in darkness.

AS WE WALK IN THE LIGHT DAY BY DAY AND CORPORATELY SHINE HIM OUT IN THIS DARK AGE AS HIS CHURCHES, THE GOLDEN LAMPSTANDS, OUR HASTENING THE DAY OF HIS COMING WHEN WE WILL BE FULLY PREPARED TO BE HIS BRIDE, THE NEW JERUSALEM, THE CITY OF LIGHT AND THE KINGDOM OF LIGHT FOR THE FULL EXPRESSION OF GOD AS LIGHT

As we walk in the light day by day and corporately shine Him out in this dark age as His churches, the golden lampstands, we will hasten the day of His coming when we will be fully prepared to be His bride, the New Jerusalem, the city of light and the kingdom of light for the full expression of God as light (Rev. 21:11, 23; 22:5).—E. M.

THE DIVINE ECONOMY IN THE BOOK OF ISAIAH

Christ as the Covenant and as the Light to Be God's Full Salvation
(Message 23)

Scripture Reading: Isa. 42:5-7; 49:6, 8b-9a; Rom. 10:3; 3:21-28; 4:22-25; 5:18; 1:16-17; 8:4

I. Christ as the Servant of Jehovah serves God by being a covenant and a light to God's chosen people that He may be the full salvation of God—Isa. 42:5-7; 49:6, 8b-9a:

　　A. Through His death and resurrection, Christ has become the new covenant as the new testament according to God's righteousness to be the base of God's full salvation—Luke 22:20; Psa. 89:14:

　　　　1. As the Servant of Jehovah, Christ serves God by being a covenant—Isa. 42:6; 49:8b:

　　　　　　a. Christ served us by dying for us; this was to serve by being a covenant.

　　　　　　b. Christ serves God by ministering life to us through His death and resurrection—Mark 10:45; John 12:24.

　　　　2. In the new covenant it seems that we have received many things, but actually we have gained only one thing—Christ—Heb. 8:10-13:

　　　　　　a. Christ is the reality of the new covenant; therefore, Christ *is* the new covenant, the new testament.

　　　　　　b. The new covenant, established by Christ through His death, gives us Christ—Luke 22:20; Matt. 26:27-28.

　　　　3. Christ as the covenant takes care of God's righteousness; hence, this covenant is the foundation of God's salvation.

　　B. God gave Christ as a light to the nations that He might be God's salvation to all the world—Isa. 42:6; 49:6:

　　　　1. This light issues in Christ as the divine life to us—John 9:5; 1:4, 9; 8:12.

　　　　2. Christ as the light carries out God's salvation to consummate God's salvation in life—Rom. 5:10.

   3. The life of this light becomes God's salvation to us in His righteousness.

C. Christ as the covenant and Christ as the light, added together, equal God's full salvation—3:21; 5:10, 18.

D. Based on the righteousness of God and in the life of God, we enjoy God as our inheritance—Acts 26:18.

II. God's full salvation is based upon His righteousness and is consummated in His life—Rom. 10:3; 3:21-28; 5:18; 1:16-17:

A. The righteousness of God is what God is with respect to justice and righteousness—10:3; 3:21-23:

   1. Because we are fallen, God must deal with us according to His righteousness.

   2. As the righteous God, He cannot forgive sinful people without meeting the demands of His righteousness—1 John 1:9.

B. Justification is God's action in approving us according to His standard of righteousness—Gal. 2:16; Rom. 3:28.

C. The proof of God's justification is the resurrection of Christ—4:22-25:

   1. The redeeming death of Christ as the ground for God to justify us has been fully accepted by God, and Christ has been resurrected as a proof of this.

   2. The resurrected Christ who sits at God's right hand is the evidence that God is satisfied with His death on our behalf and that we have been justified—1 John 2:1.

   3. Now that Christ has died and has been raised from among the dead, it is impossible for God to change His mind about forgiving us; He is bound by His righteousness to forgive us—1:9.

D. God has given Christ to us as the righteousness of God—1 Cor. 1:30.

E. Our experience of Christ rests upon the foundation of God's righteousness—Psa. 89:14.

F. Whereas God's righteousness justifies us through the death of Christ, God's life germinates us by Christ as the life-giving Spirit—Rom. 10:3; Gal. 2:16, 21; Rom. 5:18; Eph. 2:5; 1 Cor. 15:45b:

   1. The condemnation of God is dissolved by Christ as the

covenant, and the death that comes from Satan is annulled by Christ as the light that issues in life—John 8:12.

2. Christ became the life-giving Spirit in resurrection to dispense the life which was in God into us to enliven us, to regenerate us, to make us children of God—3:3-6; 1 John 3:1; John 1:12-13; Rom. 8:15.

III. The New Jerusalem is the embodiment of God's full salvation, and God's full salvation is a composition of God's righteousness as the base and God's life as the consummation—Rev. 21:2, 10, 19-20, 23; 22:1-2:

A. The foundation of the New Jerusalem is the righteousness of God with God's faithfulness—21:19-20.

B. The content of the New Jerusalem is life, which issues from light—v. 23:

1. The entire New Jerusalem is a matter of life built on the foundation of righteousness—22:1-2.

2. Life is the consummation of righteousness, and righteousness is the base, the foundation, of life.

IV. The way to receive and enjoy the full salvation of God is to exercise our spirit, live according to our spirit, and remain in our spirit, with which is Christ, by calling on the Lord's name—Rom. 8:4; 10:12-13; 2 Tim. 4:22.

V. God's full salvation is full of springs, and we need to learn to draw water out of these springs by calling on the Lord's name—Isa. 12:2-6.

CHRIST AS THE COVENANT AND AS THE LIGHT
TO BE GOD'S FULL SALVATION

Prayer: Lord Jesus, open Your Word, open our eyes, and open our minds that we may see You as the covenant and the light, that we may know You as righteousness and life, and that we may experience and enjoy You as God's full salvation. Amen.

In the previous two messages we have considered the revelation and experience of Christ as the covenant and as the light, respectively. This message rests upon those previous two messages as a foundation so that we might see the relationship between Christ, the covenant, the light, righteousness, life, and God's full salvation. Actually, the entire Bible of sixty-six books is involved in the revelation of Christ as the covenant, issuing in righteousness for our justification and of Christ as light, bringing in life for our regeneration that we may become God's building, His corporate expression.

Isaiah 42:6 says, "I am Jehovah; I have called You in righteousness; / I have held You by the hand; / I have kept You and I have given You / As a covenant for the people, as a light for the nations." *You* here refers to Christ Himself, indicating that God has given Christ to His people as the covenant and as the light. Isaiah 49:6 says, "I will also set You as a light of the nations / That You may be My salvation unto the ends of the earth." Then verse 8 says, "I will preserve You and give You for a covenant of the people." These verses emphatically state that God has given Christ, the Servant of Jehovah, as a covenant and as a light. Romans 5:18 says, "So then as it was through one offense unto condemnation to all men, so also it was through one righteous act unto justification of life to all men." In this verse we have one righteous act, justification, and life. Then 1:16 and 17 say, "I am not ashamed of the gospel, for it is the power of God unto salvation to everyone who believes, both to Jew first and to Greek. For the righteousness of God is revealed in it out of faith to faith, as it is written, 'But the righteous shall have life and live by faith.'" In Isaiah we have the covenant and the light, in Romans we have righteousness and life, and in both we have God's salvation.

Before we consider the diagram below, we need to ponder two questions, which are closely related, and then open to receive the divine answer. The first question is, "Why is the gospel the power of God?" In the New Testament three things are designated the power of God: Christ (1 Cor. 1:24), the word of the cross (v. 18), and the gospel (Rom. 1:16). The second simple yet vital question is even more crucial for our entire Christian life: "What is the foundation for our experience of Christ?" We want to experience and to enjoy Christ, but we need to understand the foundation for our experience and enjoyment of Christ. We need to see what is our basis, our ground, and our right to seek the experience and enjoyment of Christ. These two matters are very much on my heart concerning all the dear saints, that there would be an unshakable foundation for our experience and enjoyment of Christ in the church life for our whole Christian life. I long that we would see that we have a foundation that is as unshakable as the throne of God is unshakable. Such a foundation is not only possible; it is an established fact because God has provided it in His economy for our full salvation.

Christ as the Covenant, Issuing in Righteousness, and as the Light, Issuing in Life, for our Full Salvation

In the diagram the arrows connecting the various words indicate both relationship and progression. At the top we must begin with the

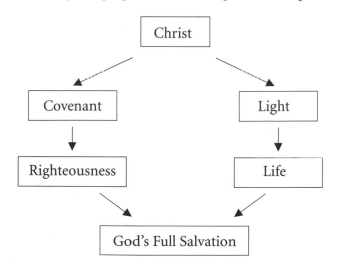

all-inclusive Christ, who is the center of God's economy. He is God, and He is man. He is righteousness, holiness, glory, kindness, patience, endurance, life, light, love, grace, mercy, strength, power, authority, and every positive thing in the universe. Christ is the one reality of all, and we are here for Christ.

God has given Christ as a covenant. This defies human logic, for a covenant is normally an agreement, a contract. How then can a person be a covenant? In order to see this, our natural mind needs to be renewed, for Isaiah 42:6 says that God has given Christ as a covenant. Christ initiated the covenant, enacted the covenant, is the Mediator of the covenant, is all the bequests contained in the covenant, and is the reality of the covenant. Without Christ there would be no covenant. Since Christ is the reality of the new covenant, in the sight of God He is the covenant.

Moreover, Christ is the light. This is easier for our minds to grasp, for the Lord Himself said, "I am the light of the world" (John 8:12). John 1 declares that He is the true light (v. 9) and that those who receive this light are born of God (vv. 12-13).

Furthermore, we need to see that the covenant is a matter of God's righteousness. The covenant is not based on love although it was love that motivated God to enter into the covenant. Neither is the covenant based on grace although God bestows grace upon us through the covenant. The covenant is a matter of righteousness. When a legal contract has been signed, the carrying out of its contents is not a matter of love, grace, kindness, or mercy but a matter of righteousness. Perhaps *righteousness* is not one of our favorite words in the Bible, for it does not sound warm. Nevertheless, it is surely marvelous that our God is a God of righteousness. Everything He says and does is according to righteousness. Nothing binds Him more than His own righteousness. He has entered into a covenant judicially, justly, and righteously according to His own righteousness, and He is prepared to carry out this covenant according to His righteousness. He wants to be bound by His righteousness so that He might fully apply the covenant to us.

Finally, we need to see that light brings in life. In the Bible and in our Christian experience, light comes first. Hence, "God said, Let there be light; and there was light" (Gen. 1:3), and then He caused the dry land to appear and said, "Let the earth sprout grass, herbs yielding seed, and fruit trees bearing fruit according to their kind with their seed in them upon the earth" (v. 11). Following this, on the fourth day

God created more definite and solid lights—the light of the sun, the moon, and the stars. Following the fourth-day lights, God brought forth higher forms of life. Thus, we see that light brings in life. Sinners have two monumental problems. One is God's condemnation because of their unrighteousness, and the other is death because of Satan. Outwardly, every unbeliever is under the righteous judgment of God, issuing in condemnation. Inwardly, every man is a victim of the devil, who is the source of death. Light exposes man's outward situation, and life annuls man's inner death. When a sinner hears the preaching of Christ as the gospel, he does not first receive life but rather light. First, the light shines on his situation, exposing him and at the same time revealing Christ. Then when he receives the light into his being, the light becomes life.

However, according to the sequence of the revelation in both John 1 and 1 John 1, life is first, and the life becomes the light. As a sinner in condemnation and death, light comes and brings in life, but as a child of God, the more we touch life, the more we have light. God wants Christ to be our full salvation. Thus, Isaiah 49:6 clearly says that He is a light for the peoples that He may be salvation. The light brings in life to match the covenant that brings in righteousness. Who is righteousness and life? The very Christ who is the covenant is righteousness, and the very Christ who is the light is life. When we have Christ as righteousness plus Christ as light, we have God's full salvation, which also is Christ. Therefore, the covenant, righteousness, light, life, and God's full salvation are all intrinsically Christ.

God only cares for Christ. He has presented Christ as a covenant righteously so that we might be justified, that is, approved by God according to the standard of His righteousness. But if all we believers had were justification, we would be merely justified corpses. If we were merely justified, believing in the doctrine of justification that Christ has been imputed to us as righteousness, we would still be dead. We may be judicially and objectively righteous, but that is not God's complete salvation. Hence, Christ is also the light to bring in life. Life regenerates us and enlivens us to make us children of God. Only then can we have Christ as our full salvation. According to Isaiah 12:3-4, the way to receive God as our salvation is to draw water from the springs of salvation, that is, to drink Him.

What we have covered thus far is an introduction to the central thought of the message. Christ is the covenant, issuing in righteousness, and Christ is the light, issuing in life, for our full salvation. Therefore, the title of this message is "Christ as the Covenant and as the Light to Be God's Full Salvation." The message outline has three main sections. In the first section we will develop the diagram on page 147 mainly along the line of the truth. In the second section we will develop the same points but mainly along the line of our experience. Then in the remainder of the outline, we will see the consummation and the practical, simple, wonderful, marvelous, and accessible application.

CHRIST AS THE SERVANT OF JEHOVAH SERVING GOD BY BEING A COVENANT AND A LIGHT TO GOD'S CHOSEN PEOPLE THAT HE MAY BE THE FULL SALVATION OF GOD

Christ as the Servant of Jehovah serves God by being a covenant and a light to God's chosen people that He may be the full salvation of God (Isa. 42:5-7; 49:6, 8b-9a). We may summarize this as follows: God gives Christ as the covenant to us for justification, and God gives Christ as light to us for life. God wants to bring us all through faith into a situation whereby we know that He approves us according to the standard of His righteousness. We need to know that God has no problem with us, and we can peacefully be in His presence. He wants to bring us continually into a situation where we may receive the dispensing of the Triune God as life.

Through His Death and Resurrection, Christ Having Become the New Covenant as the New Testament according to God's Righteousness to Be the Base of God's Full Salvation

Through His death and resurrection, Christ has become the new covenant as the new testament according to God's righteousness to be the base of God's full salvation (Luke 22:20; Psa. 89:14). Here we have a partial answer to the question regarding the gospel being the power of God. God's righteousness is the base. According to Luke 22:20, this base is afforded to us through the covenant established in the Lord's blood, which is related both to the covenant and to righteousness.

Why does God forgive us of our sins when we confess? Why does the blood of Jesus cleanse us from every sin when we walk in the light? First John 1:9 says, "If we confess our sins, He is faithful and righteous to forgive us our sins and cleanse us from all unrighteousness." To be sure, God is loving, merciful, gracious, and kind, but 1 John 1:9 does not say that He forgives us because He is kind, loving, gracious, and merciful. This verse says that He forgives because He is righteous and faithful to His righteousness. Hence, forgiveness is a matter of the covenant and righteousness.

As the Servant of Jehovah, Christ Serving God by Being a Covenant

As the Servant of Jehovah, Christ serves God by being a covenant (Isa. 42:6; 49:8b). This is not a human thought but a divine thought. God gave Christ to be a covenant. Christ serves Jehovah by being a covenant, and the center of His service is to die. Mark 10:45 says, "The Son of Man did not come to be served, but to serve and to give His life as a ransom for many." He served God by giving His life as a ransom through His death on the cross for us. He served God by dying for our redemption. The ministers of the new covenant also serve God by dying, not for redemption but for the release of life. Serving God according to the covenant required the death of God's Son for our redemption and requires the ministers of the new covenant to participate in the life releasing aspect of His death so that life may flow into the churches. Without such a death there can be no service in the sight of God.

Christ Serving Us by Dying for Us; This Being to Serve by Being a Covenant

Christ served us by dying for us; this was to serve by being a covenant. On the night in which He was betrayed, He had the Passover with His disciples. Following that, He established the Lord's table, and in presenting the cup, He said, "This cup is the new covenant established in My blood, which is being poured out for you" (Luke 22:20). In effect He was saying, "This cup is the new covenant established in My blood. Soon I will die as My service and shed My blood righteously to establish this covenant." He drank the cup of suffering that the Father gave Him so that we may drink the cup of blessing, the cup of salvation. What a service!

Christ Serving God by Ministering Life to Us through His Death and Resurrection

Christ serves God by ministering life to us through His death and resurrection (Mark 10:45; John 12:24).

In the New Covenant It Seeming That We Have Received Many Things, but Actually Our Having Gained Only One Thing, That Is Christ

In the new covenant it seems that we have received many things, but actually we have gained only one thing, that is Christ (Heb. 8:10-13). If there were no Christ, there would be no forgiveness. If Christ had not died righteously for us, on what basis could God forgive us? We may respond by saying that God loves us or that He is kind. Surely He is a God of love and kindness, but if God would take any action without caring for His righteousness, Satan would accuse Him, saying, "How could You do that? Yes, You are loving, kind, and merciful, but what about Your righteousness? Does not Psalm 89:14 say that righteousness is the foundation of Your throne?" May our eyes be opened to see the basis on which God forgives sinners. In order for God to forgive any one of us, who do not deserve anything from Him, His righteousness must be satisfied according to the law decreed by Him. Thus, forgiveness is really Christ Himself, for it is based upon Christ as righteousness. The law of life is Christ as the Spirit within us. The new covenant is a person.

Christ Being the Reality of the New Covenant; Therefore, Christ Being the New Covenant, the New Testament

Christ is the reality of the new covenant; therefore, Christ *is* the new covenant, the new testament. The new covenant, established by Christ through His death, gives us Christ (Luke 22:20; Matt. 26:27-28). Eventually, we will reach the point in our experience where Christ is all we want. All we need is Christ, God wants to give us Christ, and we only want Christ. If you are new to the church life in the Lord's recovery, I want to tell you that we have only one thing to offer you—the wonderful all-inclusive Christ. We want to enjoy the Christ that you have, and we want to pursue Christ together with you.

Christ as the Covenant Taking Care of God's Righteousness; Hence, This Covenant Being the Foundation of God's Salvation

Christ as the covenant takes care of God's righteousness; hence, this covenant is the foundation of God's salvation. A simple human illustration may be apt. Every year all United States citizens must file an income tax return, which is a matter of conscience and of righteousness before the government ordained by God. This is not a matter of love. We do not file out of love, nor does the IRS evaluate our returns out of love. The tax we owe is the amount due to the government according to righteousness. If we file correctly and pay the required amount, we are right with the IRS. One year I received a letter from the IRS, pointing out that I had made a mistake on my tax return and indicating the additional amount due according to righteousness. I realized that they were correct, and therefore I promptly sent them a check for the additional amount. The check was then endorsed, cashed, and deposited by the government according to righteousness, and I was once again fully right with the IRS. This is an example of contractual, judicial relationship.

When the Spirit of reality comes to convict a person, every sinner will realize that he is not right with God and that if he were to meet Him, he would need to be right with Him. The prodigal son did not have such a realization when he was reduced to eating carob pods. He only realized his hunger, saying, "How many of my father's hired servants abound in bread, but I am perishing here in famine!" (Luke 15:17). He did not have the theological understanding that he had a judicial problem related to righteousness and that he must first return and be reconciled with his father. He was driven merely by hunger. But the father knew that before he could give his son the fattened calf, he had to cover him with his best robe. Surely the son was overjoyed that his father ran to meet him and embraced him, and surely he would not dispute the father's action in covering him first. Our Father runs to meet every repentant sinner even though he may not know why he is repenting. The first thing He does is to cover him with a robe, that is, with Christ as his righteousness. Thus, the first thing Christ is to us is righteousness. First Corinthians 1:30 says, "Of Him you are in Christ Jesus, who became wisdom to us from God: both righteousness and sanctification and redemption." God must first take care of His righteousness. In Luke 15 after the father had put the best robe on his son, he says, "Bring the fattened calf; slaughter it, and let us eat and be merry" (v. 23). Once God's righteousness has been taken care of, we can enjoy Christ as the fattened calf. This is to enjoy God's full salvation.

God Giving Christ as a Light to the Nations
That He Might Be God's Salvation to All the World

God gave Christ as a light to the nations that He might be God's salvation to all the world (Isa. 42:6; 49:6). This light issues in Christ as the divine life to us (John 9:5; 1:4, 9; 8:12). Christ as the light carries out God's salvation to consummate God's salvation in life (Rom. 5:10). The life of this light becomes God's salvation to us in His righteousness.

Righteousness is our foundation, whereas life is our consummation. God's salvation has a consummation in life. Romans 5:10 says, "If we, being enemies, were reconciled to God through the death of His Son, much more we will be saved in His life, having been reconciled." To be saved in Christ's life is to be sanctified, renewed, transformed, conformed, and glorified. We all want the growth in life and to have more experiences of life, but we may unintentionally not have a solid foundation for our entire life experience. We may take our progress or the process of organic salvation as our foundation, when the foundation of our Christian experience is not life but Christ as righteousness to us from God. Christ as light carries out God's salvation based on His righteousness.

Christ as the Covenant and Christ as the Light,
Added Together, Equaling God's Full Salvation

Christ as the covenant and Christ as the light, added together, equal God's full salvation (3:21; 5:10, 18). There is a divine logic here. God is a very deep Thinker and the most reasonable of beings. Everything He does is principled, well thought out, and is actually quite marvelous. Not only the reality but also the logic of God's salvation has two aspects. The first aspect is Christ as the covenant for justification. If God could not justify us, He would have no way to impart life to us. We are defiled and buried under heaps of sins. Suppose an unsaved man who is fifty years of age has sinned only once a day since the age of accountability. What would be the weight of the accumulation of sins recalled in his conscience? Surely for a person to only sin once a day is an unreasonably low estimate. Imagine how much all those sins would weigh on a fifty-year-old man! Certainly God could not put His life into such a filthy, sinful human being. God first must have a righteous basis, a righteous standing, to give life. Hence, God first takes care of

His righteousness by giving us Christ as a covenant, as the One who served God by dying for our sins. Because Christ paid the price for our sins and because God has accepted the death of Christ for our sins, God can righteously forgive us. This is His logic. Then He brings forth Christ in the aspect of light. Now based on righteousness, which issues in our justification, the light shines into our being. Second Corinthians 4:6 says, "The God who said, Out of darkness light shall shine, is the One who shined in our hearts." His light comes into the deepest, darkest abyss of our being, and we are born of God. Therefore, Romans 8:10 says that the spirit, the human spirit, is life because of righteousness.

Based on the Righteousness of God and in the Life of God, Our Enjoying God as Our Inheritance

Based on the righteousness of God and in the life of God, we enjoy God as our inheritance (Acts 26:18). In God's heart there is the desire for a mutual inheritance involving Himself and His children. God wants to have a people who inherit God Himself. *Hymns,* #608 says, "How rich the source, the Father as the fountain. / And all this wealth He wants man to enjoy!" God wants to have a people who even today are heirs of God with Christ, inheriting on the basis of the covenant all the wealth of God's eternal Being. God Himself also would like an inheritance. He wants something precious as a treasure to be His inheritance. Ephesians 1:13-14 reveals, on one hand, that we have the Spirit as a seal, as a guarantee, that God is our inheritance, but on the other hand, that in Christ and with Christ as our content, we become precious to God. God can inherit us because we are constituted with Christ; thus, we become God's inheritance. Then in and for eternity as the New Jerusalem, we will enjoy God as our inheritance and God will enjoy us as His inheritance.

Eventually, in the Song of Songs the Beloved, Christ Himself, sees in His seeker, as a garden, the reproduction of Himself (4:12). She has been constituted with Him. She invites Him, saying, "Awake, O north wind; / And come, O south wind! / Blow upon my garden: / Let its spices flow forth; / Let my beloved come into his garden / And eat his choicest fruit" (4:16). In other words, she says, "My Beloved, enjoy Yourself wrought into me." In the divine romance we inherit the infinitely rich Triune God, and the Triune God inherits those who are constituted with Christ to be most precious to Him. What a salvation it is that He can make sinners, lepers, rebels against God, and enemies of God not only righteous, forgiven, enlivened, children of God, and heirs of God but even God's very inheritance. The Father will enjoy such a mutual inheritance.

GOD'S FULL SALVATION BEING
BASED UPON HIS RIGHTEOUSNESS
AND BEING CONSUMMATED IN HIS LIFE

The Righteousness of God Being What God Is
with Respect to Justice and Righteousness

God's full salvation is based upon His righteousness and is consummated in His life (Rom. 10:3; 3:21-28; 5:18; 1:16-17). The righteousness of God is what God is with respect to justice and righteousness (10:3; 3:21-23). If we had not fallen, righteousness would not be an issue; we would never have had a problem with God's righteousness.

Because We Are Fallen,
God Needing to Deal with Us
according to His Righteousness

Because we are fallen, God must deal with us according to His righteousness. In Genesis 3:24 the way to the tree of life was closed by a cherubim and a flaming sword. The cherubim signifies God's glory, the flame signifies God's holiness, and the sword signifies God's righteousness. That the way to God as a tree of life was closed in such a way indicates that the demands of God's glory, holiness, and righteousness must first be fulfilled. Righteousness being signified by a killing sword indicates that if anyone were to come to God without Christ as his righteousness, God must righteously kill him. Such a person has no standing, no right, no ground, and no basis to receive anything but death. God must deal with us according to His righteousness, not mainly for our sake but for His sake. The Old Testament type of this is the blood of the sin offering being brought by the high priest into the Holy of Holies and sprinkled before God. The blood is not mainly for us; it is for God. When God sees the blood, He can pass over us, for He knows that His righteousness has been fulfilled. Then the blood is for the enemy. If the enemy accuses us, we can answer him, overcome him, conquer him, and defeat him by the blood of the Lamb. Finally, the blood is for us; it is for our conscience so that we can have fellowship with God. Praise the Lord!

As the Righteous God, His Not Being Able to Forgive Sinful People without Meeting the Demands of His Righteousness

As the righteous God, He cannot forgive sinful people without meeting the demands of His righteousness (1 John 1:9). God loves us, and He is full of mercy and grace. He wants to and intends to forgive us. But forgiveness is not based on God's love, God's mercy, or God's grace; it is based on God's righteousness. Only if there is a way for God's righteousness to be satisfied with respect to us can He righteously forgive us.

Let us consider why the gospel is the power of God unto salvation. In Romans 1:16 Paul says, "I am not ashamed of the gospel, for it is the power of God unto salvation to everyone who believes, both to Jew first and to Greek." Why is the gospel so powerful? The answer is in verse 17: "For the righteousness of God is revealed in it." Now we must consider how the righteousness of God is revealed in the gospel. As sinners we are among other things indebted to God. According to the righteous law of God, the wages, the penalty, of sin is death. Thus, a sinner must die. If the sinner does not die, righteousness is not fulfilled because God Himself in His law has established capital punishment for every sin. Since we have sinned and deserve death, only by our deaths is God's righteousness fulfilled. But if we all died, God would not have an inheritance or a family, and Christ would not have a church or a bride. God would be righteous, but His heart's desire would be lost.

Hence, there was a counsel among the three of the Godhead, and it was determined that the second of the Godhead, the Son, would die according to the eternal, determined counsel of God. For this reason, Revelation 13:8 speaks of "the Lamb who was slain from the foundation of the world." We were chosen *before* the foundation of the world, but the Lamb was slain *from* the foundation, the existence, of the created universe. Then God became man; that is, the Word became flesh to be the Lamb of God to take away the sin of the world as a totality (John 1:14, 29).

During the first three hours on the cross, Christ was persecuted and tormented by man for doing God's will. But in the second three hours there was darkness all over the land, and God made Christ sin for us as the fulfillment of the type of the bronze serpent and placed on Christ's body all the sins of man. First Peter 2:24 says that He "bore up our sins in His body on the tree." The number of sins committed by God's people is beyond calculation. When God looked at Christ in those three hours, He considered Him as sin in the flesh. According to Romans 8:3, God sent His Son "in the likeness of the flesh of sin and concerning sin, condemned sin in the flesh." On the cross the entire debt of sin was paid once and for all by the Son of God as the Lamb of God. When He was about to breathe His last breath, He said, "It is finished!" (John 19:30) and "Father, into Your hands I commit My spirit" (Luke 23:46). Then the atmosphere immediately changed, for Christ had died righteously. First Peter 3:18 says, "Christ also has suffered once for sins, the Righteous on behalf of the unrighteous."

By His death the debt was paid. How do we know that God has accepted Christ's payment? Romans 4:24 and 25 say, "For [our sakes] also to whom it is to be accounted, who believe on Him who has raised Jesus our Lord from the dead, who was delivered for our offenses and was raised for our justification." We were hopelessly in debt and under the sentence of death. When Christ died on the cross, He paid God our entire debt. We may say that He gave God a "check" for the full amount. Christ came and died in our place vicariously as our Representative. It is as if He said, "Father, they cannot pay, but You require the payment of death. I will die in their place. I will shed My blood for them." His blood is the blood of God as the blood of the God-man. It is human blood, which qualifies Him to die for human beings, yet it is also the blood of the Son of God with eternal, unlimited efficacy. Thus, God killed Him by the sword of His righteousness and smote Him by the scepter of His law, fulfilling all the requirements of His righteousness.

When did God endorse the "check" by which Christ paid our debt at the cross? When did the payment become irrevocable? Once one endorses a check and cashes it, it cannot be revoked. God "endorsed the check" by raising Christ from the dead. If Christ had not been resurrected, we would have no proof that God was really satisfied with His death on our behalf. But God raised Christ from among the dead and set Him at His right hand in the heavens as a declaration to the whole universe that He has accepted the death of His Son for our justification (Eph. 1:20). Praise the Lord! Today we can tell Satan, "Look who is at the right hand of God. Our Savior is there, our Redeemer!"

We were in debt, Christ paid the debt, and God accepted that payment by endorsing and depositing the check. Now our debt has been paid in full. Since God is righteous, when we fail and sin, He cannot come to us to require a payment. If He did that, He would not be righteous. It would be good to spend some time with the Lord and sing *Hymns*, #1003: "For me forgiveness He has gained, / And full acquittal was obtained, / All debts of sin are paid; / God would not have His claim on two, / First on His Son, my Surety true, / And then upon me laid."

What then should we do when we sin? Some of us have had to learn this experientially through huge, shocking, heart-breaking failures. After such a failure we may wonder, "What do I do now? How do I go on? If anyone knew about this, they would be shocked. How can I approach God? I do not know how He feels about me. He may not love me. He may be angry with me. What should I do?" Should we suffer and waste days and weeks of our life? Should we beat and accuse ourselves to impress God? On the contrary, we should simply invoke the covenant, which includes forgiveness as a bequest. Although we may feel terrible and condemned, although Satan may be accusing us, and although we do not know whether we are loved by God, 1 John 1:9 clearly states, "If we confess our sins, He is faithful and righteous to forgive us our sins and cleanse us from all unrighteousness." This is our solid foundation. If our eyes are enlightened and if our faith has been increased a little bit, we can tell God, "I do not know how You feel about me, but You must forgive me of this sin. You have no right and no standing to not forgive me. You are bound by the covenant to forgive me. Christ paid for this. I do not have to pay, and I cannot pay. Moreover, You did not ask me to pay but only to confess." In Greek *to confess* means "to speak the same thing." When we sin, God comes and enlightens us. By confessing, we are simply speaking what God is saying. If He says, "You were wrong in this matter," our response should be, "Lord, I agree with You. I was wrong in that matter." Our God is righteous. Christ already died for this particular sin. The only thing that God asks us to do is first to confess and then to simply believe that God is righteous and that He is bound by His righteousness to forgive us. I was thrilled and released when I first heard a word like this from Brother Lee in 1969. Later I would have the privilege of polishing that very message in the *Life-study of Romans* (msg. 2). At the time, I had the light and the revelation but little experience until, under the discipline of the Spirit, I suffered a particular kind of failure. There was no way to excuse it or justify it, yet the Spirit was there to begin to work out the word. I told the Lord, "I am sorry I did this, but one thing I know: You must forgive me, or You are not righteous. The real issue is not my forgiveness, but whether You want Your throne to be shaken. You have to uphold Your government by being righteous."

In 1 John 2:1 John says, "My little children, these things I write to you that you may not sin. And if anyone sins, we have an Advocate with the Father, Jesus Christ the Righteous." Whenever we commit a sin, it is fully under observation. The heavens know all things, yet Jesus Christ the Righteous, as our defense Attorney, immediately begins to plead on our behalf, saying, "Father, this is a matter of righteousness. I died for this one. I am his Advocate. He can hardly lift his head; he feels so ashamed. He can hardly pray, but I can lift up My head. This is a family matter. I am Your righteous Son. I took care of this already, and now I am the Advocate based on righteousness." Christ is not only our Advocate but also our High Priest and our Intercessor who is praying for us. As a result of His intercession, we get a feeling just to turn back to God and simply confess, believing in the blood of Jesus, His Son, that cleanses us from every sin.

Charles Wesley must have received such a revelation in order to write *Hymns*, #296:

> No condemnation now I dread;
> Jesus, and all in Him, is mine!
> Alive in Him, my living Head,
> And clothed in righteousness Divine,
> Bold I approach the eternal throne,
> And claim the crown, through Christ my own.
> Bold I approach the eternal throne,
> And claim the crown, through Christ my own.

God approves us according to His own standard of righteousness. Even right now God does not see us in ourselves; He has put us in Christ, and Christ is our garment of righteousness. Christ is righteousness to us from God, and we are in an organic union with Him. Thus, when God looks at us in Christ, He sees no unrighteousness. He can say, "I approve you. I justify you according to My standard of righteousness. I evaluate you and approve you according to the righteousness that I am. I have no problem. Let us eat, drink, and be merry. Let us rejoice. Now I can open My being to you and flood you with life. Just exercise a little faith in the kind of God that I am and in the Christ that I have provided for you. Based upon righteousness, your spirit is life. Now I do not have to hold Myself back, nor do you have to close yourself off. Let us open to one another. Let Me flood you with *zoe*. Let Me dispense My life into you. Let Me usher you into the reality of being saved much more in My life." Praise the Lord!

Justification Being God's Action in Approving Us according to His Standard of Righteousness

Justification is God's action in approving us according to His standard of righteousness (Gal. 2:16; Rom. 3:28). No human being can be approved by God out of the works of the law. We all need to stop trying, for we could never match the standard of God's righteousness by our own effort. Righteousness is Christ, and God first gives Christ to us to be our righteousness as the foundation of His full salvation.

Like the prodigal son, we may have come to the Father because we were starving and empty, but the righteous Father knows that before He can give us the fattened calf, He must give us the covering robe. We need to simply take Christ and let Him envelope us. We should not be too quick to proceed to the subjective things such as our constitution, our inner being. We must take things one step at a time. We will eventually be made the very righteousness of God in Christ through our experience of God's organic salvation, but first, we need to have the basis for such an experience, which is Christ as our robe of righteousness.

The Proof of God's Justification Being the Resurrection of Christ

The proof of God's justification is the resurrection of Christ (4:22-25). The redeeming death of Christ as the ground for God to justify us has been fully accepted by God, and Christ has been resurrected as a proof of this. The resurrected Christ who sits at God's right hand is the evidence that God is satisfied with His death on our behalf and that we have been justified (1 John 2:1). Now that Christ has died and has been raised from among the dead, it is impossible for God to change His mind about forgiving us; He is bound by His righteousness to forgive us (1:9).

God is not capricious or double-minded. In a sense, before Christ died on the cross, the Triune God could have called the whole thing off. When He was arrested, the Lord said, "Do you think that I cannot beseech My Father, and He will provide Me at once with more than twelve legions of angels? How then shall the Scriptures be fulfilled which say that it must happen this way?" (Matt. 26:53-54). When He was on the cross, the people mocked Him, saying, "Save Yourself and come down from the cross!" (Mark 15:30), but He made a fundamental choice, deciding not to save Himself but to save us. Hence, He did not come down, even though He had the power to do so. He did not pray for angelic intervention, even though He had the ground to pray. He chose to die there as the sin offering and as the trespass offering under the righteous judgment of God. Then God resurrected Him, and now it is impossible for God to change His mind. Therefore, we can pray, "My Father God, You are bound by Your righteousness to forgive me of everything. You are the God of the covenant—Your beloved Son." God is bound by His righteousness to forgive us.

God Having Given Christ to Us
as the Righteousness of God

God has given Christ to us as the righteousness of God (1 Cor. 1:30).

Our Experience of Christ Resting
upon the Foundation of God's Righteousness

Our experience of Christ rests upon the foundation of God's righteousness (Psa. 89:14). Now we can answer the question: "What is the foundation of our experience of Christ?" Every day I begin with this as a foundation: "Lord, cleanse me with Your precious blood. Apply the blood on my behalf according to Your evaluation of it, according to Your understanding of its power, worth, value, and effectiveness. I do not know what the blood is worth, but You, Father, know the value of the blood of Jesus, Your Son. I confess that I need a thorough cleansing. If there is anything that I need to confess, I am open to confess under Your light, but I will not waste my time condemning myself and wallowing in guilt. I believe in the God of righteousness. I believe in the Christ who is the covenant. I believe in the blood of Jesus the Son of God." Romans 3:25 speaks of "faith in His blood." I am able to speak this message because I have faith in the blood of Jesus. No matter what happened today or at any time in our life, God is righteous, and His forgiveness is ours as our right of inheritance. Hallelujah!

Whereas God's Righteousness Justifying Us through the Death of Christ, God's Life Germinating Us by Christ as the Life-giving Spirit

The Condemnation of God Being Dissolved by Christ as the Covenant, and the Death That Comes from Satan Being Annulled by Christ as the Light That Issues in Life

Whereas God's righteousness justifies us through the death of Christ, God's life germinates us by Christ as the life-giving Spirit (Rom. 10:3; Gal. 2:16, 21; Rom. 5:18; Eph. 2:5; 1 Cor. 15:45b). The condemnation of God is dissolved by Christ as the covenant, and the death that comes from Satan is annulled by Christ as the light that issues in life (John 8:12). What good news! We can declare that our condemnation has been dissolved by righteousness, by Christ as the covenant, and that the power of death in our being has been annulled by Christ as the divine life.

Christ Becoming the Life-giving Spirit in Resurrection to Dispense the Life Which Was in God into Us to Enliven Us, to Regenerate Us, to Make Us Children of God

Christ became the life-giving Spirit in resurrection to dispense the life which was in God into us to enliven us, to regenerate us, to make us children of God (3:3-6; 1 John 3:1; John 1:12-13; Rom. 8:15). This full salvation consummates in the New Jerusalem.

THE NEW JERUSALEM BEING THE EMBODIMENT OF GOD'S FULL SALVATION, AND GOD'S FULL SALVATION BEING A COMPOSITION OF GOD'S RIGHTEOUSNESS AS THE BASE AND GOD'S LIFE AS THE CONSUMMATION

The Foundation of the New Jerusalem Being the Righteousness of God with God's Faithfulness

The New Jerusalem is the embodiment of God's full salvation, and God's full salvation is a composition of God's righteousness as the base and God's life as the consummation (Rev. 21:2, 10, 19-20, 23; 22:1-2). The foundation of the New Jerusalem is the righteousness of God with God's faithfulness (21:19-20). We can say this based upon verses 19 and 20: "The foundations of the wall of the city were adorned with every precious stone: the first foundation was jasper; the second, sapphire; the third, chalcedony; the fourth, emerald; the fifth, sardonyx; the sixth, sardius; the seventh, chrysolite; the eighth, beryl; the ninth, topaz; the tenth, chrysoprase; the eleventh, jacinth; the twelfth, amethyst." The layered foundations of the wall are in the appearance of a rainbow. According to Genesis 9:13-17, the rainbow is a sign of God's faithfulness, yet God's faithfulness itself must have a basis. God's faithfulness is founded on His righteousness. Only a righteous person can be faithful. One who is unrighteous can easily be unfaithful. Therefore, in order for God to be faithful as testified by the rainbow foundations, He must be righteous. The stones that form the foundations of the wall are laid upon the foundation of God's righteousness.

The Content of the New Jerusalem Being Life, Which Issues from Light

The content of the New Jerusalem is life, which issues from light (Rev. 21:23). Revelation 22:1-2 indicates that the river of water of life bearing the tree of life is spiraling down in the middle of the golden street to reach every part of the city, making it a city of water, a city of righteousness, and a city of *zoe,* a city of life. The source of the life is the light; hence, 21:23 says, "The city has no need of the sun or of the moon that they should shine in it, for the glory of God illumined it, and its lamp is the Lamb." Therefore, in the New Jerusalem we see the fulfillment of the covenant and the light.

The Entire New Jerusalem Being a Matter of Life Built on the Foundation of Righteousness

The entire New Jerusalem is a matter of life built on the foundation of righteousness (22:1-2). May we all let righteousness be the foundation of our daily Christian life, no matter what happens. Nothing can shake such a foundation. We should not try to build our growth in life upon our feelings, upon self-improvement, upon our experience, or even upon life itself. Only God's righteousness can be our foundation. Nevertheless, we are not remaining passively on the foundation of God's righteousness, but based upon this foundation, we need to build a structure of life, an organic building.

Life Being the Consummation of Righteousness, and Righteousness Being the Base, the Foundation, of Life

Life is the consummation of righteousness, and righteousness is the base, the foundation, of life.

THE WAY TO RECEIVE AND ENJOY THE FULL SALVATION OF GOD BEING TO EXERCISE OUR SPIRIT, LIVE ACCORDING TO OUR SPIRIT, AND REMAIN IN OUR SPIRIT, WITH WHICH IS CHRIST, BY CALLING ON THE LORD'S NAME

The way to receive and enjoy the full salvation of God is to exercise our spirit, live according to our spirit, and remain in our spirit, with which is Christ, by calling on the Lord's name (Rom. 8:4; 10:12-13; 2 Tim. 4:22).

GOD'S FULL SALVATION BEING FULL OF SPRINGS, AND OUR NEEDING TO LEARN TO DRAW WATER OUT OF THESE SPRINGS BY CALLING ON THE LORD'S NAME

God's full salvation is full of springs, and we need to learn to draw water out of these springs by calling on the Lord's name (Isa. 12:2-6). Verses 2 through 6 say,

> God is now my salvation; / I will trust and not dread; / For Jah Jehovah is my strength and song, / And He has become my salvation. / Therefore you will draw water with rejoicing / From the springs of salvation, / And you will say in that day, / Give thanks to Jehovah; call upon His name! / Make His deeds known among the peoples; / Remind them that His name is exalted. / Sing psalms to Jehovah, for He has done something majestic! / Let it be made known in all the earth! / Cry out and give a ringing shout, O inhabitant of Zion, / For great in your midst is the Holy One of Israel.

We can draw water with rejoicing from the springs of salvation by calling on the Lord's name! We need to see this governing vision of Christ as the covenant, issuing in righteousness and of Christ as the light, issuing in life. The covenant, the righteousness, the light, and the life are all the very Christ who is in our spirit. We simply need to come back to Him by turning to Him. He becomes our springs of salvation whenever we call on His name.—R. K.

THE DIVINE ECONOMY IN THE BOOK OF ISAIAH

Enjoying Christ as the New Covenant
for His Expansion within Us
(Message 24)

Scripture Reading: Isa. 49:1-9; 42:1-7; 50:4

I. Isaiah as the servant of Jehovah typifies Christ as a covenant of the people to restore the land—Isa. 49:1-9; 42:1-7:

A. The good land of Canaan with all of its riches typifies the all-inclusive, unsearchably rich Christ, who has been bequeathed to us as the reality of the new covenant—vv. 5-7; 49:8-9; Col. 1:12; 2:6.

B. In the believers' experience, to restore the land is to have Christ as the land enlarged or expanded; the more we experience Christ as the new covenant and occupy Him as the land, the more we sense that He is expanding within us and the more God's kingdom is established with God's temple as His testimony—v. 19; Phil. 3:8-10; Mark 4:26-27; Eph. 2:21-22.

II. In order for Christ to expand within us, we need to enjoy Him as the bequests of the new covenant in its four major aspects:

A. "I will be propitious to their unrighteousnesses, and their sins I shall by no means remember anymore"—Heb. 8:12:

1. The precious and all-efficacious blood of Christ resolves all of our problems so that we can remain constantly in fellowship with God to continually enjoy His organic salvation—1 John 1:7-9; 2:1-2; Heb. 9:12, 14; Psa. 51:2.

2. Once God forgives us, He erases our sins from His memory and remembers them no longer:

a. No sin that has been repented of, that has been confessed and put under the blood of the Lord Jesus, can ever raise its head at the judgment seat—1 John 1:7, 9; *Hymns*, #295, #1003, #1008.

b. When God forgives us of our sins, He causes the sins that we have committed to depart from us—Psa.

103:12; Lev. 16:7-10, 15-22; John 3:18; 5:24; cf. Psa. 130:4; Luke 7:47.

B. "I will impart My laws into their mind, and on their hearts I will inscribe them"—Heb. 8:10:

1. The law of life, the law of the Spirit of life, is the processed Triune God as the spontaneous power and automatic function of life—Rom. 8:2; Phil. 2:13.

2. The function of the law of life is to free us from the law of sin and of death (Rom. 8:2), to dispense the processed Triune God into us to make us men of life in our entire tripartite being (vv. 10, 6, 11), to shape us into the image of the firstborn Son of God so that we may become His corporate expression (vv. 28-29), and to constitute us the members of the Body of Christ with all kinds of functions (Eph. 4:11-12, 16).

C. "I will be God to them, and they will be a people to Me"—Heb. 8:10:

1. For God to be our God means that He is our inheritance, and for us to be God's people means that we are His inheritance—Eph. 1:11, 14, 18; 3:21:

   a. God created man as a vessel to contain Him (Gen. 1:26; Rom. 9:21, 23-24); therefore, God is man's possession, just as the content of a vessel is its possession.

   b. It is by having God wrought into us that we are being constituted into God's inheritance—Eph. 1:13; 3:16-21.

2. God is ours and we are His by the divine life's enabling us to participate in the enjoyment of God in fellowship with Him—1 Cor. 1:9.

D. "They shall by no means each teach his fellow citizen and each his brother, saying, Know the Lord; for all will know Me from the little one to the great one among them"—Heb. 8:11:

1. In the new covenant we have the privilege of knowing God experientially, inwardly, and personally with His intimate counsel and sweet, satisfying companionship—Psa. 25:14; Exo. 33:11; Phil. 3:10a; 1:19-21a; 2 Cor. 2:10.

2. We can know God subjectively from within by the sense of life, which is the feeling, the consciousness, of the divine life within us—Rom. 8:6.

III. In order for Christ to expand within us, we need to enjoy Him as the Servant of Jehovah in the following aspects:

A. As the Servant of Jehovah, Christ was never discouraged— Isa. 42:1-4; cf. 53:2.

B. As the Servant of Jehovah, Christ was constituted with the Spirit of Jehovah—48:16; 11:2; cf. Matt. 12:18; Luke 4:14-22.

C. As the Servant of Jehovah, Christ was the Prophet of Jehovah to be His mouthpiece to speak forth His word—Isa. 49:1-4; Acts 3:22-23; John 3:34; 14:10; cf. 1 Cor. 14:31-32:

1. As typified by Isaiah, Christ's mouth was like a sharp sword, and He was a polished arrow hidden in Jehovah's quiver—Isa. 49:2; Rev. 12:10-11; 6:2; cf. 2 Cor. 2:17; 13:3.

2. As the Servant of Jehovah, Christ did not speak His own word, but spoke according to God's instructions—Isa. 50:4; John 14:24; Matt. 12:42; Eph. 6:17-20:

a. We should be one with Christ to speak as learners, as trainees, as instructed and taught ones—1 Cor. 2:13; Prov. 25:15, 20.

b. We need to be awakened by the Lord morning by morning, having our ears opened to hear the voice of our Master—Mark 1:35; Exo. 21:1-6.

D. As the Servant of Jehovah, Christ did not cry out, lift up His voice, or make His voice heard in the street—Isa. 42:2; Matt. 12:19; 2 Tim. 2:24; Prov. 27:14.

E. As the Servant of Jehovah, Christ will not break the bruised ones or quench the smoking ones—Matt. 12:20; Isa. 42:3; cf. 61:1-2; Eph. 4:11-12.

F. We can be one with Christ as the Servant of Jehovah to make God happy in the releasing and raising up of His elect to build up the church as the house of God and the kingdom of God—Matt. 16:18-19; Eph. 4:11-12, 15-16; Rom. 14:17.

ENJOYING CHRIST AS THE NEW COVENANT
FOR HIS EXPANSION WITHIN US

Prayer: O Lord, we open our whole being to You. We pray that You will grow in us. We pray for one another, and we pray for all the saints in Your recovery—intensify Your growth within us in these days. We give You our time together. Praise You for Your prevailing and cleansing blood. Thank You that Your blood washes away our sin. Praise You that by Your pure blood we have the right to enjoy You as the tree of life. May all of us enjoy You to the uttermost. Lord, unveil us to see more of You, and bring us into more precious experiences of You. Use this message to build up Your Body and to build up Your kingdom. We are here to hasten Your coming.

In this message we will speak more concerning enjoying Christ as the new covenant. In the previous message we presented the great revelation that Christ Himself is the new covenant, the new testament. He did not merely give us the new testament; He has given us Himself as the new testament. Through His death Christ has enacted the new covenant, making it a testament. Hebrews 9:16-17 says, "Where there is a testament, the death of him who made the testament must of necessity be established. For a testament is confirmed in the case of the dead, since it never has force when he who made the testament is living." These verses clearly say that for a testament to have force, the death of the testator is required. Christ made a covenant with His people, and when He died on the cross, that covenant became a testament. What Christ bequeathed to us was Himself with all His unsearchable riches. His death enacted the new testament. Then in His resurrection He became the new testament.

Humanly speaking, when a person bequeaths something, that person is gone after he dies. Therefore, what he has bequeathed is something apart from himself. However, Christ died and resurrected. In resurrection He became the life-giving Spirit, and now He is giving Himself to us with His unsearchable riches as all the bequests of the new covenant in our whole being. Thus, in His resurrection He became the new covenant. Furthermore, in His ascension He is carrying out the new covenant. He is making sure that we enjoy Him as the reality of all the bequests conveyed in the new covenant. Not only is He the reality of the new covenant, He is also the Executor of the new covenant. He is now in our spirit making sure that all the reality of what He is as the new covenant with all of His riches is being dispensed into our being.

He is not only the Executor of the new covenant in our spirit; He is the surety of the new covenant (7:22). He is the living guarantee in our spirit of what we will inherit. Not only do we enjoy Him today as the foretaste of our inheritance in our spirit; He is the guarantee that we will enjoy Him as the full taste in the coming age. He is therefore God's living guarantee, or warranty, in our spirit. This warranty will never expire. He is also our great High Priest (4:14) who is praying for us this very moment. Day and night Christ is continually interceding for each one of us (7:25). He can intercede for every one of us at the same time because He is God. He is not only praying for each one of us individually and personally; He is also praying for all of us corporately as His people, that we would be built up to be His church, that we would be prepared as His bride, that we would become the reality of His kingdom, and that consequently we would become the New Jerusalem in a marriage union with Him forever and ever. He is not only praying for us, but according to Hebrews 8:2, He is the Minister of the holy places. His job is to minister the processed God into our being day and night. He is continually ministering God into us. If we open our whole being to Him, He will minister Himself into us in a fresh way.

In this message we want to see more of Christ as the new covenant. The title of this message is "Enjoying Christ as the New Covenant for His Expansion within Us." My hope and prayer is that the Lord would shine on the truth contained in the words of this message and convey a vision into our being. I hope that these matters would become a heavenly vision to us and that we would see Christ in all these points.

ISAIAH AS THE SERVANT OF JEHOVAH TYPIFYING CHRIST AS A COVENANT OF THE PEOPLE TO RESTORE THE LAND

Isaiah as the servant of Jehovah typifies Christ as a covenant of the people to restore the land (Isa. 49:1-9; 42:1-7). Isaiah was a servant of Jehovah, and as such, he is a type of Christ. Christ is the Servant of Jehovah. Therefore, Isaiah typifies Him. As the reality and fulfillment of the type, Christ is a covenant of the people to restore the land (49:8). Today we are in the new testament reality; we are enjoying Christ as our reality. Therefore, we need to see what it means to enjoy Him as the new covenant to restore the land.

The Good Land of Canaan with All of Its Riches Typifying the All-inclusive, Unsearchably Rich Christ, Who Has Been Bequeathed to Us as the Reality of the New Covenant

The good land of Canaan with all of its riches typifies the all-inclusive, unsearchably rich Christ, who has been bequeathed to us as the reality of the new covenant (42:5-7; 49:8-9; Col. 1:12; 2:6). In order to understand what we mean by the phrase *to restore the land,* we first need to see what the good land is. The good land of Canaan was God's goal for the children of Israel. He redeemed them, He became their Passover, and He brought them out of Pharaoh's usurpation and slavery. When the children of Israel were about to leave Egypt, they were instructed to kill a lamb and put the blood on the doorposts. They were also told to eat the lamb inside the house. Eating the passover lamb energized them to get out of Egypt.

The children of Israel then passed through the Red Sea, which was a type of baptism (1 Cor. 10:2). When we believed in Christ, the blood cleansed us from every sin (1 John 1:9), and then the living Lamb, Christ Jesus, entered into our spirit in order to energize us to pass through the waters of baptism to escape the world's satanic tyranny. We are now no longer under Satan's usurpation and tyranny.

Next in our Christian experience, the Lord brings us into the wilderness where there is manna. It seems that there should be nothing in the desolate wilderness. Some of us visited Israel, and after passing through the wilderness, we realized why the Bible calls it "a howling desert waste" (Deut. 32:10). There is nothing in that wilderness. Yet God purposely took them to that place, apart from everything, so that He could reconstitute them with Christ. The only thing they had to eat for forty years was manna. That was all they ate. Although the children of Israel had moved out of Egypt, they were still Egyptian in their constitution. We know this because they still longed for the food of Egypt. They were saying, "We're tired of this manna. We're tired of the same thing day after day." They fondly longed for the food of Egypt, saying, "We remember the fish which we used to eat in Egypt for nothing, the cucumbers and the melons and the leeks and the onions and the garlic" (Num. 11:5). A man will long for that with which he is constituted. The children of Israel were constituted with Egypt, so they desired the food of Egypt, which signifies the enjoyment of the entertainment and pleasures of this world. God has brought us out of Egypt, out of the world, in order to constitute us with Christ as the heavenly manna.

The children of Israel also drank the living water out of the smitten and cleft rock. According to 1 Corinthians 10:4, the rock was Christ. Christ was smitten on the cross, and He gushed out living water for us to drink. In type, the children of Israel ate Christ and drank Christ. However, the wilderness was not God's ultimate goal. His goal was to bring them across the Jordan to enter into the good land where the temple would be built. God's goal was that they would enter into the good land and enjoy all the riches of the good land. By enjoying and being constituted with those riches, they could then offer something to God, the temple could be built up for God's glory, satisfaction, and expression, and the city of Jerusalem could be built up for God's kingdom. This is God's goal. His goal is to have a built-up kingdom and a built-up temple, which are types of the church as the Body of Christ for His expression and authority in this universe. God's goal is the good land, for the good land of Canaan with all its riches typifies the all-inclusive, unsearchably rich Christ.

Colossians 1:12 reveals to us that Christ is the reality of the type of the good land. Paul says, "Giving thanks to the Father, who has qualified you for a share of the allotted portion of the saints in the light." When we pray, we need to thank the Father for qualifying us through Christ's redemption. Through redemption we have been cleansed by the blood of Christ, and He has become our righteousness. All the debt of sin has been paid on the cross. We are now qualified for a share of the allotted portion of the saints in the light. God allotted a portion of the good land to every Israelite. When they entered into the good land, an allotted portion of the land was given to each of them. Now in the New Testament age, we received Christ as our life and our Savior when we opened to Him. He has been allotted to each one of us, and now we can enjoy Christ as the portion of the saints. He is our good land on whom we can labor. We can enjoy all the produce of Christ in our spirit as the good land. Colossians 2:6 says, "As therefore you have received the Christ, Jesus the Lord, walk in Him." In the same way that the children of Israel walked in the good land to possess it, we also need to walk in Christ every day. Whatever territory we tread upon, we will possess (Deut. 11:24). We want to possess and gain more of Christ for God's kingdom.

To walk in Christ is to walk according to the Spirit (Rom. 8:4; Gal. 5:16, 25), for the Spirit is the reality of Christ. The all-inclusive Christ as the Spirit is the reality of the good land for us to enjoy in the New Testament age (3:14). We need to walk in the Spirit who is the pneumatic Christ, the reality of Christ. Therefore, we need to walk according to our mingled spirit, which is one spirit with the Lord (1 Cor. 6:17). This is the central point of the entire New Testament. We need to enjoy Christ who is the all-inclusive Spirit as the all-inclusive land so that He can expand and grow in us. The growth of Christ in us is the building up of the church as the house of God and as the kingdom of God (Eph. 2:21; Col. 2:19).

In the Believers' Experience, to Restore the Land Being to Have Christ as the Land Enlarged or Expanded; the More We Experience Christ as the New Covenant and Occupy Him as the Land, the More Our Sensing That He Is Expanding within Us and the More God's Kingdom Being Established with God's Temple as His Testimony

In the believers' experience, to restore the land is to have Christ as the land enlarged or expanded; the more we experience Christ as the new covenant and occupy Him as the land, the more we sense that He is expanding within us and the more God's kingdom is established with God's temple as His testimony (v. 19; Phil. 3:8-10; Mark 4:26-27; Eph. 2:21-22). This is the meaning of Christ being given as a covenant of the people to restore the land. We need to experience Christ as the new covenant. We are occupying more of Him as the land within us. He is the good land, and He is unsearchably rich. He is unsearchably expansive. Not one of us can say that we have possessed all of Christ. Not one of us can be confident that we have possessed the entire territory of Christ. Therefore, we should never be satisfied. We need to enjoy Him more fully as the bequests of the new covenant to restore the land. To restore the land is to gain more of Christ as the land. To restore the land is to possess more of Christ as the land. To restore the land is to have Christ as an expanded and expanding land within us. As He expands and grows within us, God's kingdom is being established with God's temple as His testimony.

Hymns, #395 says, "O Jesus Christ, grow Thou in me." This needs to be our daily aspiration, longing, and desperate prayer. It would be a great tragedy if at any point in our Christian life or church life, we would stop growing in life. It is possible for the growth to stop if we become contented, self-satisfied, distracted, or proud. We need to beware of thinking like those in Laodicea. The general condition among the church in Laodicea was that they considered themselves to be rich, needing nothing. This is a terrible attitude to have. Their attitude was, "We have become wealthy. We know so much. We have the biblical and doctrinal knowledge. We don't need anything. No one can tell us anything because we already know everything." Theirs was a most pitiful state. In Revelation 3:17-18 the Lord says to them, "Because you say, I am wealthy and have become rich and have need of nothing, and do not know that you are wretched and miserable and poor and blind and naked, I counsel you to buy from Me gold refined by fire that you may be rich, and white garments that you may be clothed and that the shame of your nakedness may not be manifested, and eyesalve to anoint your eyes that you may see." The Lord was saying, "You don't realize it, but you are blind, miserable, wretched, and naked. Therefore, I counsel you to buy from Me. I counsel you to pay the price in your experience to buy gold, white garments, and eyesalve." We need to be desperate to gain Christ as the all-inclusive land. We should never be contented.

In Colossians 2:19 Paul speaks of our "holding the Head, out from whom all the Body, being richly supplied and knit together by means of the joints and sinews, grows with the growth of God." To hold Christ as the Head is to regard Him as the Head of the Body, honoring Him and allowing Him to be the Head of the Body. May we have this prayer in us, "Lord, I want You to be my Head. I would consult You in everything. I want to honor You. I want to exalt You. I want You to be the preeminent One in my being." The rich supply by means of the joints and sinews in the Body implies that we need to give the Lord a free way to dispense Himself into us. Verse 19 says that "the Body...grows with the growth of God." This does not mean that God in Himself grows. God does not grow in Himself, but He grows in us. We need for Him to grow in us every day. We should pray, "Lord, grow in me. I want this day's growth in life. Grow in me today." We grow with the growth of God in Christ as life to us.

Philippians 3:8-10 says, "Moreover I also count all things to be loss on account of the excellency of the knowledge of Christ Jesus my Lord, on account of whom I have suffered the loss of all things and count them as refuse that I may gain Christ and be found in Him, not having my own righteousness which is out of the law, but that which is through faith in Christ, the righteousness which is out of God and based on faith, to know Him and the power of His resurrection and the fellowship of His sufferings, being conformed to His death." Paul wanted Christ to expand within him. He was not satisfied, so he said that he counted all things as refuse so that he could gain Christ, be found in Christ, and know Christ. The book of Philippians was written approximately twenty-six years after Paul's conversion. Many believers who have been saved for such a long time do not have the kind of desperate seeking that Paul had. They may say, "I am saved. I am now waiting to go to a happy place. I will try to live a good Christian life." Paul was not like this. He was saying, "Yes, I was converted many years ago, but I would like to tell you that everything is trash to me so that I may gain Christ. I want to win Christ today. Christ is my prize. I want to know Him. I don't fully know Him yet. I want to lay hold of Him. I want to gain Christ. Not only so, I do only one thing; every day of my life on this earth 'I do not account of myself to have laid hold; but one thing I do: Forgetting the things which are behind and stretching forward to the things which are before, I pursue toward the goal for the prize'" (vv. 13-14). I hope the Lord will react within all of us. We need to forget the things that are behind. Forget them! They are over. We do not have yesterday, and we do not have tomorrow. All we have is right now. We can enjoy the Christ now. We can be those who forget the things that are behind and stretch forward to the vast territory of Christ as the land that is before us. We pursue toward Him as our goal and our prize in the millennial kingdom. This should be our sole pursuit.

Christ as the reality of the kingdom was sown into us as a seed to make us the kingdom. He is the King, and we are the "dom." The more the King grows within us, the more we become the reality of the kingdom. He was sown into us as a seed, and we need to give Him the way to grow in us. His growth in us is our growing into a holy temple in the Lord (Eph. 2:21-22).

IN ORDER FOR CHRIST TO EXPAND WITHIN US, OUR NEEDING TO ENJOY HIM AS THE BEQUESTS OF THE NEW COVENANT IN ITS FOUR MAJOR ASPECTS

In order for Christ to expand within us, we need to enjoy Him as the bequests of the new covenant in its four major aspects. Christ has bequeathed Himself to us. We are in the Triune God's will, and He has given Christ to us in His will. This is a legal document enacted by the death of Christ by the shedding of His blood. All the things in this document are now ours. Even if we say, "I don't want them," they are still ours.

We need to know what is in the will. That is the reason we read the Bible. We have to read our will. If a person wants to know how much he is worth, he has to read the will. Humanly speaking, if I have many millions that have been willed to me, how am I going to know what is mine? I may think that I am poor. I may not realize that I am a million-aire; so I have to read the will. I need to read what has been bequeathed to me. I am speaking in a human sense. This is the reason we must read the Bible and say Amen to what is in the Bible. *Amen* means "let it be so." There are many bequests in the Bible. The way they become a real-ity is by means of all prayer. We need to take this word by means of all prayer (Eph. 6:17-18). We need to pray-read the bequests, and then the bequests are converted from the letter of the Word into the spirit of the word, and they become our reality.

"I Will Be Propitious to Their Unrighteousnesses, and Their Sins I Shall by No Means Remember Anymore"

Hebrews 8:12 says, "I will be propitious to their unrighteousnesses, and their sins I shall by no means remember anymore." This is one of the four bequests in verses 10 through 12. The word *propitiate* indicates that there are two parties and that one party owes something to the other. To reconcile these two parties, the demands of the one party must be met, or appeased. Let us say that one party owes the other party many millions of dollars without any hope of repaying the debt. How can they be reconciled? God is the party to whom the debt is owed, and we are the other party. We owe God what we cannot pay. However, God is righteous; He cannot simply forgive us because His righteousness demands justice. He wants to forgive us, but He has to be righteous in the way that He forgives us.

We may illustrate in this way. One person owes billions of dollars to a second person. Can they be reconciled? Can the second party be appeased? The party to whom the debt is owed is absolutely righteous. For him to righteously forgive this debt, the billions of dollars must be fully paid. We have sinned against God, and God is righteous. According to Romans 6:23, "The wages of sin is death." Therefore, according to God's righteousness, we are condemned to die. The wages of sin is death, and thus, our death is the payment that we owe. How can this debt be paid? In our case, this debt was paid with the death of another. The wages of sin is death, but another has received these wages on our behalf.

God loves us, and He wants to dispense Himself into us to make us His bride. He wants to regenerate us, grow in us, sanctify us, transform us, and glorify us. So what did God do? He became a man, He passed through human living, and He went to the cross to die in our place, receiving the wages for our sin. On the cross, all the sins of the entire world were laid on Him. All our iniquity was laid upon Him. Through His death on the cross, He fulfilled all the demands of God's righteousness, and He took away the sin of the world. The debt of sin has been fully paid! Now God has been appeased because the debt has been fully paid. Now He can dispense Himself into us because the demands of His righteousness have been satisfied. Since the debt of sin has been paid, God cannot require any further payment from us. Because the debt has been paid, He must forgive us when we confess our sins. He is legally bound by His own righteousness. The second half of Hebrews 8:12 says, "Their sins I shall by no means remember anymore." He does not even remember our sins because the debt of sin has been paid. With regard to our sins, God has divine amnesia. God is all-knowing and remembers everything. He is everything, and He can do everything, yet when we repent and receive Him, He no longer remembers our sins. On the cross, He eternally cleansed us from all our sin; we have the eternal forgiveness of sins.

Although we have an eternal forgiveness, we live in time. The Bible says that whenever we sin in time, we need to confess (1 John 1:9). When we confess, we are agreeing with God. It is as if we were saying, "Yes, God, I confess that this is sin. I agree with You." Because of Christ's eternal redemption and His eternal payment of the debt, God is faithful to His word. He is also righteous because of His cleansing blood to forgive us of our sins and to cleanse us from all unrighteousness. He does not remember our sins anymore. This is a bequest of the new covenant. This is how the forgiveness of sins is the forgetting of sins.

The Precious and All-efficacious Blood of Christ Resolving All of Our Problems So That We Can Remain Constantly in Fellowship with God to Continually Enjoy His Organic Salvation

The precious and all-efficacious blood of Christ resolves all of our problems so that we can remain constantly in fellowship with God to continually enjoy His organic salvation (1 John 1:7-9; 2:1-2; Heb. 9:12, 14; Psa. 51:2). We have the precious, all-efficacious, and eternally effective blood of Christ that resolves all of our problems and maintains us in the enjoyment of Christ. We enjoy the cleansing of His blood all day. He has cleansed us once for all eternally (Heb. 9:12-14). Therefore, His redemption is eternal. He has cleansed us once for all eternally, but in our conscience in our daily life we need the instant application of the constant cleansing of His precious blood to maintain our fellowship with the Lord. We can enjoy the instant application of the constant and eternal cleansing of the precious blood of Christ by confessing our sins. Then we can enjoy more of Him as life, have more fellowship with Him, and receive more light. When we receive more light, we realize that we have more sins, which causes us to make further confession.

This is a wonderful "cycle in our spiritual life, a cycle formed of four crucial things—the eternal life, the fellowship of the eternal life, the divine light, and the blood of Jesus the Son of God. Eternal life issues in its fellowship, the fellowship of eternal life brings in the divine light, and the divine light increases the need for the blood of Jesus the Son of God that we may have more eternal life. The more we have of eternal life, the more of its fellowship it brings to us. The more fellowship of the divine life we enjoy, the more divine light we receive. The more divine light we receive, the more we participate in the cleansing of the blood of Jesus. Such a cycle brings us onward in the growth of the divine life until we reach the maturity of life" (1 John 1:7, footnote 3). Eventually, by this cycle we become the bride of Christ and the New Jerusalem.

God must forgive us of every sin. The blood of Jesus cleanses us from every sin. He cleanses us even from the sins that we think cannot be forgiven. If we confess, the blood cleanses us from every sin. If we confess, He is faithful and righteous to forgive us of all our sins and to cleanse us from all unrighteousness.

Once God Forgives Us, His Erasing Our Sins from His Memory and Remembering Them No Longer

Once God forgives us, He erases our sins from His memory and remembers them no longer. We may try to remind Him, but He has erased them from His memory. Sometimes we confess our sins and say, "Lord, forgive me," but then we try to go back and remind Him of them again. The enemy will come again and again to accuse us. However, once we have confessed our sin, any reminder of that sin comes from Satan and is an accusation of the devil. When we confess our sins, He is immediately faithful and righteous to forgive us of our sins and to cleanse us of all unrighteousness. This is what the Bible says (1 John 1:9). This is the preciousness of the blood of Jesus, God's Son.

We overcome the accuser because of the blood of the Lamb (Rev. 12:11). We do not overcome him because of our perfection. We are under the perfect blood of Jesus. His blood is our perfection. We simply need to agree with Him and confess our sins.

In the world men keep records of many things. For example, we have learned through several political scandals that high officials often keep tape recordings of nearly every conversation. Some people like to keep a record of the failures of others. We should never do this. We should never keep a record of the failures of the brothers and sisters in the back of our mind. We need to forgive them. When God forgives us, He forgets; we should be the same. Do you want a recording of your personal history? We need to take all the "tapes" and throw them in the lake of fire. When you confess, you are pressing the "erase button." When we confess a sin, it is fully erased.

No Sin That Has Been Repented of, That Has Been Confessed and Put under the Blood of the Lord Jesus, Ever Being Able to Raise Its Head at the Judgment Seat

No sin that has been repented of, that has been confessed and put under the blood of the Lord Jesus, can ever raise its head at the judgment seat (1 John 1:7, 9; Hymns, #295, #1003, #1008). This is our bequest. We need to pray over the hymns referred to in this point and sing them to the Lord. I enjoyed these hymns very much, especially today. *Hymns*, #1008 says,

> What can wash away my sin?
> Nothing but the blood of Jesus;
> What can make me whole again?
> Nothing but the blood of Jesus.
>
> > Oh! precious is the flow
> > That makes me white as snow;
> > No other fount I know,
> > Nothing but the blood of Jesus.
>
> For my cleansing this I see—
> Nothing but the blood of Jesus!
> For my pardon this my plea—
> Nothing but the blood of Jesus!
>
> Nothing can my sin erase—
> Nothing but the blood of Jesus!
> Naught of works, 'tis all of grace—
> Nothing but the blood of Jesus!
>
> This is all my hope and peace—
> Nothing but the blood of Jesus!
> This is all my righteousness—
> Nothing but the blood of Jesus!

This hymn does not say, "What can wash away my sin? / Nothing but my great conduct" or "Nothing but my perfect record in the training." The blood of Jesus is all our hope and peace. The blood of Jesus is all our righteousness. Satan hates for us to say, "Nothing but the blood of Jesus!"

When God Forgives Us of Our Sins,
His Causing the Sins That
We Have Committed to Depart from Us

When God forgives us of our sins, His causing the sins that we have committed to depart from us (Psa. 103:12; Lev. 16:7-10, 15-22; John 3:18; 5:24; cf. Psa. 130:4; Luke 7:47). This is the foundation of our Christian experience. We need such a foundation. He has caused the sins that we have committed to depart from us. Psalm 103:12

says, "As far as the east is from the west, / So far has He removed our transgressions from us." He sends away our sins as far away as the east is from the west.

Leviticus 16 speaks of the Day of Expiation, which is the Day of Atonement. It is a wonderful type of what happened when Christ died on the cross for our sins. The Day of Atonement in the Old Testament took place once a year. It did not cleanse man of his sins once for all, but merely covered them until the time when Christ would die on the cross. His death and His redemption were once for all time, both past and present. Now if we confess our sins, He causes our sins to leave us and depart from us. He erases our sins and forgets them. He forgives us of our sins, and we enjoy Him as the law of life.

Leviticus 16 shows us the type of the Day of Atonement or the Day of Expiation. Verses 7 through 10 say,

> He shall take the two goats and set them before Jehovah at the entrance of the Tent of Meeting. And Aaron shall cast lots on the two goats: one lot for Jehovah and the other lot for Azazel. And Aaron shall present the goat on which the lot for Jehovah fell, and offer it as a sin offering. But the goat on which the lot for Azazel fell shall be made to stand alive before Jehovah to make expiation over it, that it may be sent away for Azazel into the wilderness.

On the Day of Atonement they were to take two goats and put them at the entrance of the Tent of Meeting. Aaron then cast lots for the two goats. One lot was for Jehovah, and the other lot was for Azazel. *Azazel* means a "goat of departure." The King James Version uses the word *scapegoat*. Azazel is the scapegoat. In human terms a scapegoat is someone to whom blame is assigned. It is usually understood that this one does not actually deserve the blame, yet the blame is put on him, making him a scapegoat. However, in the type of the Day of Atonement, this goat actually does deserve the blame, and he is sent away.

Aaron then took the goat on which the lot for Jehovah fell and offered it as a sin offering. This goat was a type of Christ. When Christ died on the cross, He was offered for a sin offering. He was made sin on our behalf, and God laid on Him the iniquity of us all (Isa. 53:6). Second Corinthians 5:21 says, "Him who did not know sin He made sin on our behalf that we might become the righteousness of God in Him." All of our sins were laid on Him, and He became the sin offering. Thus, He took away the sin of the world (John 1:29).

The other lot was for Azazel. Azazel signifies Satan. The sin offering was for Jehovah to satisfy the demands of His righteousness. The other goat is for Satan, and it goes to Satan. Satan was destroyed on the cross. Leviticus 16:10 says, "The goat on which the lot for Azazel fell shall be made to stand alive before Jehovah to make a expiation over it, that it may be sent away for Azazel into the wilderness." This means that it was sent away for Satan into the wilderness. The wilderness typifies the lake of fire. Verse 21 says, "Aaron shall lay both his hands on the head of the live goat and confess over it all the iniquities of the children of Israel and all their transgressions, even all their sins; and he shall put them on the head of the goat, and shall send it away into the wilderness by means of the man who has been appointed." Aaron was to lay his hands on the head of this goat and confess all the sins and iniquities of the children of Israel. All the sins of God's people were laid on this goat. He put them on the head of the goat and sent it away into the wilderness. Satan, typified by Azazel, is the source and the origin of sin. On the cross Christ took away all the sins of God's redeemed once for all as a sin offering. He sent all those sins back to Satan, and He sent Satan away with all those sins into the lake of fire. On the cross He took away the sin of the world (John 1:29) and destroyed the devil (Heb. 2:14). Thus, God put all the sins back on the author of sin, the one who is the source of sin, and sent him away with all the sins of mankind into the wilderness, the lake of fire.

We can apply this every day by taking Christ as our sin and trespass offering. This means that we confess our sins and remind Satan, saying, "Satan, all my sins came from you. I confess them. I agree with God that they are sins and that they came from you. I confess and agree with God that I have sinned, and He is faithful and righteous to forgive me of my sins. Now you, Satan, are in the lake of fire with all my sins, and I am enjoying God."

Psalm 130:4 says, "With You there is forgiveness, / That You would be feared." Luke 7:47 says, "For this reason I say to you, her sins which are many are forgiven, because she loved much; but to whom little is forgiven, he loves little." These two verses indicate that when we are forgiven of our sins we do not become more audacious; rather, the more we are forgiven of our sins, the more we fear God and love Him. Beginning every morning and throughout each day, we are those who confess our sins. This means that we open to the Lord, allow Him to shine on us, and confess our sins to Him, acknowledging that we are fallen. Then we are filled with Him, and have a reverence for and awe of God. We do not want to offend Him, and we do not want to lose His presence.

Furthermore, our love for Him increases. According to Luke 7:47, he who is forgiven much, loves much. If we realize how much we have been forgiven, we will love the Lord to the uttermost. Mary Magdalene and those who followed the Lord realized how much they had been forgiven, so they loved Him very much. Our eyes need to be opened. In our daily life the more we enjoy His forgiveness, the more we love Him.

"I Will Impart My Laws into Their Mind, and on Their Hearts I Will Inscribe Them"

"I will impart My laws into their mind, and on their hearts I will inscribe them" (Heb. 8:10). This is the next bequest. We devoted a whole conference to the matter of living an overcoming life by the law of the Spirit of life (published in *The Ministry,* vol. 7, no. 7).

The Law of Life, the Law of the Spirit of Life, Being the Processed Triune God as the Spontaneous Power and Automatic Function of Life

The law of life, the law of the Spirit of life, is the processed Triune God as the spontaneous power and automatic function of life (Rom. 8:2; Phil. 2:13). This law of life is like a scientific principle that works spontaneously and automatically in the same way as the law of gravity and the law of electricity. To enjoy electricity we need only to flip the switch. If we "turn on the switch" of the law of life, we will be electrified with the Spirit of life. There are many ways to turn on the switch. First Thessalonians 5 lists several. The first way to turn on the switch is to "always rejoice" (v. 16). This verse does not say that we should rejoice every day or when we feel like it; it says to *always* rejoice. When we say, "Praise the Lord!" we are turning on the switch. Verses 17 and 18 say, "Unceasingly pray, in everything give thanks." We can say, "Thank You, Lord Jesus." It is not a small thing to exercise to thank Him every day. We need to be reminded to thank the Lord. This is to exercise our spirit. Whether we are in the full-time training, serving full time, at our job, or at home, we can thank the Lord.

The Function of the Law of Life Being
to Free Us from the Law of Sin and of Death,
to Dispense the Processed Triune God into Us to Make Us
Men of Life in Our Entire Tripartite Being,
to Shape Us into the Image of the Firstborn Son of God
So That We May Become His Corporate Expression,
and to Constitute Us the Members
of the Body of Christ with All Kinds of Functions

The function of the law of life is to free us from the law of sin and of death (Rom. 8:2), to dispense the processed Triune God into us to make us men of life in our entire tripartite being (vv. 10, 6, 11), to shape us into the image of the firstborn Son of God so that we may become His corporate expression (vv. 28-29), and to constitute us the members of the Body of Christ with all kinds of functions (Eph. 4:11-12, 16). These are the major functions of the law of the Spirit of life. We can contact Christ in our spirit by calling on the Lord. We can say, "Lord Jesus, I love You." We can also open the Bible and spend time to pray-read His Word. We can fellowship with the saints, preach the gospel, and drink the living water. There are many ways to open ourselves to the Lord. We can say, "Lord, I open my whole being to You. I open to You without any reservation." In this way He is switched on within us. Then spontaneously, automatically, and effortlessly we are freed from the law of sin and death, and He is dispensed into our tripartite being. In this way we are being shaped into His image, and He is constituting us the living members of His Body with all kinds of functions for the building up of the Body.

"I Will Be God to Them,
and They Will Be a People to Me"

For God to Be Our God Meaning
That He Is Our Inheritance,
and for Us to Be God's People Meaning
That We Are His Inheritance

"I will be God to them, and they will be a people to Me" (Heb. 8:10). For God to be our God means that He is our inheritance, and for us to be God's people means that we are His inheritance (Eph. 1:11, 14, 18; 3:21). He is not just God in a general way; He is God *to us*. He is our inheritance, our heart's treasure. For this reason Paul says, "We have this treasure in earthen vessels" (2 Cor. 4:7). Paul also said that he preached the unsearchable riches of Christ as the gospel (Eph. 3:8). We inherit God in Christ as the Spirit in all of His unsearchable riches. We inherit Him, and we enjoy Him as all the real wealth in this universe. He is being dispensed into us, making us a treasure. The New Jerusalem is the wife of Christ as a miraculous structure of treasure in the universe. We are filled with the Triune God as the unique treasure in the universe. We are filled with gold, typifying God the Father and His nature, with silver, typifying God the Son as our Redeemer, and with precious stones, typifying God the Spirit as our Transformer. He is thus filling us and constituting us with Himself to become His inheritance. God will inherit Himself in us and with us.

God Creating Man as a Vessel to Contain Him; Therefore, God Being Man's Possession, Just as the Content of a Vessel Is Its Possession

God created man as a vessel to contain Him (Gen. 1:26; Rom. 9:21, 23-24); therefore, God is man's possession, just as the content of a vessel is its possession. God created man as a vessel to contain Him in the same way that a vessel contains water. God is man's possession just as the content of a vessel is its possession. The possession of a glass is the water it contains. We have God within us, and God is filling us. Therefore, God is our portion and our inheritance. We are vessels of "liquid mercy." We are also vessels unto honor and glory. God is our mercy, God is our honor, and God is our glory. He is our inheritance.

By Having God Wrought into Us We Are Being Constituted into God's Inheritance

It is by having God wrought into us that we are being constituted into God's inheritance (Eph. 1:13; 3:16-21). We are being filled with God. When we are fully filled with Him, He will inherit us; that is, He will inherit Himself in us and with us. In the New Jerusalem God will enjoy His full inheritance, and we will enjoy Him as our inheritance. It is by our having God dispensed into us that we are constituted God's inheritance. This happens by His sealing Himself into us (1:13). We were sealed with God in the same way that a paper is stamped with a seal; we were stamped with God as a living seal. When ink is stamped onto a piece of paper, the ink absorbs into the paper. Not only does the ink get into the paper, but the image of the seal is stamped onto the paper. When we were saved, God stamped Himself into our spirit. God in Christ as the Spirit became the heavenly ink in us (cf. 2 Cor. 3:3). Now His image has been and is being stamped on us. For example, if I were to have a stamp with my name on it and I stamped my name in my Bible, the Bible now has my seal and my name on it.

You have been sealed by the Triune God. His name has been imprinted on your being. You belong to Him. You bear His image. When you were saved, He sealed you. You may have grown up in the church, but one day you said, "Lord Jesus," and He sealed you. Perhaps you were like me, a wild man, running around everywhere; but finally God caught you. You said, "Lord Jesus," and you were sealed. You then began to turn to the Lord, and He sealed you again and again. Then you came to the full-time training, and you were stamped some more. Then when you are married, you will experience more stamping. If you have children, you will be stamped some more. All of your experiences with the church life, the elders, and the brothers and sisters—every experience—simply causes you to be sealed more. Now when people look at you, they can see God in you.

God Being Ours and Our Being His
by the Divine Life's Enabling Us
to Participate in the Enjoyment of God
in Fellowship with Him

God is ours and we are His by the divine life's enabling us to participate in the enjoyment of God in fellowship with Him (1 Cor. 1:9).

"They Shall by No Means
Each Teach His Fellow Citizen
and Each His Brother, Saying, Know the Lord;
for All Will Know Me from the Little One
to the Great One among Them"

"They shall by no means each teach his fellow citizen and each his brother, saying, Know the Lord; for all will know Me from the little one to the great one among them" (Heb. 8:11). If we have been regenerated, we have God in Christ as the Spirit in our spirit as the living seal. This means that we know God. We may be impressed by someone who has met the president of the United States, but we are those who have met God and know God.

In the New Covenant Our Having the Privilege of Knowing God Experientially, Inwardly, and Personally with His Intimate Counsel and Sweet, Satisfying Companionship

In the new covenant we have the privilege of knowing God experientially, inwardly, and personally with His intimate counsel and sweet, satisfying companionship (Psa. 25:14; Exo. 33:11; Phil. 3:10a; 1:19-21a; 2 Cor. 2:10). It is wonderful having God's sweet and satisfying companionship. Others may think that we are all alone, but we have Him. I remember a brother's testimony. He was out in an empty parking lot after work; he thought he was the last one to leave his place of work, so he was talking to the Lord in the parking lot, saying, "O Lord Jesus, I love You. I'm open to You." Then one of his colleagues overheard him and asked, "What are you doing?" It is a mystery to others, but we are enjoying the sweet, satisfying companionship of the Triune God.

I once worked in the security department for a large company. They not only hired security people; they also hired police officers from the city. I was sitting in a room with all these police officers. One of them was a homicide detective. Homicide detectives in that city were known to be tough guys. They were there playing cards, and I was reading my Bible. I had just been saved, so I began to pray for them. I was not even conscious of what I was doing, but I was enjoying the Lord and saying, "Lord, save these guys. I prayed that each one of them would be saved." When I looked up, they were all staring at me. One of them asked, "What are you doing?" I said, "I was praying for you guys." Eventually, that homicide detective was saved. That was a mysterious, sweet, and satisfying companionship.

I remember the testimony of another brother who worked on a construction site. His co-workers were big, rough, tough, strong guys. One day, because they started work so early, they were all admiring the sunrise. Then this brother said, "You see that sun. The very God who created that sun lives in me." It is a mystery that we can have His companionship. Moses spoke to the Lord face to face as a man speaks to his companion (Exo. 33:11). Paul did everything in the face of Christ (2 Cor. 2:10 and footnote 3).

Being Able to Know God Subjectively
from within by the Sense of Life,
Which Is the Feeling, the Consciousness,
of the Divine Life within Us

We can know God subjectively from within by the sense of life, which is the feeling, the consciousness, of the divine life within us (Rom. 8:6). We need to do everything according to the inner sense of life and peace. When we are in God's presence, we are in our spirit and we have life and peace. When we are not in our spirit, we have the sense of warning, urging us to turn back to the Lord in our spirit.

IN ORDER FOR CHRIST TO EXPAND WITHIN US,
OUR NEEDING TO ENJOY HIM AS THE SERVANT OF JEHOVAH
IN THE FOLLOWING ASPECTS

As the Servant of Jehovah,
Christ Being Never Discouraged

In order for Christ to expand within us, we need to enjoy Him as the Servant of Jehovah in the following aspects. As the Servant of Jehovah, Christ was never discouraged (Isa. 42:1-4; cf. 53:2). We may be discouraged often, but there is a person in our spirit who is never discouraged. When we contact Him, He is never discouraged. If we say to Him, "O Lord, I feel bad; I'm wiped out," He does not respond in kind. Instead, He will say, "Cheer up." This was Paul's experience. He was on a ship in a terrible storm, yet he said to those on the ship, "Cheer up, men." All the men were fearing for their lives, but Paul said, "Now I advise you to cheer up, for there will be no loss of life among you, but only of the ship. For this very night an angel of the God whose I am and whom I serve stood by me, saying, Do not fear, Paul; you must stand before Caesar. And behold, God has granted you all those who are sailing with you. Therefore, cheer up, men, for I believe God that it shall be so, even in the way in which it has been spoken to me" (Acts 27:22-25). In reality, that ship belonged to Paul, and all those men were saved because Paul was on that ship.

The Lord Jesus was never discouraged because He did not look for anything in His environment to satisfy Him. We need to be one with the Lord in this. We should not look for anything in our environment to satisfy us, for nothing in our environment can satisfy us. The only One who can satisfy us is Christ as the living water. We are disappointed because we hope in things other than Christ. Perhaps those who are attending the full-time training expected something else, but in the full-time training, the trainees receive only one thing—Christ plus nothing. The Lord told the Samaritan woman, "Everyone who drinks of this water shall thirst again." (John 4:13). *This water* signifies the water of this world. When we drink of the world's water, we are never satisfied. Even as a believer, we might look for something to satisfy us. Perhaps it is our family. Eventually, Christ is the only One who will never disappoint us. He is the only One who can satisfy us.

We need to know that we can touch the One who is never discouraged. Some tried to make the Lord a King (6:15), but that did not affect Him; that was not what He was about. As long as the Father was happy with Him, He was happy. It did not matter whether He was rejected or accepted. He lived in the presence of God the Father continually. That was all He cared for. Isaiah says that He was a root out of dry ground (53:2). This means that in His eyes, the whole environment was dry. Nothing in His environment was able to sustain Him. What sustained Him was the fact that He was rooted in God the Father. God the Father was His supply, His satisfaction, and His unique goal. God the Father was His everything. If we enjoy Christ above everything else, He will become our everything. We need to be reduced to Christ. This is what the Lord does as we go on with Him.

As the Servant of Jehovah, Christ Being Constituted with the Spirit of Jehovah

As the Servant of Jehovah, Christ was constituted with the Spirit of Jehovah (48:16; 11:2; cf. Matt. 12:18; Luke 4:14-22). These verse references confirm this point. We need to be one with Christ to be filled with the Spirit of Jehovah every day. In Isaiah this is the Spirit of wisdom and understanding, the Spirit of counsel and might, and the Spirit of the knowledge and the fear of Jehovah. When we are filled with the Spirit, we have wisdom. We have Christ as wisdom, we have understanding, we have the counsel of the Triune God, and we have the power of the Triune God. We have the Triune God inwardly, and we fear Him. We are filled with the Spirit of the fear of Jehovah. We regard Him, we revere Him, we stand in awe of Him, we love Him, we adore Him, we worship Him, we gaze on Him, and we behold Him. This is why we need to be filled with such a Spirit.

As the Servant of Jehovah,
Christ Being the Prophet of Jehovah
to Be His Mouthpiece to Speak Forth His Word

As the Servant of Jehovah, Christ was the Prophet of Jehovah to be His mouthpiece to speak forth His word (Isa. 49:1-4; Acts 3:22-23; John 3:34; 14:10; cf. 1 Cor. 14:31-32). When we contact Christ within us, we all become prophets. All of the Lord's children should be prophets. We should not think that only some should be prophets. Every member of the Body of Christ should be a prophet. Paul said, "You can all prophesy one by one" (1 Cor. 14:31). Moses also said, "Oh that all Jehovah's people were prophets, that Jehovah would put His Spirit upon them!" (Num. 11:29). That was God's desire from the beginning. Predicting the future is but a minor aspect of being a prophet. To be a prophet is primarily to speak God's word into people.

As Typified by Isaiah,
Christ's Mouth Being like a Sharp Sword,
and His Being a Polished Arrow
Hidden in Jehovah's Quiver

As typified by Isaiah, Christ's mouth was like a sharp sword, and He was a polished arrow hidden in Jehovah's quiver (Isa. 49:2; Rev. 12:10-11; 6:2; cf. 2 Cor. 2:17; 13:3). Jehovah has a quiver, and within His quiver is a polished arrow. That arrow is Christ. The polished arrow is like a cruise missile that goes right to the heart of the enemy. If we are one with Christ, we also become a polished arrow in Jehovah's quiver. Any time the Lord wants to slay the enemy and the demons, He pulls us out of His quiver and shoots us at the enemy.

Revelation 6:2 speaks of the white horse, which signifies the glorious gospel of Christ. The One who sits on the horse has a bow, but there is no arrow because it has already been shot into the heart of God's enemy. This indicates that the victory has already been won. Now the victory needs only to be executed by the overcomers. We are being perfected to be polished arrows, to execute God's sentence on His enemy by our speaking. We simply speak to Him. We would not let the enemy shut our mouth. As *Hymns,* #1095 says, "Our mouth shut up defeats us / And wins the Devil's smile; / So why not open battle / And chase him all the while."

As the Servant of Jehovah, Christ Not Speaking His Own Word, but Speaking according to God's Instructions

As the Servant of Jehovah, Christ did not speak His own word, but spoke according to God's instructions (Isa. 50:4; John 14:24; Matt. 12:42; Eph. 6:17-20). Isaiah 50:4 says, "The Lord Jehovah has given me / The tongue of the instructed, / That I should know how to sustain the weary with a word. / He awakens me morning by morning; / He awakens my ear / To hear as an instructed one." I would encourage you to use this marvelous verse in your time with the Lord in the morning.

Have you ever been weary? Did the Lord ever speak to you when you were weary? Surely, that speaking sustained you. Sometimes a brother or sister speaks something of Christ to you when you are weary, and you are encouraged by the Lord's speaking through them. Perhaps you receive a phone call from a brother or sister that shepherds you.

The Lord was awakened by God the Father morning by morning. We should tell the Lord, "I would like You to wake me up. Lord Jesus, I want to be awakened by You morning by morning. I do not want to be awakened simply by my alarm clock. I want You to wake me up." This indicates that the Lord Jesus had morning revival. He had a time with God the Father morning by morning. Mark 1:35 says, "Rising very early in the morning, while it was still night, He went out and went away to a deserted place, and there He prayed." A crucial part of the full-time training is to spend time with the Lord in the morning. We should treasure this time.

Our Needing to Be One with Christ to Speak as Learners, as Trainees, as Instructed and Taught Ones

We should be one with Christ to speak as learners, as trainees, as instructed and taught ones (1 Cor. 2:13; Prov. 25:15, 20). We should never be proud. When we go to speak to others, we should not have the attitude that we are so knowledgeable or that we know everything. Isaiah 50:4 says, "He awakens my ear / To hear as an instructed one." We are learners; we are instructed ones. All of us are trainees. We never cease to be trainees. We will be trainees until we bring the Lord back.

Proverbs 25:15 says, "A soft tongue can break the bone." Perhaps we are with someone who is very hard. First, we need to be one with the Lord to pray for that person. Then we need to speak with a soft tongue, speaking with God as our kindness, our wisdom, our person, and our love. We thus will have God in Christ as the Spirit as a soft tongue to break all of the bone-like resistance in their being. The soft tongue breaks a bone.

Proverbs 25:20 says, "He who sings songs to a troubled heart / Is like one who takes off a garment on a cold day, / Or like vinegar on soda." Suppose a brother is very troubled, downcast, and out of it. I know that I should shepherd him. However, if I come to him and say, "Turn to your spirit!" and begin to sing a joyful song to him, that will make matters worse. Romans 12:15 says, "Rejoice with those who rejoice; weep with those who weep." If a brother has a troubled heart, I should not be super spiritual or hyper excited. If I sing songs to his troubled heart it is like taking off his garment on a winter day. He is wearing a coat because he is cold. If I say, "Turn to your spirit," I am just ripping off his coat. That is not the way to shepherd people. We must be one with the Lord to shepherd others in the appropriate way.

*Our Needing to Be Awakened by the Lord Morning by Morning,
Having Our Ears Opened to Hear the Voice of Our Master*

We need to be awakened by the Lord morning by morning, having our ears opened to hear the voice of our Master (Mark 1:35; Exo. 21:1-6). Exodus 21:5 describes a slave who says, "I love my master, my wife, and my children; I will not go out free." The master will then take that slave to the door or the doorpost and bore his ear through with an awl. We also may say to the Lord, "I love You, Lord Jesus. I love the church, and I love the saints. I open to You. I give myself to You. I consecrate myself to You. I want to be Your slave for the rest of my life." The Lord will then bring us to the door, and we will receive the infusion of His living instructions.

As the Servant of Jehovah, Christ Not Crying Out, Lifting Up His Voice, or Making His Voice Heard in the Street

As the Servant of Jehovah, Christ did not cry out, lift up His voice, or make His voice heard in the street (Isa. 42:2; Matt. 12:19; 2 Tim. 2:24; Prov. 27:14). We should not be ones who cry out or lift up our voice. Second Timothy 2:24 says, "A slave of the Lord ought not to contend but be gentle toward all, apt to teach, bearing with wrong." We should not contend with people; instead, we need to be gentle toward them. To "be gentle toward all, apt to teach, bearing with wrong" means that we take the Lord as our meekness, as our forbearance, and as our generosity. We should never argue with people. Verse 23 says, "Foolish questionings and those arising from an untrained mind refuse, knowing that they beget contentions." Because they come from an untrained mind and result in quarrels, we should not even try to answer these kinds of questions. We should not contend with anyone but pray for them and minister Christ to them. We should inwardly pray, "Lord, I would like to take You as my wisdom. What are You saying to this person? Are You saying anything to this person?" We would simply be one with Him.

Proverbs 27:14 says, "He who blesses his friend with a loud voice, / Arousing him early in the morning, / It will be reckoned as a curse to him." Suppose it is very early in the morning, my wife is sleeping, and she is not feeling very well. If I go to her and shout, "Praise the Lord, dear!" That would be like a curse to her. We need the humanity of Jesus. We should not go out in the street and pray-read with a loud voice early in the morning; otherwise, the police will come and ask us to be quiet. We should have the humanity of Jesus. We should be quiet at the appropriate time, and we should shout at the appropriate time. It is so wonderful that these things are in the Bible.

As the Servant of Jehovah,
Christ Not Breaking the Bruised Ones
or Quenching the Smoking Ones

As the Servant of Jehovah, Christ will not break the bruised ones or quench the smoking ones (Matt. 12:20; Isa. 42:3; cf. 61:1-2; Eph. 4:11-12). In the ancient times flutes were made of reeds. When the reed was bruised and the flute no longer made a musical sound, the reed was broken and thrown away. We are often like bruised reeds that do not produce a musical sound, yet Christ does not break a bruised reed; rather, He perfects the bruised reed, heals the bruised reed, and causes the bruised reed to give off the beautiful music of the Triune God.

The Lord also does not quench a smoking flax. Flax was used to make torches. If the flax began to smoke, they would simply quench it. We also are like smoking flax; sometimes we do not burn brightly. Sometimes we burn very dimly and are full of smoke. Nevertheless, Christ does not quench us, the smoking ones; instead, He adds oil to us and causes us to burn brightly.

Our Being Able to be One with Christ
as the Servant of Jehovah
to Make God Happy in the Releasing
and Raising Up of His Elect to Build Up
the Church as the House of God
and the Kingdom of God

We can be one with Christ as the Servant of Jehovah to make God happy in the releasing and raising up of His elect to build up the church as the house of God and the kingdom of God (Matt. 16:18-19; Eph. 4:11-12, 15-16; Rom. 14:17).—E. M.

THE DIVINE ECONOMY IN THE BOOK OF ISAIAH

Enjoying Christ as the Arm of Jehovah, the Reigning God, and the Exalted Christ in the Principle of the Restoration of Life for a New Revival

(Message 25)

Scripture Reading: Isa. 51:9-11; 52:7-15; 53:1

I. We can enjoy Christ as the holy arm of Jehovah, signifying the strength of Jehovah, the dynamic might of Christ in His divinity, for the restoration of Zion—Isa. 51:9-11; 52:8-12; 53:1; cf. Exo. 3:13-14; John 8:58:

A. Because of Christ as Jehovah's arm, the dynamic Redeemer, the ransomed of Jehovah will return and come to Zion with a ringing shout, and eternal joy will be upon their heads; they will lay hold on gladness and joy, and sorrow and sighing will flee away—Isa. 51:9-11; cf. Luke 18:24-27; 19:1-10; 15:23-24.

B. Christ as the arm of Jehovah is a root out of dry ground, having the power to live in any kind of environment for His magnification, and a grain of wheat falling into the earth to die, having the power to live under any kind of limitation for His propagation—Isa. 53:1-2; John 12:24, 37-43; Phil. 4:13.

C. In Exodus 14:19 the arm of Jehovah was the Angel of Jehovah, supplying, protecting, and guiding God's people out of all of the enemy's tyranny, oppression, captivity, deception, and usurpation—3:2, 6; Isa. 52:8-12; cf. Rev. 18:4; Gen. 19:16-29; Rom. 1:24-27; Exo. 1:11-14; 5:1; Acts 5:31.

D. We need to pray that the Lord would set us permanently as a seal upon His heart of love and indelibly as a seal upon His arm of power—S. S. 8:6:

1. Our love for the Lord is the basic factor, element, and essence of our having the Lord as our power and authority—John 21:15-17.

2. All of our hopes are in His keeping love and holding

power; whether we can endure to the end does not depend upon our own endurance but on the Lord's preservation; everything depends on God and His preserving power—cf. Exo. 28:9-12, 21, 29-30; Jude 24-25.

II. We can enjoy Christ as the reigning God—Isa. 32:1; 52:7-10; cf. 40:9:

A. When we are under God's throne, God's golden administration is within us, and we enjoy the divine light in the redeeming God for the application of God's judicial redemption with the life-river and the life-tree for the enjoyment of God's organic salvation—Rev. 21:23; 22:1-2; 2 Pet. 1:4; cf. 1 Kings 10:18.

B. According to the scene presented in Ezekiel 1, in our inward being we must have Christ as the Man-God on the throne with a clear sky like awesome crystal, with nothing between us and the Lord; the throne in Ezekiel is in the likeness of a sapphire stone of blue, a heavenly color indicating the heavenly situation, condition, and clearness of God's presence— vv. 22, 26; Exo. 24:10; Acts 24:16; 2 Tim. 1:3; Col. 1:18b; Rev. 2:4.

C. We need to receive the abundance of grace and the abundance of the gift of righteousness in order to allow grace to reign in us that we might reign in life over Satan, sin, and death—Rom. 5:17, 21; Rev. 3:21.

D. We need to allow Christ as the life-giving Spirit to rule within us, remaining in the restriction of the divine life in our spirit—cf. 4:2; Matt. 5:3, 8; 8:9.

E. The Lord is enthroned upon and inhabits the praises of His people, the sacrifice of praise—Psa. 22:3; 115:17-18; 119:162, 164; Heb. 13:15.

III. We can enjoy Christ as the exalted One, the extolled One who is very high, the One who has the preeminence in all things—Isa. 52:13; Col. 1:18:

A. Christ has been exalted far above all to transmit Himself into the church, which is His Body—Phil. 2:9; Heb. 4:14; 7:26; 8:1; Eph. 1:19-23.

B. From the day that He came out to minister on earth and since His ascension, the Lord Jesus has been acting prudently and

wisely on earth, and He has prospered in God's good pleasure—Isa. 52:13a; 53:10b; Matt. 11:19:

1. For the Lord Jesus to prosper in God's good pleasure was
for Him to fall into the ground to die to accomplish His
judicial redemption and to be resurrected for the reproduction, duplication, and glorification of God in His
organic salvation—Isa. 52:13; 53:10; John 12:24; Eph. 1:5;
Matt. 3:17; Heb. 10:5-10; Rom. 5:10.

2. The Acts is a record of the acts of Christ in His heavenly
ministry through the apostles in their spirit, carried out
wisely and prosperously for the propagation of the resurrected Christ as the wisdom and power of God—Isa. 52:7;
Rom. 10:14-15; Acts 1:8; 1 Cor. 1:22-24; 2:6-10.

C. The exalted Christ will surprise many nations, and kings will
shut their mouths, because what He is, is altogether different
from what they imagined—Isa. 52:15; Acts 8:26-39; 26:19-29:

1. People are surprised to hear that such a great One as
Christ was actually a small man who lived in the despised
region of Galilee, in the despised city of Nazareth, in the
poor home of a carpenter, and that He was rejected and
put on the cross and crucified—Isa. 53:2-10a.

2. Instead of majesty, Jesus had poverty, and instead of an
attractive form and a beautiful appearance, He had a
visage and a form that were marred (disfigured); when
we see Him, there is no beauty that we should desire
Him—52:14; 53:2; Matt. 13:55-57; cf. 2 Cor. 6:10.

3. Men would have expected that when the Redeemer came,
His countenance would surely be desirable to them, just
as Moses and David were handsome in appearance, yet
He had no comeliness, but appeared worn and old; He
was a man of thirty, but people took Him for a man of
fifty—Acts 7:20; 1 Sam. 16:12; John 8:57-58.

4. In reality, He was altogether lovely and entirely handsome; but this is invisible to our natural eyes and can only
be seen through our spiritual eyes—Isa. 52:15b; S. S. 5:10,
16; 1:15; Eph. 1:17-18; Psa. 27:4; Phil. 3:8-9.

ENJOYING CHRIST AS THE ARM OF JEHOVAH,
THE REIGNING GOD, AND THE EXALTED CHRIST
IN THE PRINCIPLE OF THE RESTORATION
OF LIFE FOR A NEW REVIVAL

Prayer: O Lord Jesus, we love You. We praise You that this love is not ours. Lord, thank You for infusing us with Yourself as love. We love You with Your love. We open our whole being to You. Thank You for another opportunity to enjoy You together. Lord, unveil us and even unload us. We want to see more of You. Reveal Yourself to us as the arm of Jehovah, as the reigning God, and as the exalted Christ. Bring Your whole recovery into a new revival. Lord, we thank You for Your cleansing blood. Wash us thoroughly from all our iniquities. Cleanse us from our sins. We take You as our sin offering and as our trespass offering. We are blessed to be able to wash our robes and thereby exercise our right to enjoy You as the tree of life. Amen.

The title of this message is "Enjoying Christ as the Arm of Jehovah, the Reigning God, and the Exalted Christ in the Principle of the Restoration of Life for a New Revival." Have you ever considered that Christ is the arm of Jehovah? We need to enjoy Christ as the arm of Jehovah, the reigning God, and the exalted Christ in the principle of the restoration of life for a new revival. These aspects of Christ are revealed in Isaiah 51—53, which speaks of the restoration of the saved Israelites in the millennial kingdom. On one hand, these chapters prophesy concerning Israel's experience of Christ as the arm of Jehovah, the reigning God, and the exalted Christ in the millennial kingdom; on the other hand, we need to realize that the New Testament believers also need to experience these aspects of Christ in the principle of the restoration of life today. We all want to be the overcomers, reigning with Christ for a thousand years in the coming age, the millennial kingdom. In order to enjoy Christ on that wedding day of a thousand years and to reign in Him, with Him, by Him, and through Him as His overcoming bride, we need to experience all that He will be in the millennial kingdom as a foretaste today.

The principle of the restoration of life is for a new revival. The Lord's burden in these last days is to bring His recovery into not just another revival but a new revival. We are speaking of a revival of which the like has never been seen—a revival in which a corporate people arrive at the highest peak of the divine revelation, living the life of a God-man and taking the God-ordained way to enter into Christ's wonderful shepherding according to God so that they can be built up as the Body of Christ, prepared to be the bride of Christ, and consummated as the city of life, the New Jerusalem.

Of course, Isaiah is prophesying concerning these aspects of Christ in their future fulfillment in the millennial kingdom, but in this message we are emphasizing our present experience of Christ as life in the principle of the restoration of life. We want to be those who change the church age from the age of grace to the age of the kingdom. We want to be God's dispensational instrument to change this age and bring the Lord back to reign on the earth. In Isaiah 51—53 we see a scene of recovery, revival, and restoration. We want this to be our own present reality so that we can become His bride and He can reign on the earth for a thousand years. Eventually, God will be expressed and reign through all of His chosen and redeemed as the New Jerusalem for eternity. Isaiah 51:9-11 says,

> Awake, awake! Put on strength, / O arm of Jehovah; / Awake as in the days of old, / As in the generations of past ages. / Was it not You who cut Rahab in pieces, / Who pierced through the dragon? / Was it not You who dried up the sea, / The waters of the great deep; / Who made the depths of the sea into a way / For the redeemed to pass through? / Therefore the ransomed of Jehovah will return / And will come to Zion with a ringing shout, / And eternal joy will be upon their heads. / They will lay hold on gladness and joy, / And sorrow and sighing will flee away.

Then 52:7—53:1 says,

> How beautiful on the mountains / Are the feet of him who brings good news, / Of him who announces peace, who brings news of good things, / Who announces salvation; / Of him who says to Zion, Your God reigns! / The voice of your watchmen! They lift up their voice; / They give a

ringing shout together; / For they will see with their very own eyes / When Jehovah restores Zion. / Break forth, give a ringing shout together, / You wasted places of Jerusalem, / For Jehovah has comforted His people, / He has redeemed Jerusalem. / Jehovah has bared His holy arm / In the sight of all the nations, / And all the ends of the earth will see / The salvation of our God. / Depart! Depart! Go out from there! / Do not touch any unclean thing! / Go out from the midst of her! Cleanse yourselves, / You who bear the vessels of Jehovah! / For you will not go out in haste, / And you will not go in flight; / For Jehovah will go before you, / And the God of Israel will be your rear guard.

Indeed, My Servant will act wisely and will prosper; / He will be exalted and lifted up and very high. / Even as many were astonished at Him — / His visage was marred more than that of any man, / And His form more than that of the sons of men— / So will He surprise many nations; / Kings will shut their mouths because of Him; / For what had not been recounted to them they will see, / And what they had not heard of they will contemplate.

Who has believed our report? / And to whom has the arm of Jehovah been revealed?

This question—"To whom has the arm of Jehovah been revealed?"— should reverberate in our being. John quotes this verse, referring to Christ as the arm of Jehovah (John 12:38). At John's time the religionists did not believe the Lord's report; hence, the arm of Jehovah was not revealed to them. It would also be a tragedy if Christ as the arm of Jehovah were not revealed to us in this message. We are here to see Him as the arm of Jehovah. Therefore, every time we read the Bible or attend a church meeting or a ministry meeting, we need to pray, "Lord, I do not trust in my natural understanding. I need You to open my eyes. I need You to open my mind to understand the Scriptures. I need You to infuse me with Your thought. Lord, I drop my concepts. I want to forget what I have learned in the past, what I know, and what I think I know so that I can see You in a new, fresh, and deeper way." In the *Life-study of Galatians* Brother Lee says, "If we would receive the revelation of the Son of God, we need to drop our concepts. Every concept, whether spiritual or carnal, is a veil. I have spent many years groping in my search to learn how to have revelation. Eventually, I discovered that to have revelation we need to drop our concepts" (pp. 35-36). Our natural concepts govern what we see. We see things according to who we are and what we like to see. Once we drop our natural concepts, we need to turn our heart to the Lord. Then, we need to pay attention to our spirit and to exercise our spirit. Lastly, we need to spend time in God's Word with prayer, in prayer, by prayer, and through prayer. Therefore, we can receive the revelation in this message by dropping our concepts, turning our heart to the Lord, paying attention to our mingled spirit, and remaining in a spirit and atmosphere of prayer to receive the word into our being.

ENJOYING CHRIST AS THE HOLY ARM OF JEHOVAH, SIGNIFYING THE STRENGTH OF JEHOVAH, THE DYNAMIC MIGHT OF CHRIST IN HIS DIVINITY, FOR THE RESTORATION OF ZION

We can enjoy Christ as the holy arm of Jehovah, signifying the strength of Jehovah, the dynamic might of Christ in His divinity, for the restoration of Zion (Isa. 51:9-11; 52:8-12; 53:1; cf. Exo. 3:13-14; John 8:58). These verses clearly state that Christ is the holy arm of Jehovah, signifying that He is the strength of Jehovah, the dynamic might of Jehovah in His divinity. Christ is the arm of Jehovah in order to restore Zion. In the Old Testament the children of Israel returned from captivity by Christ as the arm of Jehovah. In the New Testament His burden is to release God's people from the captivity of Babylon, of Satan, of sin, and of the world in order that they would return to Jerusalem, the unique ground of oneness. God's intention is that on the unique ground of oneness (Jerusalem) His people would build up the temple as the house of God and the city, especially its walls, as the kingdom of God. Our returning to Jerusalem, our coming back to meet on the genuine ground of oneness, the ground of the church, is for the Lord to gain Zion, the overcomers. God desires and is calling for overcomers in all the local churches, those who will live the life of a God-man in the reality of the Body of Christ. For this Christ is the arm of Jehovah. The name *Jehovah* literally means "I AM WHO I AM." Exodus 3:13-14 says, "Moses said to God, If I come to the children of Israel and say to them, The God of your fathers has sent me to you, and they say to me, What is His name? what shall I say to them? And God said to Moses, I AM WHO I AM. And He said, Thus you shall say to the children of Israel, I AM has sent me to you." What a name! Our God is Jehovah,

I Am Who I Am. Hence, Christ is the arm of the great I Am, the Triune God, and the God of Abraham, Isaac, and Jacob to be everything to us in order to make us today's Zion.

Because of Christ as Jehovah's Arm, the Dynamic Redeemer, the Ransomed of Jehovah Returning and Coming to Zion with a Ringing Shout, and Eternal Joy Being upon Their Heads; Their Laying Hold on Gladness and Joy, and Sorrow and Sighing Fleeing Away

Because of Christ as Jehovah's arm, the dynamic Redeemer, the ransomed of Jehovah will return and come to Zion with a ringing shout, and eternal joy will be upon their heads; they will lay hold on gladness and joy, and sorrow and sighing will flee away (Isa. 51:9-11; cf. Luke 18:24-27; 19:1-10; 15:23-24). We need to see this divine and mystical "arm" in our spirit. When we contact Christ, we are contacting the arm of the Triune God, that is, the dynamic power and might of the Triune God in Christ in His divinity. Christ as the arm of Jehovah is not merely an inward matter. As the arm of Jehovah, Christ is also the Angel of Jehovah (Exo. 3:2, 14:19). The terms *arm of Jehovah, Angel of ,Jehovah,* and *Angel of God* are synonymous. As the Angel of God, Christ supplied, protected, empowered, guarded, was behind, and led the children of Israel out of Egyptian captivity. Hence, as God's holy arm Christ is not only the dynamic power of the Triune God within us; He is also working in His people's environment to save them out of Satan's captivity, bringing them out of all kinds of Babylonian captivity back to God's original intention to have the church as the house of God, the kingdom of God, the Body of Christ, the new man, and eventually the prepared bride of Christ to bring Him back.

Isaiah 51:11 says, "Therefore the ransomed of Jehovah will return / And will come to Zion with a ringing shout, / And eternal joy will be upon their heads. / They will lay hold on gladness and joy, / And sorrow and sighing will flee away." When we initially received the Lord, especially if we were saved in dynamic way, we rejoiced with a ringing shout. There should be at least one time in our Christian life when we praise the Lord with a ringing shout! In the course of our contact with the Lord, there should be a time when we become ecstatic. Of course, we also need to be Jesusly human in taking care of others. For instance, we should not give a ringing shout early in the morning when others are resting. There is a place and a time to give a ringing shout.

Many Christians can testify that when they first received the Lord they were filled with gladness and joy, and their sorrow and sighing fled away. Some of the children of Israel were born in the good land, whereas others were born in captivity. Likewise, some believers were saved into the church life, in Zion, while others were saved in Christianity, in captivity. Blessed are those who were saved in Zion, yet many of those who were not saved in Zion were also filled with gladness and joy. Sadly, many were then led out of that joy by being brought out of their spirit into their mind. God wants to bring all His saved ones out of every kind of mixture, hypocrisy, compromise, and leaven back to His original intention. Thus, many can testify that when they came into the church life it was as if they were saved all over again.

John 1:45-46 says, "Philip found Nathanael and said to him, We have found Him of whom Moses in the law, and the prophets, wrote, Jesus, the son of Joseph, from Nazareth. And Nathanael said to him, Can anything good be from Nazareth? Philip said to him, Come and see." Phillip was inaccurate in saying that the Lord Jesus was the son of Joseph and from Nazareth. Jesus was not born of Joseph but of Mary, and He was born in Bethlehem in Judea, not Nazareth. This illustrates how, when some of us first came into the church life, we made many doctrinal mistakes. But the best thing that Philip said to Nathanael was, "Come and see." Likewise, the best way to testify concerning the church life to a new one is to say, "Come and see. Come to a meeting." Before my wife and I were married, I had told her about the church life. At first I spoke a long message concerning Acts 9. Eventually, I said, "You should just come and see." She came for a visit, saw the truth, and entered into the church life. After we were married, we continued to enjoy the church life.

Verses 47-49 say, "Jesus saw Nathanael coming to Him and said concerning him, Behold, truly an Israelite, in whom there is no guile! Nathanael said to Him, How do You know me? Jesus answered and said to him, Before Philip called you, while you were under the fig tree, I saw you. Nathanael answered Him, Rabbi, You are the Son of God; You are the King of Israel." What a revelation! Surely we would have been filled with great joy to see such a revelation. However, "Jesus answered and said to him, Is it because I told you that I saw you under the fig tree that you believe? You shall see greater things than these. And He said to him, Truly, truly, I say to you, You shall see heaven opened and the angels of God ascending and descending on the Son of

Man" (vv. 50-51). The Lord's word here refers to Jacob's vision of Bethel, the house of God, which is today's church life (Gen. 28:10-22). When we come into the church life, we see "greater things." No matter who we may be, whenever we are in the house of God on the genuine ground of oneness, we will receive much light. This is because, by His mercy, the Lord has brought us back to Bethel, where Christ as the Son of Man, in His humanity, is the ladder that brings heaven (God) to earth (man) and joins earth and heaven as one.

As the arm of Jehovah, Christ works not only within people but also in their environment. Christ as the arm of Jehovah has carried out many things throughout history. For example, it is Christ as the arm of Jehovah who opened up the former Soviet Union and brought down the Berlin wall. Luke 18 indicates the power of the dynamic salvation of Christ as the arm of Jehovah and how He can cause a dynamic response within people in order to save them. After speaking to the rich young ruler, who was unwilling to sell all that he had in order to follow Him, and seeing that he became very sorrowful, the Lord said, "How difficult it is for those who have riches to go into the kingdom of God. For it is easier for a camel to enter through the eye of a needle than for a rich man to enter into the kingdom of God. And those who heard said, Then who can be saved? But He said, The things that are impossible with men are possible with God" (vv. 24-27).

In the very next chapter, we read of a man named Zaccheus who was small in stature and who also was rich. Luke 19:1-2 says that the Lord "entered and was passing through Jericho. And behold, there was a man whose name was called Zaccheus." The Lord did not go to Jericho to hold a great gospel campaign in the way that Christianity does today. Rather, the Lord Jesus went to Jericho for one person— Zaccheus—as an illustration of how that which is impossible for man is possible for God. The Lord went to a lot of trouble to save each one of us. He first had to come to where we were. He arranged world events and even world history in order to save us. For example, He arranged the economy so that I would move to Houston, Texas, where it was easy to get a job. I thought that I had moved there for a job, but actually it was the arm of Jehovah that moved me to Houston so that I would be saved.

Because Zaccheus was small in stature, he could not see the Lord because of the large crowd. Therefore, in order to see the Lord, who was about to pass through that way, he climbed up in a sycamore tree.

Verse 5 says, "As He came to the place, Jesus looked up and said to him, Zaccheus, hurry and come down, for today I must stay in your house." Zaccheus joyfully received the Lord and was dynamically saved, even to the extent that he no longer loved money. He said, "Behold, the half of my possessions, Lord, I give to the poor, and if I have taken anything from anyone by false accusation, I restore four times as much" (v. 8). By giving half of his possessions to the poor, Zaccheus did much more than tithe. Moreover, he restored four times the amount to anyone from whom he had taken something by false accusation. Hence, the Lord said, "Today salvation has come to this house, because he also is a son of Abraham. For the Son of Man has come to seek and to save that which is lost" (vv. 9-10). This illustrates that the arm of Jehovah seeks, saves, and recovers what is lost and brings it back to God's original intention.

We are familiar with the parable of the prodigal son in Luke 15, in which a profligate and wayward son "squandered his estate by living dissolutely. And when he had spent all, a severe famine occurred throughout that country, and he began to be in want" (vv. 13-14). Eventually, he came to his senses and decided to return to his father. We may wonder what caused him to come to his senses. Why was there a famine in that country? We may say that the famine was the work of Christ as the arm of Jehovah in that prodigal's environment, and his coming to his senses was the operation of Christ as the arm of Jehovah in his inner being. Sometimes when we pray for someone to be saved, that one's situation becomes worse. We may wonder why, instead of answering our prayer, the Lord turns their situation from bad to worse. Actually, the Lord is answering our prayer in a way that will cause that one to come to his senses. The famine in Luke 15 caused the son to come to his senses and to return to his father. Upon returning home the father gave him the best robe and a ring and killed the fattened calf to feast with him. This signifies that he was clothed with Christ as his righteousness, sealed with the eternal Spirit, and satisfied with the riches of Christ for his nourishment and enjoyment. The fattened calf signifies the rich Christ killed on the cross for our enjoyment. The robe signifies that the lost son was redeemed, and his eating the fattened calf signifies his being regenerated by the life-giving Spirit in his spirit. Furthermore, he was brought into the father's house, which signifies the church, where they could eat and be merry. The genuine church life is a life of eating the Lord, enjoying the Lord, and being merry in the Lord. The church life is not a place of sorrow but of joy. Thus, when the older son came to the house, he heard music and dancing (v. 25). In a spiritual sense the church life is a place of "music and dancing." One of the hallmarks of the Lord's recovery and one of the central matters in God's economy is our enjoying Christ in the church.

Christ as the Arm of Jehovah Being a Root out of Dry Ground, Having the Power to Live in Any Kind of Environment for His Magnification, and a Grain of Wheat Falling into the Earth to Die, Having the Power to Live under Any Kind of Limitation for His Propagation

Christ as the arm of Jehovah is a root out of dry ground, having the power to live in any kind of environment for His magnification, and a grain of wheat falling into the earth to die, having the power to live under any kind of limitation for His propagation (Isa. 53:1-2; John 12:24, 37-43; Phil. 4:13). How marvelous to see that the Lord Jesus, who is the Triune God-man, God incarnated to be a man, is the arm of Jehovah. According to our religious concept and to the concept of the Jewish religionists at that time, the arm of Jehovah, the Messiah, is a great warrior and king who would conquer the whole earth. However, when God was incarnated, He lived as a small Nazarene from a despised village. He was born in a manger and eventually was crucified on the cross. He was a root out of dry ground, which is a difficult environment. This means that although the Lord lived in a difficult environment, He was rooted elsewhere; that is, He did not look to His environment to sustain Him, supply Him, or be a source of encouragement. In fact He did not expect anything from His environment. We all need to confess that we are easily disappointed. The reason we get disappointed is because we are expecting something other than Christ. We may be expecting something in our environment to satisfy us—such as our wife, our children, our degree, our job, or even the full-time training. The trainees may be enjoying the training, but they will be disappointed if they expect something other than Christ from the training. We should expect nothing other than Christ. We need to be rooted in Him as our unique source of satisfaction. He is the arm of Jehovah in whom we have the power to live in any kind of environment. To live Christ in any kind of environment and to magnify Christ in any kind of environment requires divine power. This great power is in Christ as the arm of Jehovah.

Christ is also the grain of wheat that fell into the ground and died. In John 12:24 the Lord says, "Truly, truly, I say to you, Unless the grain of wheat falls into the ground and dies, it abides alone; but if it dies, it bears much fruit." Then in verses 37 and 38 John says, "Though He had done so many signs before them, they did not believe into Him, that the word of the prophet Isaiah which he said might be fulfilled, 'Lord, who has believed our report? And to whom has the arm of the Lord been revealed?'" These verses indicate that Christ as the grain of wheat is the arm of Jehovah. We need to consider this. The arm of Jehovah, that is, the strength and dynamic power of Christ in His divinity, is a grain of wheat. This is against our natural concept. The arm of Jehovah as a grain of wheat points to His power to live under any kind of limitation. The grain of wheat in verse 24 signifies the limited Jesus. We all are a duplication of Christ in His resurrection. He was the one grain of wheat, and in His resurrection He produced us to be the many grains of wheat. A grain of wheat exists to be buried in the ground and surrounded by soil, that is, to be forced to live in an extremely limited environment. The more we go on with the Lord, the more limitations we will have and the more limited we will become. According to our natural concept, the more we grow in life, the stronger and the freer we should be, but according to God's economy, the more we grow in life, the more limited and restricted we become. For example, no one knew God's New Testament economy more than the apostle Paul. The apostle Paul knew the truths in the Scriptures better than anyone else. His Epistle to the Hebrews is an amazing exposition of Leviticus. Nevertheless, the Lord sovereignly allowed such an apostle to be imprisoned. The natural concept is that if we are in a limited situation, such as prison, we should seek to be released. However, Paul testified that he was "the prisoner of Christ Jesus" (Eph. 3:1). He did not say that he was a prisoner of the Roman Empire. Then he spoke of himself as "I, the prisoner in the Lord" (4:1). To some, the full-time training may be a "prison" from which their natural man wants to break out. When prisoners break out of a real prison, there are many searchlights shining to find the escapees. Spiritually speaking, if we try to escape from our limitations, there will be a light searching us from within.

Thus, Paul not only considered himself to be the Lord's prisoner; he also considered that the Lord was his prison. Paul was in a "maximum security prison," which was the Lord Himself as his dwelling place. The Lord is our prison. In 6:20 Paul said, "I am an ambassador in a chain." Footnote 2 says that the word *chain* here denotes "a coupling chain, a chain that bound the prisoner to his guard." The Lord even allowed Paul to be chained to a guard. In the full-time training the trainees may feel as if they are chained to their roommates, to their gospel partners, to their trainers, and to their service. Paul is implying that we are all ambassadors in a chain. This means that we can magnify Christ, display Christ, live Christ, enjoy Christ, and propagate Christ in the midst of all our limitations.

In Exodus 14:19 the Arm of Jehovah Being the Angel of Jehovah, Supplying, Protecting, and Guiding God's People out of All of the Enemy's Tyranny, Oppression, Captivity, Deception, and Usurpation

In Exodus 14:19 the arm of Jehovah was the Angel of Jehovah, supplying, protecting, and guiding God's people out of all of the enemy's tyranny, oppression, captivity, deception, and usurpation (3:2, 6; Isa. 52:8-12; cf. Rev. 18:4; Gen. 19:16-29; Rom. 1:24-27; Exo. 1:11-14; 5:1; Acts 5:31). The Angel of Jehovah in Exodus 14 and the arm of Jehovah in Isaiah 51—53 are synonymous. All these reference verses show that as the arm of Jehovah, signifying the strength of Jehovah and the dynamic might of Christ in His divinity, Christ wants to bring us out of the enemy's tyranny, oppression, captivity, deception, and usurpation.

Jerusalem typifies the church as the Body of Christ. Consummately, the New Jerusalem will be the bride and the wife of Christ. In the Old Testament three cities stand in opposition to Jerusalem. The first is Babel. We need to be delivered from everything of Babel, which is Babylon; thus, we need to be delivered from idolatry. Idolatry is not merely the worship of a graven image or a statue; it is to put anything in our life above Christ. Whatever or whomever we place above Christ is an idol to us. Whenever we give a person, matter, or thing the first place in our life, that is idolatry. We need to come out of all kinds of idolatry, mixture, and compromise. If we see that this is the Lord's way, then we should take this way with our entire being. We need to follow the Lord by taking Him as our absoluteness. Babel eventually consummates in Babylon the Great (Rev. 17:5).

The second city that opposes Jerusalem is Sodom. We need to come out of everything of Sodom. We are in a dark age. We must never compromise with religious mixture or sin, for both are leaven in the eyes of God. We need to confess our sins. Although we are sinners, we can confess our sins and be cleansed, but we can never excuse ourselves with regard to sin. Sodom was an enemy in Genesis 19. Abraham had given Lot his choice of where he would dwell, and Lot chose the plains of Jordan and eventually settled in Sodom (13:12). Genesis 19:1 even indicates that Lot was considered as one of the leaders in Sodom. According to typology, Lot signifies the New Testament believers who are trapped in the world and in sin.

Lot should have remained with Abraham, who was the Lord's servant and His minister of the age. Since the Lord was with Abraham, to remain with Abraham was to remain in the Lord's move. Nevertheless, Lot chose to leave the person who was in the center of the Lord's move in that age. Eventually, he settled in the evil city of Sodom. In Romans 1:24-27 Paul speaks of some of the evil practices for which Sodom was known. We must realize that what today's world regards as an "alternative lifestyle" is evil and utterly condemned by God. The only truly proper lifestyle is the God-man living. Today this so-called alternative lifestyle is seeping into our society, especially into the mentality of the young people in the schools and universities. Of course, we love the sinners, for we ourselves are saved sinners; we must love those in every kind of situation. In 1 Corinthians 6 Paul speaks concerning the different backgrounds of some of the believers in Corinth. Verses 9 through 11 say, "Do not be led astray; neither fornicators nor idolaters nor adulterers nor effeminate nor homosexuals nor thieves nor the covetous, not drunkards, not revilers, not the rapacious will inherit the kingdom of God. And these things were some of you; but you were washed, but you were sanctified, but you were justified in the name of the Lord Jesus Christ and in the Spirit of our God." Believers should not remain in their sinful situation once they have been washed, sanctified, and justified. As believers we cannot condone such a lifestyle. The so-called alternative lifestyle is of Satan. Romans 1:25-27 says that such ones "exchanged the truth of God for the lie...Therefore God gave them up to passions of dishonor; for their females exchanged the natural use for that which is contrary to nature; and likewise also the males, leaving the natural use of the female, burned in their craving toward one another, males with males committing unseemliness and fully receiving in themselves the retribution of their error which was due."

They exchanged the proper, holy matrimony for perverted passions. They exchanged what is natural for that which is unnatural. How terrible! I am very concerned for the young people. In today's society and in the universities in particular the so-called alternative lifestyle is being taught as something acceptable, and this evil concept is seeping into the minds of the young people. All sin is unacceptable, including the sins of Sodom. Romans 1 indicates that for one to enter into such a sin is an indication that he has fully given up God. However, a person can be saved from this kind of sin by being forgiven, cleansed, and transferred into the kingdom of God. Nevertheless, we must be clear that as believers, we must come out of Sodom and hate Sodom.

The third city in the Old Testament that opposed Jerusalem was, collectively, the treasure cities of Egypt. The treasure cities of Egypt represent worldliness, which Satan uses to occupy us. When we are worldly, we will compromise the church life. Satan tries to bring elements of the world, such as entertainment, into the church life in order to compromise the church life. For example, Satan may bring in the thought that our goal is just to gain people. If our goal is merely to gain more people, we may resort to worldly means that compromise the purity of the church. We should always treasure purity, especially as it concerns the nature of the church. Although we surely want to gain people for the building up of the church, we must never sacrifice the pure nature of the church. We must treasure and protect the purity of Christ and the purity of His recovery.

Therefore, we must come out of all these negative cities. We need to come out of Sodom. We must reject Sodom and anything of sin. Whenever we sin, we need to confess and repent. Whenever we confess, we are immediately forgiven. It is good to confess our sins, but it is terrible to compromise our church life by claiming that this or that behavior is acceptable in today's society. We must forsake the treasure cities of Egypt, which signify worldly pleasure and entertainment, for this is how the enemy occupies people. Even after we are saved, the enemy may come in to deceive us and occupy us. To those in the full-time training he may say, "You could be out with your friends. You were having such a good time, but now you are in the training. Look at your classmates who have good jobs." According to Exodus, when we are in the world, when we forsake the Lord, and when we put pleasure, entertainment, and money first, we will know only harshness, bitterness, and hard labor. We have observed many who were deceived by the enemy with things of the world. I have even witnessed dear brothers in the Lord's recovery who have been distracted with the desire to make money. No matter how successful they may be, their countenance reveals that they are sad. Seemingly they are enjoying the pleasures of the world, but actually Satan is forcing them to make bricks without straw. Thus, in pursuit of riches many work overtime. On one hand, they are making money, but on the other hand, their health is deteriorating. They may live in large houses, but eventually they will end up in a wooden box. Surely that is not the meaning of our human life. On the contrary, our home should be the Triune God.

Needing to Pray That the Lord Would Set Us Permanently as a Seal upon His Heart of Love and Indelibly as a Seal upon His Arm of Power

We need to pray that the Lord would set us permanently as a seal upon His heart of love and indelibly as a seal upon His arm of power (S. S. 8:6). We need to pray, "Lord, set me as a seal upon Your heart and upon Your arm." The heart is the seat of love, while the arm is the seat of power. For the Lord to set us as a seal on His heart implies that we become an organic part of His heart. We cannot put a seal on our physical heart, but we can be set as a seal on God's heart. To be set as a seal on God's heart means that we have been indelibly imprinted on His heart and that we can never be erased from His heart. Likewise, we want to be set as a seal on His arm, that is, to become an organic part of His arm, as we are of His heart.

Our Love for the Lord Being the Basic Factor, Element, and Essence of Our Having the Lord as Our Power and Authority

Our love for the Lord is the basic factor, element, and essence of our having the Lord as our power and authority (John 21:15-17). Love and power go together. Christ is the heart as well as the arm of Jehovah. Songs of Songs 8:6 says, "Set me as a seal on your heart, / As a seal on your arm; / For love is as strong as death, / Jealousy is as cruel as Sheol." Our love for the Lord makes us powerful. When He shows us His love and infuses us with His love, we become His crazy lovers. When He opens His heart to us and infuses us with His heart of love, we will love Him with that heart of love, and we will spontaneously have Him as the arm of Jehovah, that is, as our power and authority.

What gives us impact when we speak to people is our love for the Lord. In our speaking others can sense whether or not we are luke-warm. Many unbelievers, especially the young people, have good "radar." They can sense whether we genuinely care for them or are like the Pharisees. However, if we love the Lord and out of this love pray for those for whom we are caring, they will be able to sense that our love is genuine. Regardless of how naughty or bad they may be, they will real-ize that we love the Lord and that we love them. In the denomination near where I grew up, there was a pastor who loved the Lord and who loved the young people. Within myself I asked, "Why would he love me? If he loves the Lord, he would not love me because I am so naughty." Although this pastor and his wife did not see the Lord's recovery, according to where they were and what they saw, they loved the Lord and they loved the young people. I still love them to this day. Once the pastor's wife told to me, "One day you are going to be like Timothy." I thanked her, but within me I thought, "I could never be like Timothy."

One time, when we were supposed to be in a church service, my best friend and I decided to sneak off to a restaurant on Eighth Avenue. Our mothers did not know that we were gone. At the restaurant, which was open twenty-four hours a day, we both had ice cream sundaes at nine o'clock in the morning. While we were enjoying our ice cream sundae, my friend suddenly stopped eating and stared behind me in disbelief. When I turned around to look, I saw the pastor behind me. He had come out of the service to look for us. When he found us, he sat down with us, looked at our sundaes, and had to struggle to keep from laughing. He said, "What are you doing here?" We said, "We are having ice cream sundaes." My point in sharing this story is that he loved us so much that he came to look for me. That touched me. Indirectly, I was saved through his care for me. Brother Lee also gave a testimony of a pastor who for a period of time visited him at his house once a week. That pastor did not say much except to invite him to the meeting on Sunday. Then he would come back again the following week to repeat his invitation. Eventually, Brother Lee said to himself, "Perhaps I should go to the church" (*Serving in the Meetings and in the Gospel*, pp. 50-51). That pastor demonstrated the Lord's heart of love. When we have such a love, there will be impact and reality when we speak to others.

All of Our Hopes Being
in His Keeping Love and Holding Power;
Whether We Can Endure to the End Not Depending
upon Our Own Endurance but on the Lord's Preservation;
Everything Depending on God and His Preserving Power

All of our hopes are in His keeping love and holding power; whether we can endure to the end does not depend upon our own endurance but on the Lord's preservation; everything depends on God and His preserving power (cf. Exo. 28:9-12, 21, 29-30; Jude 24-25). When we pray that the Lord would set us permanently as a seal upon His heart of love and indelibly as a seal upon His arm of power, we are admitting that we are helpless. Our natural love for the Lord does not last. We may think that we are absolute in our love for Him or that we are strong. Actually, our love is undependable and our strongest grip is weak. We cannot preserve ourselves by our own strength. Even if we could preserve ourselves until His coming by our own strength, it would be a shame to Him. Therefore, we need to pray, "Lord, my only hope is Your heart of love. I give myself to become an object of Your love. Set me as a seal on Your heart of love. Your heart of love keeps me. Set me as a seal on Your arm of power. Your arm of power preserves me." What preserves us is the Lord as our love and power, not our natural strength.

ENJOYING CHRIST AS THE REIGNING GOD

When We Are under God's Throne,
God's Golden Administration Being within Us,
and Our Enjoying the Divine Light in the Redeeming God
for the Application of God's Judicial Redemption
with the Life-river and the Life-tree
for the Enjoyment of God's Organic Salvation

We can enjoy Christ as the reigning God (Isa. 32:1; 52:7-10; cf. 40:9). When we are under God's throne, God's golden administration is within us, and we enjoy the divine light in the redeeming God for the application of God's judicial redemption with the life-river and the life-tree for the enjoyment of God's organic salvation (Rev. 21:23; 22:1-2; 2 Pet. 1:4; cf. 1 Kings 10:18). In the New Jerusalem the golden street is linked to God's throne. The river of water of life proceeds out of the throne in the middle of the street that is constituted of pure gold.

Hence, by being under God's throne, we are also walking on the way of life and partaking of His divine nature. On both sides of the street in which flows the river of water of life grows the tree of life. The throne is the throne of God and of the Lamb. God is the light, and the Lamb is the lamp, and out of the God-light-Lamb-lamp flows the Spirit as the river of water of life in the middle of the golden street with the tree of life. Therefore, whenever we are under the Lord's headship and lordship and He is the preeminent One in our being, He shines in, through, and out of us as the light. He is in the Lamb as the lamp, and God is the light shining in the Lamb. The light exposes and convicts us, but the blood of the Lamb cleanses us from every sin as the application of God's judicial redemption. Then we are able to open to Him to partake of His holy, golden nature. By partaking of His divine nature, we enjoy the life-river flowing in us and the life-tree supplying us in order to become men of life to constitute the city of life.

According to the Scene Presented in Ezekiel 1, in Our Inward Being Our Needing to Have Christ as the Man-God on the Throne with a Clear Sky like Awesome Crystal, with Nothing between Us and the Lord; the Throne in Ezekiel Being in the Likeness of a Sapphire Stone of Blue, a Heavenly Color Indicating the Heavenly Situation, Condition, and Clearness of God's Presence

According to the scene presented in Ezekiel 1, in our inward being we must have Christ as the Man-God on the throne with a clear sky like awesome crystal, with nothing between us and the Lord; the throne in Ezekiel is in the likeness of a sapphire stone of blue, a heavenly color indicating the heavenly situation, condition, and clearness of God's presence (vv. 22, 26; Exo. 24:10; Acts 24:16; 2 Tim. 1:3; Col. 1:18b; Rev. 2:4). We need to maintain our Christian life and our church life by having nothing between us and the Lord. We need to pray, "Lord, I do not want there to be anything between You and me. I want to open my being to You. If there is anything between You and me, I want to confess it right now. I want to open to You so that I can confess anything You shine upon." Whenever we confess, there will be a clear sky in our being.

The sky between us and God is connected to our conscience. What kind of sky do we have? How is the weather in our being? Above Los Angeles there is a layer of smog covering the city. On the contrary, the sky over Seattle or Vancouver is clear and blue. Spiritually speaking, it is a great thing to have a clear sky. Ezekiel 1:22 says, "Over the heads of the living creature there was the likeness of an expanse, like the sight of awesome crystal, stretched forth over their heads above." The word *awesome* is scriptural. In addition to *crystal* the Amplified Bible also translates the same word as *ice*. Hence, the sky over the living creature is like awesome ice. It is awesome because it is clear and transparent.

Furthermore, verse 26 says, "Above the expanse that was over their heads was the likeness of a throne, like the appearance of a sapphire stone; and upon the likeness of the throne was One in appearance like a man, above it." Every day we need to pray, "Lord, I give You the preeminence in my being. I want You to have the highest and the most prominent position in my life. I want to have a clear sky, a good conscience. I want nothing between me and You or between me and any brother or sister. Moreover, give me a pure conscience so that You are my only goal. If I have any goal other than You, my conscience is not pure. Lord, I want You to be my only goal, and I would like You to be the preeminent One in my being." When we pray such prayers, we will experience the sapphire throne. A sapphire is a blue precious stone. When we are under God's throne, when there is nothing between us and the Lord, we will experience Him as a blue sapphire, which is a heavenly color indicating the heavenly situation, condition, and clearness of God's presence within us. This should be the situation in all the churches.

Needing to Receive the Abundance of Grace and the Abundance of the Gift of Righteousness in Order to Allow Grace to Reign in Us That We Might Reign in Life over Satan, Sin, and Death

We need to receive the abundance of grace and the abundance of the gift of righteousness in order to allow grace to reign in us that we might reign in life over Satan, sin, and death (Rom. 5:17, 21; Rev. 3:21). Romans 5:17 says, "Much more those who receive the abundance of grace and of the gift of righteousness will reign in life through the One, Jesus Christ." Every day we should open to the Lord to receive the abundance of grace and of the gift of righteousness. We first need

Christ as our righteousness. Since God is righteous, He must forgive us whenever we confess our sins. The Lord has paid the debt for all of our sins; therefore, if we fail and confess our sins, He immediately forgives us and cleanses us of our sins. This is the abundance of the gift of righteousness. Having been cleansed, we can receive the abundance of grace, the abundance of the enjoyment of God. By enjoying the abundance of grace, we will spontaneously reign in life, not over our spouse or our children but over Satan, sin, and death.

Needing to Allow Christ as the Life-giving Spirit to Rule within Us, Remaining in the Restriction of the Divine Life in Our Spirit

We need to allow Christ as the life-giving Spirit to rule within us, remaining in the restriction of the divine life in our spirit (cf. 4:2; Matt. 5:3, 8; 8:9).

The Lord Being Enthroned upon and Inhabiting the Praises of His People, the Sacrifice of Praise

The Lord is enthroned upon and inhabits the praises of His people, the sacrifice of praise (Psa. 22:3; 115:17-18; 119:162, 164; Heb. 13:15). If we desire to enthrone the Lord, if we want God to reign, we should be those who habitually praise the Lord. We need to treasure the words *Praise the Lord!* and build up a habit of exercising our spirit to praise Him day by day. Praising the Lord should not be limited to our meeting life. We need to praise the Lord in our daily life in many matters and for many things. If we cannot think of anything to praise the Lord for, at least we can praise Him that we are alive and that we have another day to live.

We need to build up a habit of praising the Lord. Psalm 115:17-18 says, "The dead do not praise Jehovah, / Nor do any that go down into silence. / But we will bless Jehovah / From now and to eternity. / Hallelujah." We should not be silent. This is not the way to worship God. Idols are silent. According to verse 5, idols have mouths but they do not speak, and verse 8 says that those who make idols are like them. Those who worship idols are likewise silent. But we do not worship a silent idol. We worship a speaking God! Therefore, we must fill our days with praising the Lord.

In Psalm 119:164 David says, "Seven times a day I praise You." David praised the Lord seven times a day. Brother Nee once said, "Do not let David beat us in his praise" (*The Collected Works of Watchman Nee*, vol. 48, p. 249). In order to beat David, we need to praise the Lord at least eight times a day. If we would praise the Lord at least eight times a day for a whole month, surely we would be changed inwardly. This does not mean that we should praise in a religious way but with the exercise of our spirit.

ENJOYING CHRIST AS THE EXALTED ONE, THE EXTOLLED ONE WHO IS VERY HIGH, THE ONE WHO HAS THE PREEMINENCE IN ALL THINGS

Christ Having Been Exalted Far Above All to Transmit Himself into the Church, Which Is His Body

We can enjoy Christ as the exalted One, the extolled One who is very high, the One who has the preeminence in all things (Isa. 52:13; Col. 1:18). Christ has been exalted far above all to transmit Himself into the church, which is His Body (Phil. 2:9; Heb. 4:14; 7:26; 8:1; Eph. 1:19-23). According to Ephesians 1:19-23, God caused His surpassing great power to operate in Christ in raising Him from the dead, and seating Him at God's right hand in the heavenlies, subjecting all things under His feet, and giving Him to be Head over all things to the church. The words *to the church* imply a transmission. Thus, when we open to the Lord, He transmits Himself and all that He has attained and obtained into us, the church, His Body.

From the Day That He Came Out to Minister on Earth and Since His Ascension, the Lord Jesus Having Been Acting Prudently and Wisely on Earth, and His Having Prospered in God's Good Pleasure

From the day that He came out to minister on earth and since His ascension, the Lord Jesus has been acting prudently and wisely on earth, and He has prospered in God's good pleasure (Isa. 52:13a; 53:10b; Matt. 11:19). Isaiah 52:13 says, "Indeed, My Servant will act wisely and will prosper; / He will be exalted and lifted up and very high."

For the Lord Jesus to Prosper in God's Good Pleasure Being for Him to Fall into the Ground to Die to Accomplish His Judicial Redemption and to Be Resurrected for the Reproduction, Duplication, and Glorification of God in His Organic Salvation

For the Lord Jesus to prosper in God's good pleasure was for Him to fall into the ground to die to accomplish His judicial redemption and to be resurrected for the reproduction, duplication, and glorification of God in His organic salvation (Isa. 52:13; 53:10; John 12:24; Eph. 1:5; Matt. 3:17; Heb. 10:5-10; Rom. 5:10). Thus, when the Lord was baptized, the Father said, "This is My Son, the Beloved, in whom I have found My delight" (Matt. 3:17). It is God's good pleasure for us to be put into the baptism of Christ's death. By living in Christ's crucifixion and in the reality of His resurrection, we are declaring that we are men in the flesh who are worthy of nothing but death and burial. If we have such a realization, God will be very happy. However, in our baptism we are not left to remain in the waters but are raised to walk in newness of life. Thank the Lord!

The Acts Being a Record of the Acts of Christ in His Heavenly Ministry through the Apostles in Their Spirit, Carried Out Wisely and Prosperously for the Propagation of the Resurrected Christ as the Wisdom and Power of God

The Acts is a record of the acts of Christ in His heavenly ministry through the apostles in their spirit, carried out wisely and prosperously for the propagation of the resurrected Christ as the wisdom and power of God (Isa. 52:7; Rom. 10:14-15; Acts 1:8; 1 Cor. 1:22-24; 2:6-10). When we preach Christ as wisdom and power, when we bring the glad tidings to others, and when we minister Christ as the depths of God, we are prospering in the divine life and in the death and resurrection of Christ. The real prosperity is not related to material riches but to Christ as the depths of God and as the riches of God.

The Exalted Christ Surprising Many Nations, and Kings Shutting Their Mouths, Because What He Is, Is Altogether Different from What They Imagined

The exalted Christ will surprise many nations, and kings will shut their mouths, because what He is, is altogether different from what they imagined (Isa. 52:15; Acts 8:26-39; 26:19-29). Isaiah 52:15 says, "So will He surprise many nations; / Kings will shut their mouths because of Him; / For what had not been recounted to them they will see, / And what they had not heard of they will contemplate." For Christ to surprise many nations and kings to shut their mouths, we must go out and preach the good news. We need to speak and propagate this exalted Christ. Verse 7 says, "How beautiful on the mountains / Are the feet of him who brings good news, / Of him who announces peace, who brings news of good things, / Who announces salvation; / Of him who says to Zion, Your God reigns!" We must be those who have beautiful feet, those who announce glad tidings of good things.

This is what the apostles did in Acts. In 8:26-39 Philip preached the gospel to an Ethiopian eunuch. That Ethiopian eunuch was a man of power and authority, for he was over all the treasure of the queen of Ethiopia. While he was coming back from Jerusalem on his chariot, he was reading Isaiah 53, but he did not understand what he was reading. The Spirit spoke to Philip to approach and join the chariot. Verse 30 says, "When Philip ran up, he heard him reading Isaiah the prophet and said, Do you really know the things that you are reading?" The eunuch said, "How could I unless someone guides me?" (v. 31). He was reading a passage from Isaiah 53, which in Acts 8:32-33 says, "As a sheep He was led to slaughter; and as a lamb before its shearer is dumb, so He does not open His mouth. In His humiliation His judgment was taken away. Who shall declare His generation? For His life is taken away from the earth." Regarding these verses the eunuch beseeched Philip, saying, "Concerning whom does the prophet say this?" (v. 34). Then Philip unveiled that those Scriptures referred to Christ, and he announced Jesus as the gospel to the eunuch (v. 35). To the eunuch Christ was altogether different from what he had imagined. Perhaps in his natural concept Christ should have been a great warrior. Isaiah 53:2 says, "He grew up like a tender plant before Him, / And like a root out of dry ground. / He has no attracting form nor majesty that we should look upon Him, / Nor beautiful appearance that we should desire Him." Verse 5 says, "He was wounded because of our transgressions; / He was crushed because of our iniquities; / The chastening for our peace was upon Him, / And by His stripes we have been healed." All the iniquities of all the people who ever lived were laid upon the Lord on the cross. Philip may have opened these verses to the eunuch; hence, when they came upon some water, the eunuch said, "Look, water. What prevents me from being baptized?" (Acts 8:36). It is as if the Lord had prepared a baptistery along the road for him. Acts 8:37-38 says, "Philip said, If you believe from all your heart, you will be saved. And he answered and said, I believe that Jesus Christ is the Son of God. And he ordered the chariot to stand still, and they both went down into the water, Philip and the eunuch, and he baptized him."

In Acts 26 Paul was giving his testimony before King Agrippa and Festus. In verse 22 and 23 he said, "Having therefore obtained the help which is from God, I have stood unto this day, testifying both to small and great, saying nothing apart from the things which both the prophets and Moses have said would take place, that the Christ would suffer and that He, being the first to rise from the dead, would announce light both to the people and to the Gentiles." In Greek the word *help* denotes an alliance, indicating that the apostle Paul was allied with God and realized God's assistance in this alliance. After Paul had given his testimony, Festus said, "You are insane, Paul. Much learning is driving you insane" (v. 24). Festus knew that Paul was scholarly and brilliant. If we had been Paul, we probably would have defended ourselves. However, Paul said, "I am not insane, most excellent Festus, but I am uttering words of truth and soberness. For the king knows about these things, to whom also I speak freely, for I am persuaded that none of these things have escaped his notice; for this has not been done in a corner. King Agrippa, do you believe the prophets? I know that you believe" (vv. 25-27). Paul was bold to speak faith into those who heard him. Hence, King Agrippa said, "By so little are you trying to persuade me to become a Christian?" (v. 28). And Paul said, "I would to God that both by little and by much, not only you, but also all those who hear me today might become even such as I am, except for these bonds" (v. 29).

People Being Surprised to Hear That Such a Great One as Christ Was Actually a Small Man Who Lived in the Despised Region of Galilee, in the Despised City of Nazareth, in the Poor Home of a Carpenter, and That He Was Rejected and Put on the Cross and Crucified

People are surprised to hear that such a great One as Christ was actually a small man who lived in the despised region of Galilee, in the despised city of Nazareth, in the poor home of a carpenter, and that He was rejected and put on the cross and crucified (Isa. 53:2-10a).

Instead of Majesty, Jesus Having Poverty, and Instead of an Attractive Form and a Beautiful Appearance, His Having a Visage and a Form That Were Marred (Disfigured); When We See Him, There Being No Beauty That We Should Desire Him

Instead of majesty, Jesus had poverty, and instead of an attractive form and a beautiful appearance, He had a visage and a form that were marred (disfigured); when we see Him, there is no beauty that we should desire Him (52:14; 53:2; Matt. 13:55-57; cf. 2 Cor. 6:10). The many so-called pictures of Jesus actually do not depict Jesus. They are idols and blasphemies. How terrible! Not only Catholicism but many of the denominations display so-called pictures of Jesus, depicting a handsome person. But Isaiah 52:14 says, "His visage was marred more than that of any man, / And His form more than that of the sons of men." Therefore, those pictures are false and are idols. Once Brother Lee shared an experience of dealing with such idols. He said,

> None of us should have a picture of Jesus in our home; that is an idol. The popular picture of Jesus today is a painting of a famous artist in the Middle Ages. However, Jesus did not look like this. Isaiah 53 tell us that while Jesus was in the flesh, He had no beauty; rather, He was despised by people (vv. 2-3). In 1936 in the province of Honan in China we dealt with the case of a sister who was demon-possessed. From our experience we knew that demon possession mostly comes from the worship of idols. Behind any kind of idol there is a demon; if someone has something related to idols in his home, he is in danger of possession by demons. Because in China there are many idol worshippers, I asked the people of that sister's house if they had idols in their home. They said they did not, but eventually I found out that in their home was a picture of Jesus. Later we came to know that the sister many times knelt down to pray to that picture of Jesus. A demon took this opportunity to possess her. I told them to burn that picture, and when they did, the demon left her. (*Enjoying the Riches of*

Christ for the Building Up of the Church as the Body of Christ, p. 200)

We do not need pictures of Jesus; we have the person of Jesus in our spirit. We do not need any leaven, which make things easier to take in; we have the Triune God as the reality within us.

Men Having Expected That When the Redeemer Came, His Countenance Would Surely Be Desirable to Them, Just as Moses and David Were Handsome in Appearance, yet His Having No Comeliness, but Appearing Worn and Old; His Being a Man of Thirty, but People Taking Him for a Man of Fifty

Men would have expected that when the Redeemer came, His countenance would surely be desirable to them, just as Moses and David were handsome in appearance, yet He had no comeliness, but appeared worn and old; He was a man of thirty, but people took Him for a man of fifty (Acts 7:20; 1 Sam. 16:12; John 8:57-58). Acts 7:20 says that Moses was "lovely to God," and 1 Samuel 16:12 says that David was "ruddy and had beautiful eyes and a handsome appearance." However, the Lord Jesus had no comeliness but appeared worn and old, though He was only a man of thirty. In John 8 the Lord said to the religionists, "Your father Abraham exulted that he would see My day, and he saw it and rejoiced" (v. 56). They said to Him, "You are not yet fifty years old, and have You seen Abraham?" (v. 57). They took him for a man who looked about fifty years of age, yet He was only thirty. This indicates that the Lord appeared worn and old.

In Reality, His Being Altogether Lovely and Entirely Handsome; but This Being Invisible to Our Natural Eyes and Only Being Able to Be Seen through Our Spiritual Eyes

In reality, He was altogether lovely and entirely handsome; but this is invisible to our natural eyes and can only be seen through our spiritual eyes (Isa. 52:15b; S. S. 5:10, 16; 1:15; Eph. 1:17-18; Psa. 27:4; Phil. 3:8-9). When we exercise our spirit, we have the insight and the understanding of the Spirit. Then we see that He is the Chief among ten thousand, that He is altogether lovely, and that He is the beauty of Jehovah. Once we have the excellency of the knowledge of Christ and we see His beauty, we will realize that all other things are dung and that we need to gain Christ alone. Let us gain Christ as the arm of Jehovah, as the reigning God, and as the exalted Christ.—E. M.

REPORT ON A CONFERENCE
HELD IN PRETORIA, SOUTH AFRICA

Over the weekend of March 11-13, 2011 the churches in South Africa held a conference in Pretoria. The two brothers from the United States who came to speak the messages brought us into the fellowship and burden concerning "The Need for a Fresh Vision of the Lord's Recovery for the Increase and Spread of the Lord's Testimony." The saints were all helped to see that God's will is a person, a person whom God wants us to enjoy as our portion so that we may be His enlargement for His expression. There was a very positive response as indicated by the prophesying of many saints after each message.

The speaking was timely and quite appropriate for those in attendance. According to our estimation, two-thirds of the attendees have been in the church life for less than two years, and for more than thirty of these, this was their first conference. The attendance was the largest yet and required that we use a different venue in order to accommodate the large number of participants. Over two hundred eighty attended the conference, an increase of more than ten percent from our last conference held in September 2010. We believe that this increase is the result of the Lord's continued gathering of many seeking, hungry ones throughout this country. Saints came together from the churches in South Africa, including Cape Town, Johannesburg, Kempton Park, Pretoria, and Roodepoort. In addition, a good number of seeking ones had contact with us through their purchase of the Recovery Version of the Holy Bible. A good percentage of these seekers were from Bloemfontein, a city for which we are burdened and have been praying that the Lord would raise up a lampstand. A few saints also paid the price to come from other countries in Africa; we were particularly cherished and encouraged by a brother who came all the way from Mauritius and by two brothers who came from Zambia. Please continue to stand with what the Lord is doing among us in these days; we covet the prayers of the Body. Please pray:

1) That the Lord would supply the hungry ones in Bloemfontein with His interpreted word through the Recovery Version Holy Bible. Pray also that the Lord would make a way for us to care for these seekers so that He could raise up a lampstand there for His testimony. Recently, the seekers in Bloemfontein have placed orders for fifty more Bibles.

2) That the word spoken in the recent conference would find the good soil, take root, and bear fruit.

3) That the Lord would use the CDs from this conference to speak to more seekers and spread the word that was spoken regarding the need for a fresh vision of the Lord's recovery.

4) That the Lord would raise up and strengthen His testimony in Cape Town, Bloemfontein, Haartbeespoort, and Centurion.

The saints in South Africa

ANNOUNCEMENTS

INFORMATION CONCERNING UPCOMING
CONFERENCES AND TRAININGS

The following is a schedule of upcoming conferences and trainings sponsored by the Living Stream Ministry. Information is also available online at:

http://www.lsm.org/upcoming-conf-info.html

Int'l Memorial Day Weekend Conference (Dallas, TX)	May 27-30, 2011
2011 Summer Training (Anaheim, CA)	July 4-9, 2011
Int'l Training for Elders & Responsible Ones (Baarlo, Netherlands)	October 6-8, 2011
Int'l Thanksgiving Weekend Conference (San Jose, CA)	November 24-27, 2011
2011 Winter Training (Anaheim, CA)	December 26-31, 2011
Int'l Chinese-speaking Conference (Taipei, Taiwan)	January 27-29, 2012
Int'l Training for Elders & Responsible Ones (Anaheim, CA)	March 30—April 1, 2012
Int'l Memorial Day Weekend Conference (Bellevue, WA)	May 25-28, 2012
2012 Summer Training (Anaheim, CA)	July 2-7, 2012

INFORMATION CONCERNING EUROPEAN CONFERENCES,
SEMINARS, AND WEEKEND TRAININGS

For information related to upcoming conferences, seminars, and weekend trainings in Europe, please consult the Amana Trust website at:

http://www.amanatrust.org.uk/events